Court of
Memory

Court of Memory

J A M E S   M c C O N K E Y

DAVID R. GODINE, PUBLISHER

Boston, Massachusetts

This is a Nonpareil Book first published in 1993 by
David R. Godine, Publisher, Inc.
Horticultural Hall
300 Massachusetts Avenue
Boston, Massachusetts 02115

Originally published in
1983 by E.P. Dutton, Inc.

Library of Congress Cataloging-in-Publication Data

McConkey, James.
Court of memory / James McConkey.
p.   cm.—(nonpareil book)
1. McConkey, James—Biography. 2. Novelists, American—20th
century—Biography.
I. Title. II. Series
ISBN 0-87923-983-2   PS3563.C3435Z47 1993
813'.54—dc20   93-5370 CIP

FIRST EDITION
Printed in the United States of America

ACKNOWLEDGMENTS

Chapters in Part I, "Crossroads," first appeared in
the following publications:
Perspective:
"A Night Stand."
The New Yorker:
"An Essay on a Premonition and Eight Heads,"
"Every Day Requires an Atlas and More."
Night Stand:
"Stromboli in Ithaca," "A Report to the Trustees."
The Sewanee Review:
"Of Brotherhood and a Dehorned Calf,"
"The Crossroads Near Frenchburg."
The Hudson Review:
"In Praise of Chekhov."

Chapters in Part II, "The Stranger at the Crossroads," first
appeared in the following publications:
Shenandoah:
"The Stranger at the Crossroads" (under the title "The Man
Who Couldn't Cry").
The New Yorker:
"Mythology, Art, and the Farming Life," "Fireflies,"
"The Idea of Hawk," "The Bullfrog Pond," "Bodiless Guests,"
"The Windows of the Mint," "The Laughter of Zeus."
The Hudson Review:
"Passages Early and Late."
The American Poetry Review:
"Visitors from the Fortunate Island."
Grapevine Weekly:
"Redefining a Word on Independence Day."

"All this I do inside me, in the huge court of my memory. There I have by me the sky, the earth, the sea, and all things in them which I have been able to perceive. . . . There too I encounter myself. . . ."

—St. Augustine

CONTENTS

FOREWORD

ONE NIGHT MORE than twenty years ago, as I sat in the basement study of my former home in Ithaca, New York, I underwent a change so radical that it transformed my apprehension both of the world and of valid modes for writing about people.

It was one of the earlier winters of our continuing cold war with the Soviet Union. I can't remember the precise event that led to my change, for it merges in my mind with so many similar ones in the late Eisenhower–early Kennedy years that the resumption of nuclear testing by the Soviet Union and then by the United States, the fear that led to the construction of family fallout shelters throughout America, and the crisis first over Berlin and then over Cuba all seem to have occurred during the daylight hours preceding that January night. The house was on a slope, so that the study was ground level, with windows facing the backyard. My children's German shepherd (now long dead) lay sleeping on a couch near my desk. It was late (when I was younger, I chiefly wrote in the hours surrounding midnight) and my wife and children also slept, two floors above. I had just finished writing a story, a fairly conventional third-person narrative in which a child assumes the cold and impervious nature of his mother in order to defeat an emotional and wholly vulnerable father. I was dissatisfied with it, though I thought it well-written. What did *that* story have to do with my present feelings? What did it have to say about a society which might destroy itself with nuclear missiles, very soon?

Always I had assumed my love for my wife and children, but not until that night did I know its extent. Everything about me had become transformed—my desk, the books on the shelf, my reflection in the dark glass. Momentarily, I turned off my lamp, so that I could see what lay beyond my window. Snow covered the ground, and was shimmering in the light of the stars. I could even see the whiteness of a little mound of it in an empty bird's nest in the bare branches of the maple. The nest possessed for me a sudden, quite extraordinary value; and so did the cold, moist nose of the dog—the meaning inherent in that nose was so intense that I will remember all my life the simple experience of touching it.

The story I had written was unsatisfactory because it was "made up," a fiction, one devoid of the sacredness I saw everywhere about me. The only way open to me to communicate the strength of my feelings was through myself—through my intimate experiences, through memory, and personal observation. I did feel kinship with a character from fiction, though, Conrad's Decoud, as he, awaiting the destruction of a city and political state, writes a long letter about his activities to his sister in France. "In the most skeptical heart," Conrad says, "there lurks at such moments, when the chances of existence are involved, a desire to leave a correct impression of the feelings, like a light by which the action may be seen when personality is gone."

At that moment in my own life, I began an autobiographical account of the meaning implicit in one of the humblest objects imaginable. A botched-up nightstand I had built as a child for my mother had come into my mind, and I believed I could use it more readily than the bird's nest or the dog's nose to communicate the value of the ordinary and commonplace. In rereading that account, I realize that I was (as I still am) held by the old truths of literature, for my words turn into a statement of the momentary victory of the imagination not only over mortality but over those aspects of the real world I had wanted to celebrate. Whatever my wish, I had not escaped fiction; I had simply made myself the central character of a story, finding in my own experiences and dreams a greater authenticity than I could in those of any character I might invent. Though I didn't know it then, that story was the beginning of a book, the first volume of which was called

Crossroads, and which is here reprinted with the second, *The Stranger at the Crossroads.*

The change I felt in myself that night was reflected in other writers at roughly the same time: it was a change wrought by a sense of desperation at the folly of public affairs, by a sense of the human irrationality demonstrated in present history and the history of the recent past, including the evil of Auschwitz. One either went inward, striving to testify to the meaning that still existed for the individual, trusting that the aspirations and emotional needs of the self so depicted would be representative of the responses of the separate individuals who read about them; or one went outward, beyond the personal truth, to the region in which the sacred apparently no longer existed: the outer world in which the individual had lost his uniqueness, that world which lacked apparent logic or causality or even substance.

More than two decades have passed since that January night, and the sphere which is literature has begun to tremble with whatever possibility that continuance allows, much like a bead of water in a blighted but still-living rose. If the sense of imminent catastrophe was the provocation of *Crossroads,* an encounter at that crossroads with a young stranger was the seed of the companion volume, begun after a lapse of ten years. In telling me of his most intimate concerns—he needed a listener, maybe for his survival, and I was the first he found—he so moved me that I saw myself as someone much like him. I became, in a sense, a stranger at my own crossroads, a man well into his middle years desiring (now that his children were grown) to understand himself all over again, to rediscover a personal order, and to communicate what he found to anybody who would listen. Perhaps wishes of this sort are the inevitable result of that displacement of self which a sudden insight into human mutuality provides.

I have discovered my plot in the relation that exists between my present and past. But the present is always changing, and the search for order and understanding must be made again and again, in a manner that alters with an altering and yet constant self. What follows is the story of a person who through much of his adult life has been attempting to use memory as a faculty capable of illuminating experience with

the truth that matters most to him. Time itself imposes the progression—but progression as we normally perceive it, a continual inter-
weaving of current happening and related remembrance, with certain
memories (those leitmotifs of our lives, the events that early on shaped
us) recurring more frequently than others. Hence, while the chronological headings refer to the years of composition, individual chapters
move between a present moment and a moment or a number of them
in an ever-enlarging past. We are what we were.

—JAMES McCONKEY
1982

≈ I ≈

Crossroads

1960

A Night Stand

1 I NO LONGER HAVE THE DESIRE, ON THIS immense and silent winter's night, to dissemble, to fabricate tales. When I turn out the little lamp on my desk and stare out my study window, at first I see only the faint whiteness of the snow in the yard: but what is it that illuminates the snow, what makes it faintly shimmer? There is not a light visible anywhere. My neighbor on the left, an elderly bachelor, a retired college dean, may still be at work in *his* study, for he keeps his interest in his profession, engineering, despite his retirement; but his windows always are darkened by heavy blinds—he is thorough in every respect, and would not possess a blind that permitted the tiniest rip of light to escape outward. My neighbors on the right are certainly asleep; the wife, who not long ago underwent her third operation for cancer, reads a great deal, mainly fiction and verse, but is allowed only the daylight hours.

As I watch from my darkened study, I see patches of snow on the dark pines, then the little white mound that rises absurdly from the deserted robin's nest in the maple; and then, above the maple, above the pines, suddenly rides Orion. Other stars appear. Mars, wondrously alive this season, follows the Seven Sisters. . . . Scattered on my desk are sheets of paper, palely shimmering like the snow. A completed manuscript, a story: words follow words across each sheet in thin little rows. Can I read those words in the light from Betelgeuse and Regel, in the glow from Orion's great nebula—that hazy spot, there, in the hunter's sword? But on the couch to my right, the dog whimpers: Black Judy, my children's German shepherd, wondering why I sit in the dark.

And so I switch on the lamp again, and reach over to stroke the dog. Immediately she stretches out her hind legs, closes her eyes and sleeps. Her coat is lustrous in its blackness, it is a pleasure to stroke her soft fur and to touch her cold nose, to listen as she slowly breathes in and out, in and out.

Mine is a most comfortable study, finished in its present state by the former owner of the house, a professor of philosophy. It is hidden away at the rear of the basement; but since the house is built on a slope in this town of hills, the study is actually higher than ground level. Two flights above me, wife and children sleep. My wife and I repainted this room, to cover the marks left by the former occupant's bookshelves. A reprint—a Miró—which he had firmly taped to the plasterboard of one wall is the only reminder that the room has belonged to another. Once the shelves in this room had countless volumes stamped in gold print with the single word: MIND. Now the shelves—the new ones, which I built of soft pine, that lumber of the novice—sag with novels good and indifferent, volumes of poetry, a broken camera, a pipe rack, a box of telescope lenses, and some odd-shaped rocks my older boy found in the creek bed.

And again I think of my neighbors.

Every afternoon for the past few months, at precisely the same moment—four o'clock—I have looked out my study window to see my neighbor the dean, cane in hand, walk the asphalt road behind our house. Our backyard adjoins a little park which is, in reality, only the landscaped grounds of the water filtration plant; the asphalt road circles the filtration plant. Seven times around, says my neighbor, is exactly one mile: and seven times around he briskly marches each winter day, scarf flying in the breeze, cane tapping the ice and snow. He smiles at the children, he dodges deftly between the hurtling sleds that slice down the slopes and across the road: his cheeks are red, his disposition jovial, and he knows that an emeritus professor must have his daily exercise. If, half an hour later on any day, I had climbed the steps for a cup of coffee and had thought to peer through the living room window while waiting for the pot to warm, I would probably have seen my other neighbor, the woman who recently has undergone surgery. For on the hill across the street is a pleasant old Irish Catholic cemetery, and here my other neighbor slowly but surely regains her health, each day climbing the path one headstone further. This week she has passed the Hersons (Patrick, 1818–1900; Catherine Morgan *His Wife*, 1834–1910; *Children*, 1854–John–1884, 1861–Patrick–1895, 1869–Mathew–1901, 1856–James–1906), and is well into the Shannons.

In these past few months I have been more deeply involved in making stories than I have been for several years. And so—until to-night—I have been aware only that my neighbors have been dwelling in another world than mine; their oddity has been their significance; I have watched them curiously, thinking, *I ought to get them both in a story some day,* and then I have turned quickly back into *my* realm, that world where the people and the paragraphs containing them are fixed forever on typing paper—as forever, at any rate, as the low rag content will permit them to be.

Where have I been these past few months? It is difficult to say; yet in recent nights—as writing slowly has become more chore than pleasure, as the glandular juices that excite one into creativity have begun to subside—I have waked to recall the identical dream, an image of a clumsy little table, a nightstand I built as a child. My writing has not been dealing with my childhood, it has not been consciously auto-biographical; nevertheless my mind must have been dipping back to an earlier period, collecting what it would. The nightstand—of what use is a nightstand in a story?—had been rejected, but there it rose into my dreams, haunting me for my neglect of it. And now that my writing has begun to ebb, it has taken precedence. Like the neighbors, the books, the dog, it has become important. Wretched little nightstand! Acting as if *its* turn has come, as if it won't be satisfied until given its due!

All right.

I had made it in the ninth grade. In the previous summer, despair had settled upon my family; sudden poverty—for the Depression had reached us at last—was the cause. I shall say only that my parents were so distracted that they moved here and there and finally to Arkansas, and that my father—a Northern businessman—seriously considered pig raising as an occupation and ordered the proper leaflet from the government. An impossibility, of course, but so was everything else; in their chaos, my parents separated. My father asked for a divorce, and soon married a widow in Texas. My brother, my mother, and I sold all the furniture for gasoline and traveled halfway across the nation in an old Packard—symbol of former opulence—to knock, without warning or invitation, one midnight upon the door of the nearest relatives too tender to deny us admission. They took us in, that most kind uncle and aunt—took not only us, the three of us prickled and small with shame, but my dog as well, a thin and ravenous German shepherd not unlike the one sleeping on the couch as I recall the past on another midnight.

For months thereafter, I was continually drowsy, my mind occupied with lassitudinous dreams. Full of humiliation and self-pity, I was pleased whenever someone spoke to me harshly for having neglected an assigned task. But let me pass over this year with my uncle and aunt simply by saying that my two semesters of ninth-grade manual training produced only that one wobbly nightstand, its legs spindlier than any previous nightstand had been known to be. For I had planed them down, down, down, day after day, with eyes shut: once I opened them to see the instructor and the rest of the class standing in a half-circle before my bench, laughing silently. The blueprint called for a drawer which I had neither the time nor the aptitude to build. Nor, after the legs had been screwed to the top, did I even have time for paint or stain. I gave the nightstand to my mother on her birthday: my gift, a year's toil; she—do you believe it?—cried.

Keep your eyes, whoever you are who may be following this reminiscence, keep your eyes on that nightstand; some sudden travels take place, but the nightstand is the theme of these chronicles in my youth; never lose sight of it. My mother, certainly, didn't. After this year with my relatives, my brother took a job in Michigan; we accompanied him. The dog, the nightstand, and my mother occupied the back of the car during the journey. Misfortune ensues once more, and once more as the result of insufficient cash. The finance company—the old opulence, after all, had been based on credit—took the Packard; a relative in Ohio, the dog. *I* cried when he was carted off in his Railway Express cage.

My mother, always strongly religious, now went with unfailing regularity to church for spiritual counsel; as one less benighted, I refused to accompany her. I would make us rich writing fiction; on Saturdays and Sundays, all weekend long, even after school during the week, I would furiously write—sometimes one story a week, sometimes two, sometimes three or even more. I would make us rich, yes—but even more than that I was playing God, creating little dream worlds in which I could impose the pattern, in which I could bring love to hate, peace to violence, unity to chaos. The paper, the pencils, and the typewriter ribbons took money from food, and the stories—ten-page thrillers, tales of suicide, rape, and murder, but all with happy endings—never sold; even I knew they were poor. Such a succession of failures only made me increasingly belligerent when my mother continued to ask me to attend Sunday services with her.

And so we would quarrel; I was incensed by her mild, even meek, determination to salvage my soul. Hiding behind the curtains of our second-story apartment—a small apartment in a frame dwelling on the fringes of the downtown area—I would watch as she stepped off the curb—*Careful of that car, little momma!*—and walked quickly, without a backward look, toward the Presbyterian church six or eight blocks away. But not until early morning—in those gray and heavy hours before sunrise when a child, awakening, can sense death waiting for others if not for himself—would I feel truly contrite, alone and frightened. I would tiptoe into her room, then wake her gently: "Mother, I'm sorry. Next Sunday I'll go." She would smile, clasp my hand and fall back into sleep. The clock by her bed stood on the miserable nightstand I had made.

This little idyll of my youth came to an end when we were no longer able to pay the modest rent for our apartment. My brother found other lodgings in town; eventually, after staying half a year in Chicago with my father and his second wife, I returned to live with my uncle and aunt; my mother—how it anguished me at the time!—took employment as a maid with still another relative, one insufferably rich and inexcusably distant in the bloodline. I need not comment on my intense loneliness, my bitterness; indeed, they soon began to vanish, for my uncle and aunt gave me the love and care of parents. And then, finally, the Depression began to retreat, to disperse the way a shrouding cloud does before the moist winds of spring; pockets slowly filled with cash again, madness departed the world, and my parents, as in my happy endings, were reunited. My father's second wife gladly resumed her widowhood, and at the second wedding of my parents I was the best man. Yet I still recall a letter from my mother, one written soon after she took her job as a maid:

> *My room is cheerful, in a separate wing above the garage, and with private bath. It is home for me though I look forward to the time our whole family can be together again. The photographs of you, your father and your brother are on my bureau; the nightstand you made is of course by the bed. . . .*

That wretched, miserable nightstand: wobbly, unpainted, without a drawer! I read the letter as many times as it was capable of imparting pain; I carried it in my pocket to my high school classes, it lay under my pillow at night. In my dreams I saw my mother's face in sleep at the moment before I had wakened her in my remorse; I had visions of tortured tables with twisted tops, with legs warped and wobbly as bent pins. And I tried to imagine her long bus trip from Michigan: where had she put the nightstand? Would the driver have argued that she couldn't take it, that it could travel with propriety neither in the luggage compartment nor in the racks? Later, I discovered that he *had* argued; and that she, in her mild perseverance, her gentle and maddening obstinacy, had won. It had occupied the seat next to her for the entire trip.

There it is.

The true adventure of a nightstand.

It is odd that I should remember it so fully this night, that all of the associations which once surrounded that nightstand should return with its image; that the nightstand should impinge so sharply on my mind that the recently completed manuscript on my desk fades in importance before it. Yet I had been wholly involved in that story while writing it. So involved that I locked my study door against my children, refused to bandage cut knees, made no response to bells, ignored my family at dinner and saw my neighbors only as characters in a proposed dream. There is a pleasure in locking out the actual world and in populating another world with bits of one's own self. It is, I have heard, a noble thing to do: to attempt an order and a pattern that will emulate God's own dream, if in smaller scope.

But one needs to escape from dreams, even though the real world may seem but a bubble in which nobility is hard to find. The dog, Black Judy, whimpers again: now she wants to go out into the night, to sniff the trees and shrubs in the park and graveyard, to relieve her bladder and intestines. Upstairs, my older boy—he is ten—may have wet the bed: though he has a wonderful pose of self-sufficiency, he is nervous and unsure at times and hence there are many sheets to hang on the line. He is deaf in one ear, the consequence of a severe case of mumps when he was five. It is, to be sure, a minor disability, one not affecting either his love for music—he practices the violin and the piano with great enthusiasm—or for such sports as ice skating and baseball. And perhaps the bad ear will keep him from military service. The younger boy, the seven-year-old, is attracted less by baseball than he is by butterflies; for that matter, he watches intently the doings of all small forms of animal and vegetable life—the flowering plants, the birds, the insects. Still, he is concerned, as is typical of children his age, with death. When spring comes, he will pick every flower he can; yet he intentionally has killed no breathing thing; last summer, on our walks in the deep gorge behind the park, he would shout loudly to scare the fish away whenever we saw in the creek the earnestly patient men with hip boots and poles. But his concern with death is not wholly unselfish. "If I am good, I will live again after I die," he says; it is a belief he has picked up at school, either from other children or from a young grade-school teacher desperate for some new means of discipline. "And if I'm good when I live again, I'll live once *again*. Three lives," and he holds up three fingers.

Black Judy jumps down from the couch and lifts her paw into my lap. I put on my coat, snap on her leash and snap out the light; I walk her first in the graveyard and then in the park. "Heel," I say, marching this way and then that, for she is wild as a puppy and must learn discipline and control if she is to survive both the busy thoroughfare before our house and the wrath of the gardener down the block. "Heel, sit, stay, come." She tugs at the leash, nearly pulling me over into the snow. *"Heel,"* I say sternly, now walking the asphalt road that circles the filtration plant.

Obedient to my cry, she trots now by my side, her front paws even with my feet; her ears up, alertly she awaits the next command. I look at the stars: Andromeda has long since vanished over the northwestern horizon, and Orion touches the land to the west. Except for the Big Dipper, the stars above me form no familiar constellation; and yet they are everywhere. The night is frigid but still, and the air hangs heavy with the cold: it magnifies the stars and makes them shimmer as through water. And as I watch, the dog pacing at my side, they form into dozens of constellations, each one a perfect table, each a flawless little nightstand. It is, I suppose, my imagination. But I marvel, and am pleased. And, as I circle the filtration plant for the second time, I think I see my neighbor the dean plodding ahead of me, his cane tapping into the ice; upon the hill across the road, ghostly in the starlight, my other neighbor glides softly among the tombstones.

1961

An Essay on a Premonition and Eight Heads

2

WE SAY OF PREMONITIONS THAT THEY are false if the sense of foreboding is not subsequently borne out by some disaster in our lives. Yet the premonition can be an experience in itself, one as true as any other kind of experience, and—for the period that it lasts—as much a horror to us as the actual dark body, its arms and legs still flailing with life, as it whistles down from the evening sky; as much a horror to us as that moment in time when the still-oblivious child steps toward the onrushing fender.

I have never observed a body fall out of the sky, nor have I seen a child hit by a vehicle. Last Easter morning, while driving to the drugstore in Ithaca, the small upstate New York community in which I live, to pick up my Sunday *New York Times,* I saw in the middle of our street the scattered jelly beans, the brilliantly green artificial grass, the smashed red-and-yellow straw of an Easter basket. The ambulance had already departed; the crowd was beginning to disperse. I am glad I was not a helpless spectator at that accident.

As for the man falling out of the sky, we have, of course, the story of Icarus; but what came into my mind was a brief newspaper account I read five or six years ago. It concerned a bride and groom from a relatively isolated and mountainous region of the mid-South. Following the wedding ceremony, the young couple boarded a plane that belonged to a small local airline. Judging from what followed, I assume it was the first time either of them had been aloft. I can imagine them seated together in that vibrating old DC-3. The bride wears an orchid, which she self-consciously hides with a gloved hand; the groom attempts to be at ease despite his wedding suit and new shoes. The flight out of the mountains is perhaps a bit rough; at any rate, the bride turns pale. The groom asks her if some water might help. She smiles at his solicitude and pats his hand gratefully. But how does one find water on an airplane? The stewardess is busy, and anyway he is not certain—for he is a hardware or grocery clerk, one who has never depended on assistance—if it is proper of him to request her aid for such a little thing. He imagines that paper cups are available in the lavatory. He rises, walking toward the rear of the plane with a careful nonchalance. There are two doors. He doesn't wish to show his ignorance by pausing in perplexity before them; he turns a handle. The door springs away from him as if God himself had commanded it to open. Before he has a chance to be surprised by the sudden roar of the motors, by the vast expanse of the wing, before he sees the faint lights flickering in the darkening void beneath—before he can respond at all—he is sucked silently out of the plane. He plummets down, down and away.

The news story told, as news stories do, of the bride's grief and prostration, and of the proposed investigation. Why was the door unlocked? Who was to blame? The examiners would seek out the answers, would find the logical explanation. But the account—much shorter than my own—also spoke of an old man, the only spectator of the tragedy. He was caretaker of a village cemetery somewhere in Tennessee or Virginia; his work completed for the day, he had just locked his mower and his shears in the shed. He is reported to have looked upward because of a faint whistling in the air. First he saw a moving star, the plane twinkling in the light of a sun already below the crest of a distant mountain, and then he saw a figure tumbling out of the evening sky—the torso somersaulting, the arms and legs swinging. The body landed just beyond the cemetery fence; it had to be dug from the earth to be removed to its proper burying place.

I have thought of this story, always unexpectedly, a number of times, and I suppose the years have altered it to suit my moods. Still, it has consistently been the caretaker whom I think of first; I can identify myself with him in a way I cannot with the bride and groom. The body fell rapidly, of course, yet it must have seemed to the old man to have been coming toward him through all eternity. He was, after all, the only person who—if he but knew *how*—might have averted the death. As I see him at that moment, he is helpless and human; he can do no more than stand where he is forever, breathing in the dampness of the evening and the scent of the grass he has cut, his hands held up not only for that impossible catch but to ward off the blow.

A premonition can fill us with the same sort of helplessness and dread that I find in this old caretaker. But since a premonition takes place wholly within the gray confines of the solitary mind, there can be no scream, no final thud. There is nothing but quietness, a quietness mitigated only by the soft and secret hum in our ears that tells us yes, we exist, we live.

I remember, as a soldier in World War II, crossing the Rhine River on a pontoon bridge soon after the far bank had been secured. As I drove across the bridge, I saw on the approaching shore what I took from the distance to be a haystack beside a farm dwelling—a serene and bucolic scene, surely, to find in the midst of warfare. The stack, however, was composed of human bodies. I felt no response. The stack could have been a dung heap, for within me there was no adequate feeling upon which I could draw. An hour or a day later, I saw a cow, one of its hind legs blasted away, lying swollen in a pasture that had become a minefield. Suddenly I felt not only pity and shock because of that animal but a kind of love as well. I report this because I believe it to be the normal response of most people; most of us are moved by what we can encompass. As civilians, we are concerned with the kind of teacher our first-grade children have, with the need for proper shelter and food for our families; we enjoy those responsibilities that we can meet.

In my own case, I like the sense of guardianship that a father has. It has something to do with my habit of taking brief after-midnight walks, for the walker is the sentry for all those in bed. There is a satisfaction in remaining awake, and alert, while the rest of the world sleeps. And even though one makes the same watchman's circuit of his house or block, there is always something to give fresh pleasure—a flurry of meteorites on one night, an impossibly bright Jupiter on another. If it is winter and snowing, the street light at the deserted corner is dimmed by the descending flakes; if the snow has been falling for a considerable period, one is apt in coming up the alley to find his feet slipping through the powder into the frozen prints made by his own boots a night or two before. I suppose that the after-midnight world can be our psychological bomb shelter; within it, we can be as protected as if we were snowmen within glass-ball paperweights.

On one clear and cold November night of the past year, the variety was provided by an exquisite auroral display. High over my head, a flaming crown drifted; a curtain of colors shimmered in the north, and on occasion a pale-red bolt would skitter up from the horizon to the perimeter of the flashing crown. I wanted quite urgently for my wife to see the display. The wish to share a spectacle in the night sky with a wife rudely awakened from slumber has its ridiculous aspects. "Whaz-zat?" she says, and before her puffed but dutiful eyes can be focused properly, the spectacle has vanished from the window. But on this night the display remained. In her nightgown, dragging a blanket behind her, my wife stumbled after me through the baby's room—our third child and third son, he had been born in March—and out upon the porch roof. We sat on the tin roof, hugging each other for warmth, the blanket wrapped around us, and we watched the colors vanish and reappear.

"Do you like it?" I asked.

"I like it," she said soberly, and I was proud.

It was very still that night, and we heard the faint honking of geese long before we saw them. And so, when we did see them, we were prepared for the patterned flight, for the high birds outlined against the pulsating streams of red and yellow and green. They entered the crown directly above us and passed into the dark, heading not due south but southeast; for they were following the waterways, and below our house, beyond the park, Six Mile Creek, heavy with autumnal rains, was rushing northwestward and over Van Nattas Dam. I had not heard the sound of the water until the geese flew by, but then the roar was steady and strong.

My wife held my hand. "I don't think I've ever been so happy," she said. "I'm happy enough to die."

And so was I; at that moment, I thought myself capable of soaring off that tin roof, to impale myself without regret on my neighbor's white-painted and most proper picket fence ten feet below.

Of the actual premonition that led me to this writing, what can I say? One sunny winter day, I was possessed with a vague terror of imminent disaster at home: a sense that my wife, or the baby, or the two older boys—perhaps all of them, even the dog—were at that instant nearing violence and death. I could hear a faint but clear voice that implored my help—and I a mile away, drinking coffee at the lodge on the campus where I teach and talking with a friend about the prospects for the arts in the Kennedy administration!

One picture came into my mind that winter afternoon. It was a picture not of any person I knew but of a series of starkly classical heads, each a dazzling white (for they were apparently illuminated by a spotlight), outlined against a background as dark green as deep water. I remember thinking, So you're not enough, you heads; you don't finally help at all—without having any conscious notion of what I meant. And then desolation flowed over and into me, and the voice of my friend (speaking, I think, of Robert Frost) rose and ebbed and sank further and further until it was gone.

I said, perhaps interrupting what I had ceased to hear, "Do you believe in all that nonsense about extrasensory perception?"

"What? Yes. No. Of course not."

"It's nothing but nonsense?"

"Utter nonsense."

"But I've just had a feeling—"

"Something at home?" His kindly face showed concern.

"Yes."

"Then you'd better go."

And I took off at a wild gallop, between the tables and past the line of students waiting for hamburgers. My car was parked a continent away, across the bridge and down the road.

Those heads can be easily explained. There is, on the black upright piano in our house, a series of cheap plaster-of-Paris busts of composers (Bach, Schumann, Liszt, and so on)—prizes awarded by piano teachers to my two older sons for the completion of certain assigned tasks. There are eight of these white busts, and they are always lined up carefully, like soldiers at attention. The wall behind them is a dark green. When one of the boys is playing, the illumination from the lamp falls upon the white pages of the music, upon the white fingers touching the white and black keys, and upon those eight white and almost indistinguishable busts on the piano top. Seated at the opposite end of the room, I have often looked up from a book or magazine, and the sight of the boy on the bench as he makes the ebony box resound with noises—sometimes fine and assured noises, sometimes poor and faltering ones—is something that in recent years I have increasingly wanted to hold on to. Perhaps it is the glass-ball paperweight all over again, my own frozen footprints before me in the snow. Whatever it is, it failed me in the lodge that sunny winter afternoon as I imagined my family dead or dying.

Running in panic, I knew that I had run precisely like this on some other sunny winter afternoon. And this is part of any real premonition—the sense that it has all happened before and that it is destined to happen again. On the other day, five years before—we were in Kentucky then—the elementary-school secretary burst into my classroom crying, "Mr. McConkey! Your son has just been hit by a car!" and I, still quite rational, still the lecturer, asked, in booming classroom tones, "Where is he?"

"In the street, by the gutter."

And then I was running, running, and thinking, Thank God there's still one! I had not far to run, for the elementary school—the training school for college students in education—was on campus. But there was no child in the street by the gutter. I looked at the crosswalk; I looked before and behind and beneath all the parked cars. No child, no crowd about—only people bundled up and carefully walking past on the ice and snow.

"Have you seen a child lying in the gutter?" I asked. "A child hit by a car?"

"No. No, I haven't." A polite and fully considered answer.

"Have *you* seen a child in the gutter?"

"Don't worry, Mr. McConkey." The elementary-school principal came up to me. "Only a nasty bump, where his head hit the curb. He bounced back from the fender. Not run over at all. He came to; you'll find him at the infirmary. Perfectly all right. Somebody had parked at the crosswalk, you see. . . ."

I should say here that the child hit down the street from our house last Easter was—luckily—also thrown back by the fender, was also only knocked unconscious against the curb. Our dog was killed in that same street, soon after we moved from Kentucky to Ithaca. He was a cocker spaniel. A year or so before our first child was born, I had decided never to own that kind of dog. For one morning I had picked up out of the road a cocker that had just been killed; the pressure of the wheel had made the large and limpid eyes bulge from the skull, and that night I awoke from a haunted slumber determined never to have a dog with eyes that would do that. But then we purchased one, and ours was eventually killed in the same manner, the tire rolling over the chest. Picking *him* up, I did not find the bulging eyes monstrous. It struck me only that I was dreadfully fond of that little dead beast. I was fond of the dog—and I had known all along that this was to be his end. It was, or so I felt, as if every new accident, each new violence, were but an extension of an earlier error, that these mistakes reverberated backward to the first accident and forward to the last. You have to accept the possibility of spilled blood when you undertake the care and feeding of a dog; there's a very clear end to it all whenever you give your affections to anything or anybody.

As I was walking with my friend to the campus lodge for coffee that winter afternoon, we were both enjoying the unexpected sunshine.

After several days of snow squalls and overcast skies, the air had quieted in the morning hours, and now the world was clear and crystalline. The powder from the most recent flurry lay on the branches of the elms and evergreens and occasionally would fall in soundless little avalanches. Dark beneath the snow-weighted evergreens, the path to the lodge was even more pleasant than usual; it drops through the woods in a leisurely curve and then, suddenly open to the sky and the sweep of the lake, crosses the gorge below the lake by means of a footbridge. At the opposite side of the bridge, overlooking the lake, is the lodge, and here the path ends.

We came out of the woods to see the sun sparkling upon the frozen lake. It had been cleared of snow along the shore, and skaters—students, young children, even a few elderly townspeople from whose frail shoulders bulky shawls were flying backward—glided in a fluid clockwise movement around and around and around. A dog flew down the ramp and sailed serenely on its haunches between two or three pairs of steel-shod feet. Laughter came up in thin and sporadic bursts; a loudspeaker emitted magnified scratching sounds and then a scratchy waltz. I recognized some neighborhood children, and I wished that I were skating with my sons. It was the kind of wish that bursts upon one, so poignant that it catches one quite by surprise.

I was sitting with my friend, and we were speaking of the presidential inauguration and of the change in attitude toward the arts that the new administration might conceivably bring; we were both quite heady with some new joy. And then I heard the faint voice calling for help, and I knew that whatever I might do it would not be enough. I felt myself become an elongated tube, no more than a drinking straw, one filled with nothing but emptiness and a hopeless love for my doomed wife and my three doomed children; yes, and even for my doomed and spayed German shepherd, who had replaced my dead cocker spaniel. It was then that I had fled, bearing in my brain eight white and classical heads and some odd sense that I had made this identical dash before.

There is but one item I wish to add, by way of possible explanation. A few nights earlier, I had attended an informal lecture in the basement of that same campus lodge. I thought the lecturer—a visitor of indeterminate age from New York City, a writer of fiction and social criticism—an odd mixture of melancholy and rapture, one whose young voice called for vigorous social and political action even as his old Jewish eyes made it clear that the game was up. That night I happened to be unusually fatigued; perhaps he was not as I saw him at all, but as he spoke I could visualize him at the Day of Judgment—a silent and motionless prophet, tears streaming from those old and pitying eyes as he saw his prophecy of destruction come to pass. The history of the past two hundred years has been a march toward annihilation, he told us. Western progress—so we know at last, looking back from the precipice in amazed recognition—has been all along the intensification of a death wish. Willfully, each age chooses its own afflictions: the neoclassicists selected gout; the romantics chose to cough themselves to their graves from tuberculosis; our inward ailments today take cancerous forms and are projected outward as a monstrous fungus, an ever-rising mushroom. Here is free will with a vengeance; as a species we wish to die, and die we shall. Is this actually what he said? I do not know. Midway in his talk, the lodge communications system—inexplicably, for but a moment—burst out from every hidden ceiling speaker with the wavering notes of a clarinet or trombone.

I do know that on my foolish drive homeward on the sunny afternoon of my premonition I tortured myself with recriminations. The car slipped on the ice as I came down the first of several hills; I nearly ended up against a lamppost. "Now, look here, James McConkey," I told myself severely. "Your fear that somebody *else* is dying—that's very cunning, isn't it? You're simply using it as an excuse; you want to kill yourself." And I slowed the car to a crawl. Then I said, "So you don't want to go home, after all. You don't want to find out that your wife and your children and your dog are perfectly all right. It's *their* death, not your own, that you lust for. You're secretly in love with Joan Kent."

The recollection of that name was odd—I hadn't thought of Joan Kent in years. Joan Kent had been a classmate of mine in the fourth grade at Pulaski Heights Elementary School, in Little Rock, Arkansas; the daughter of a clergyman and the terror of the playground, she had once lifted the bully of the class—a tough urchin, usually barefooted, who swore and smoked cigarette butts—and tossed him easily over her shoulder. I had always felt myself stronger than that bully (for I didn't smoke), and capable of handling Joan Kent. In the name of all boys, I had challenged her; but she had tossed me just as easily. The wind had been completely knocked out of me. I can still remember my inability to move, the look of the gravel at eye level, and the laughter of the children around me.

And so, driving home, I accused myself of wishing for the death of those whom I loved so that I could marry that little amazon! Such an accusation could only increase the sense of my loss, and tears of self-indulgence trickled down my cheeks. I *knew* what I was doing. I despised the bulging eyes and white face I saw in the rear-view mirror, and said in anger and hostility, "You stupid, self-pitying fool! You grotesque clown!"

At home, of course, nothing was wrong. The dog met me at the top of the cellar stairs (from the carport, one enters our house by way of the basement) and licked my face as I ascended, a trick she delights in; my wife was feeding the baby in the kitchen; the two older boys, watching television in the back room, ignored my greeting. Apparently, one of them had just finished his practicing, or—more likely—had stopped in the middle of it, for in the living room the gooseneck lamp illuminated the disordered sheet music on the piano and the little row of plaster-of-Paris busts. I picked one of them up and was looking at it when my wife came into the room.

"What's wrong?" she asked quietly.

"Nothing, thank God," I said. "I thought, at the lodge, ten or fifteen minutes ago—I thought that maybe you and the boys were dead, or were about to die. Something of that sort, I guess." I was ashamed.

But she understood, and without another word we held each other tightly. From the back room came the magnified clatter of hoofs and gunfire; from the kitchen the rising wails of an indignant and still-hungry baby.

Well, that is my experience, my premonition. It is the premonition of a fairly stable citizen, one who pays his taxes and is in debt only for his car and house. If my sleep is disturbed on occasion by the figure tumbling and whistling down from the sky, still I am never the person falling through space from that distant and moving star; I am no more than the old caretaker standing solidly, if helplessly, on the ground. The only time, to my knowledge, that I *honestly* wished for death was that moment I sat on the tin roof with my wife, watching the geese outlined against the aurora borealis and hearing—after their last faint honk had vanished—the seasonal rush of water over Van Nattas Dam.

The moment or eternity of panic has done nothing to alter such a habit as my nightly walks. Returning from them, I always look at the eight white busts of the composers on the piano top before I switch off the light and go upstairs. Whatever part they play in the psychological bomb shelter, I know now that they offer no real escape, no total illusion; the moment of panic and loss has told me that, and in a way I am glad to acknowledge this fact. Lying in bed, sometimes I see them, shining in their whiteness, patterned not in a row but in a V, flying high above, one with the geese; and then I fall asleep.

Stromboli in Ithaca

3   I AM FOND OF STEWART PARK, A MUNICIPAL
recreational area at the head of Cayuga Lake.
The park has a golf course, a beach and bath-
house, tennis courts, a children's zoo with peacocks and monkeys and
goats and deer, a pool for fishing and another that is a home for local
ducks as well as a resting spot for those in transit, a picnic pavilion, a
ball field, swings, and seesaws. In addition there is a small merry-go-
round operated under franchise by a man from out of town who sets
it up every spring and takes it down every fall, and who, during the
summer season, lives in a little trailer behind the bathhouse. From
most places in the park one gets a view of the lake as far as Portland
Point, five miles away; here the lake bends to the left. At Portland Point,
a grouping of white grain elevators rises against the green hills like a
monastery or a hotel on the Mediterranean. And in the summer, no
matter where one happens to be in the park, the merry-go-round
music can be heard.

Late one Saturday afternoon in September of last year, I thought
that my children might like to visit the park once more before cold
weather set in. My oldest son, who had entered the seventh grade a
week before, lay on the living room couch, munching an apple and
reading his social science text in the pale afternoon light. "Do you want
to go to Stewart Park?" I asked.

"What for?" he replied, without looking up.

He had never answered that familiar question in such a manner before, and I didn't know what to say. "To *see* it, I suppose," I finally replied.

"Swimming's over," he said. "Rob says the monkeys are gone for the winter. Who wants to look at a duck?"

"*I* do, Lawrence Clark," I answered. "And I imagine your mother does, and your brothers John Crispin and James Clayton as well." Whenever one of my children irritates me, my language takes a formal quality, and I refer to all of my boys by their first and middle names in an attempt at counterirritation. "I never knew that you *liked* homework so much it would keep you from Stewart Park," I said. "You *could* do it tomorrow."

"For Pete's sake, Jim," Larry said, "don't you want me to get into college? I promised Rob I'd play football tomorrow."

Rob is a boy in the neighborhood. Larry preferred football with him on Sunday to a Saturday visit to Stewart Park with me. Immediately there came to my mind one of my most pleasant memories. I had spent a morning with Larry at the Brookside Zoo in Cleveland, Ohio, when he was not quite three and was still our only child. My wife and I were spending a week with relatives in Cleveland, but that morning she had an appointment to have something done to her hair; she had suggested that Larry and I visit the zoo—for the day was a grand one, bright and crisp—while she was occupied at the hairdresser's. As parents do, I enjoyed Larry's excitement and pleasure at the monkeys, the performing elephant, the walruses, and the bears. He wanted to ride a pony so badly that I lied to the attendant about his age; he trotted the pony around the ring with all the assurance of a six-year-old, and I was inordinately proud. And he rode the miniature train for six trips, while I waved goodbye to him from the toy depot as many times; we pretended he was off to some remote region, in another state or another country. "Goodbye, Jim!" he would shout. "Goodbye! Goodbye!" and, though he was bound only for a tunnel beyond the bushes before looping back to me, I felt sad each time the little train honked and chugged away, and I greeted him with delight on his return. Now it was more than nine years later, and how could I expect him to remember any of the events of that day enough to wish to relive them with me at Stewart Park?

"Study away, then," I said. "Keep your shoes off the couch, put the apple core in the garbage, and don't turn on the television as soon as we're out the door. Your brothers are going to have Popsicles at the refreshment stand."

"Oh, cut it, Jim," Larry said, laughing. "The stand is closed for the season."

By the time my wife had changed and dressed eighteen-month-old Jimmy and I had located Cris, who was nine, playing by himself in his little village behind the carport, the sun was falling rapidly behind West Hill. Clearly it was the hour for dinner, not for a visit to the park; but my conversation with Larry had made me inflexible. We were off for a frolic, no matter how much we suffered.

Stewart Park was deserted, and dark beneath its large elms and willows; a sharp autumn wind swept in from the lake. Above Portland Point the sky was gold, but the sun had already vanished. "Where is the bread?" Cris asked; he always fed the ducks on our visits.

"Did you bring the bread?" I asked my wife.

"Did you?" she asked me.

"The merry-go-round's still up," I said.

"Shhh," she said, meaning that I shouldn't raise hopes that would be dashed; for it was without lights and the operator was not in view. "I'd rather feed the ducks," Cris said; but we wandered aimlessly toward the merry-go-round. Suddenly all its colored bulbs blazed on, cymbals crashed and horns blared, and the operator emerged from the darkness of the central machinery. "You folks want a ride?" he asked cheerfully. "The very last ride of the season."

"Why, yes," I cried: it seemed a little miracle. Cris, who had ridden that merry-go-round for five seasons, climbed upon the horse that always had been his favorite. I helped Jimmy straddle another, and then stood by his side; my wife watched from the entrance gate. The bell clanged, the little merry-go-round trembled and slowly began to revolve.

"Ay-eeh, ay-eeh," Cris shouted, bouncing in the saddle; his legs, much too long for the stirrups, nearly touched the floor. "You stop that jumping, hear?" the operator said in a bored voice; after collecting the fares and starting the machinery, he had climbed from the platform to stand by my wife. Jimmy laughed as his horse began to rise and fall; it was his first ride on the merry-go-round, and his eyes glowed. He gently touched the red plastic of his horse's mane, he looked from one colored bulb to the next, he stared at the glittering mirrors and listened intently to the scratchy thumpings of the drum. For a moment I was back at Brookside Zoo, and Jimmy was Larry astride his pony. As the platform revolved, I saw dark stretches of the park, the white faces of my wife and the merry-go-round operator, and the open expanse of the lake, blue and speckled with gold all the way to Portland Point. The sharp wind and the deserted park told of autumn, the grain elevators at Portland Point were no longer white but a ghostly gray as they began to merge into the blackness of the distant hill; and yet, as I rode that turning and vibrating platform, one arm around my son and the other raised to wave as the smiling face of my wife drifted again and again out of the dark toward me, it seemed that everything that mattered was free from time and that "The Tennessee Waltz" was the loveliest, most liberating carousel tune I ever had heard.

But Jimmy was too young for the little merry-go-round and Cris too old. Jimmy suddenly began to scream, and I held him in my arms until his fright ended and I could sit him beside me in one of the gaudy chariots. Cris, needing to make of the ride a game, cried again, "Ay-eeh, ay-eeh," a television Indian; and once more—for he rarely remembers commands—he bounced wildly in his saddle. "Didn't I say stop that?" the operator said in the same bored voice; and then a timing device shut off the motor and the merry-go-round slowed and stopped. As I dismounted from the platform, holding Jimmy, the operator was saying to my wife, "The older boys *always* bounce and the babies *always* cry"; and, as I released Jimmy and he began to toddle briskly right back to the platform, the operator added, "And cry or not, back they always go. See you folks next year."

We had moved no more than half a dozen steps when the colored bulbs were abruptly extinguished; we were left in a black and silent park, and I was fatigued and nearly forty. Driving homeward, I thought the experience odd, but destined for some dim mental bin. Yet a re-membered merry-go-round—something so trivial as that—can be to the mind a glowing seed, a whirling nebula which, drawing to it a series of other experiences, gradually becomes the world as we know it.

Toward the end of the school year, I quarreled with my oldest son. The quarrel came about as a result of an assignment—a theme on the subject "Why I Should Buy U.S. Government Bonds"—given to Larry by his seventh-grade English instructor. He was at work on it, in my study, when I came home one day; he completed it by supper time, and brought it to the table for me to read. It began: "Not long ago our country faced a dilema"; and I pointed out to him that he had mis-spelled a word in his opening sentence.

"Never mind," he replied. "It's the content I'm interested in."

And so I read on. The dilemma concerned the resumption of nuclear testing, a subject much in the news at the time. The United States had not wanted any more tests, but Russia—though *she* was also on record as opposing tests—had resumed them. As a consequence of this betrayal, the United States had been forced to test again, too. Only by improving our nuclear missiles could we maintain our freedom. Since it takes a great deal of money to build and test new nuclear weapons, Americans should invest in government bonds.

"What do you think of it?" Larry asked. He and I were the only ones who had not started to eat.

"The handwriting is good," I replied. "The ideas are clearly ex-pressed. I guess I would have to say, though, that I disagree with it."

"Why?"

"I disagree with it *wholly*. I think it's wrong from beginning to end." Whenever I become emotionally involved, my voice begins to tremble in a manner I detest, and I make sweeping condemnations.

"I don't see why you think that," Larry said. He had become shy, as he does when he is hurt; and he spoke hesitantly. "Isn't our way of life good, Jim? Don't we have to defend our freedom?"

"Yes," I said, "but listen. You listen to me. I read about this Nobel Prize winner—"

"You don't need to get angry at me," Larry said, for I was shouting.

"I'm not angry at you," I shouted. "I'm angry at this Nobel Prize winner, this man I thought so fine and humane. He said—it was in the paper—he had been opposed to further testing *before,* because we had been ahead of the Russians and it was to our *military advantage* to press for a ban. But now that they've caught up, he gives his blessings to such activities as Easter tests on Christmas Island. And if it's to our military advantage to blow up Easter Island next Christmas, he'll approve of *that.* Does this represent our policy? Is this why you want me to buy government bonds?"

"But suppose we hadn't tested, and suppose then that Russia got ahead of us?"

"The trouble with your essay, Lawrence Clark," I said, "is that it represents a gross simplification of the problem. Look at what you've written"; but before I could read anything aloud, he had grabbed the paper from my hand and was running upstairs to his bedroom.

My wife said, "Now he won't eat any dinner."

"Neither will I," I said.

Jimmy was laughing from his high chair at all the disturbance I had made; Cris was looking dreamily out the window as if he hadn't heard anything.

By the time I came down for breakfast next morning, Larry had already left for school. "He woke up at six," my wife told me. "I heard him go down to your study. He rewrote his whole essay."

"Did you see it?"

"No," she replied. "He wouldn't let me look."

"I suppose he would have gotten a better grade with his first version."

"He may not want to play with you so much these days," my wife said slowly, "and he may argue more, but he respects you. He respects your judgments."

"Oh my God," I said, "*my* judgments. What good are judgments when there are no valid answers?" And it seemed to me then as if I were not a real father—one who establishes some guiding principle or truth for his family—but rather a character in some domestic drama whose actions and words are intended simply to reveal his nature as the play works out to some predetermined end. I asked my fellow character, "Did Larry eat his breakfast?"

"He had an egg."

"Well," I said, "thank God for that."

As a father, I am a confusion of opposing impulses. If I would like Larry to be two or three once again, a child on a zoo train, still I have often been irritated that Cris seems such a free spirit, one unaffected by adult notions of practicality. In the weeks following my quarrel with Larry, Cris dreamed away for hours in the miniature village he painstakingly had constructed in the hidden strip between our carport and the neighbor's barberry bushes. He wanted, he told me, to soak seed in some chemical solution so that in the tiny gardens of his village he could grow stalks of corn four or five inches high and tomato plants with fruit the size of peas; but the *idea* of diminutive plants was enough for him, and he could spend an afternoon sitting motionless by the bushes and contemplating such a marvel.

Normally, he didn't want adults trespassing in his village. Soon after lunch one Saturday, however, he sought me out to show me some temporary inhabitants of one of his buried houses. "Breathe soft, they tremble easy," he whispered as I bent down to peer into a doorway; and I saw a pair of timid eyes peering back at my own. "Mrs. Hall let me take care of Doug's guinea pigs for the afternoon," Cris said. "The Halls have gone out to look at their new house."

"That's fine," I said. "I'm glad Doug and his mother trust you that much. But do you think you ought to spend an entire afternoon guarding two guinea pigs? You *could* put them back in their pen after a while and ride your bike or play ball."

"Well," he said, "I thought I'd stay here until supper and watch them and read my letters." Cris, who mails in box tops and writes for free offers, is constantly receiving brochures advertising rose bushes, African masks, tropical fish, microscopes, and Florida home sites. His mail, all second class, exceeds the total received by the rest of the family.

He reached under the rock that served as his village post office. "You'll be amazed at this very unusual coincidence," he said, showing me a smudged envelope. "For only fifteen dollars I can get a three-volume set illustrated in full color telling how to remodel old houses."

"Why is that such a coincidence?"

"Don't you *know?*" He showed his dismay at my ignorance by looking at me above his horn-rimmed glasses, a mannerism learned from some teacher. "The Halls have just bought an old farmhouse they want to remodel."

"And you want to buy the set for them?"

"I think it would give them a very *distinct* pleasure."

"How much money do you have? Five dollars?"

"I'll raise the rest with a carnival or a flower show." His eyes gleamed, for he likes to plan such affairs as much as he likes to dream of tiny gardens.

"No," I said. "You couldn't possibly earn enough from a carnival. Besides, you had one last week. Besides again, it is much too expensive a present for a child to give to adults in the neighborhood."

"But Mrs. Hall has always been good to me. She trusts nobody else with the guinea pigs."

"It's completely out of the question."

"I'll make this one a combination show: flower exhibits, magic tricks, *and* a carnival."

"No."

"It *would* make Mrs. Hall very happy, don't you think? I know if *I* were buying an old beat-up farmhouse *I'd* be happy if somebody gave me a three-volume set illustrated in full color telling me how to remodel it."

I sighed. "Why don't you go play baseball? I can hear the boys down at the diamond."

"I think," Cris said thoughtfully, "I'll stay here and watch the guinea pigs and look at this letter some more. I'll figure some way out of this problem."

One Saturday night in early summer my wife and I watched—at least we made the attempt to watch it—the late show on television, an old Italian movie starring Ingrid Bergman, *Stromboli*. Larry was sleeping overnight in a tent in Rob's backyard, Jimmy had been asleep for hours, but Cris kept climbing out of bed to patter around the house. During an early commercial, he and I had quarreled in the kitchen once again about the three-volume set. Though the Halls had moved, he wanted to mail it to them as a surprise; and he wanted me now to advance him ten dollars against his 50-cent-a-week allowance. I had refused.

Since there are no television stations in our town, most residents—we are among them—pay a fee for use of a cable; the cable is connected to an antenna on a nearby hill. Cable-users thus can see and listen to the greater world beyond Ithaca through the choice of any of five channels. The channel bearing Lawrence Welk is always sharp, but the one bringing whatever it is I have been waiting all week to view is often blurred. Snow fell constantly on Stromboli, and errant voices peddling detergent spoke out, apparently from behind rocks or walls of houses on that tiny Mediterranean island; but my wife and I, encouraged by beverages, concentrated on Ingrid.

As well as I could determine, her role was that of an American who somehow finds herself in a camp for displaced persons in Italy after World War II and who marries a Stromboli fisherman in order to escape the barbed wire. But the tiny island is impoverished, the inhabitants nourished by traditions alien to the bride. Ingrid, who has known the luxury and culture that can come by calculation to a beautiful woman, is miserable. Neighbors gossip to her husband about her behavior; and nobody can understand the sophisticated décor, abstract wall designs and a potted tree, that she brings to her little cottage. To intensify her desperation, the island is volcanic and intermittently rumbles away, breathing out steam and fire and dropping boulders upon the village. Ingrid, soon pregnant, declares her need for liberation; her husband nails the door shut to keep her where he thinks she belongs while he's off fishing. She escapes through a window, determined to climb the volcano in order to flee by ship from the seaport at the opposite side of the island. As she climbs, the volcano roars, obscuring her perilous path with its smoke and steam; as darkness descends, she faints near the summit. But morning revives her; the volcano is now passive and she has a grand view of the sunrise, the encircling Mediterranean, and the village she has left. Suddenly a vibrant voice—not one escaping from another channel, but a narrator affixed to the *Stromboli* sound track—exclaims upon all the beauty Ingrid sees. He is abetted by suitable background music and Ingrid's lovely smile. The narrator goes on to say—what follows is the roughest of paraphrases—that she has learned what we all must learn, that escape is impossible and that we must all accept with humility and joy the kind of life which is ours. Ingrid, apparently listening to the voice, nods, smiles again, and trudges back down the path to the village and her husband, and the movie comes to an end.

Long after I had snapped off the television set, my wife continued to stare at the screen. "Why was it," she finally asked, "that we wanted to watch *Stromboli* so much?"

"I heard a great deal about it when it first was released," I said. "I thought it was one of those classic Italian films everybody is *supposed* to see."

"Maybe," she said, "people talked about it back then because of Ingrid. Wasn't she making this film when she decided to leave her husband, the doctor? She fell in love with the director and they had a baby."

"Roberto Rossellini? I guess that's so."

"And finally she left the director for another."

"Yes," I said. "Poor Ingrid."

"Why do you say that?"

"I *like* her, that's why. I don't know why. Why did that movie have to be so crummy? I feel sad."

"So do I," my wife said. We finished our last drinks in the darkness. Out of our sunroom window, we could see the distant lights of West Hill winking off one by one as other residents of the little city turned off their television sets and went to bed. Our own house was completely silent—Cris, after working away at some project at the kitchen table while we had been watching the movie, had finally gone upstairs. At such an hour I am conscious of the exact whereabouts of my children:

Cris in the lower bunk in the north bedroom, Jimmy curled up at the foot of his crib in the south bedroom, Larry down the block in a backyard tent with a friend.

I suppose that when my wife and I brought our glasses into the kitchen, we were in an unusually responsive mood for the letter we found on the table. It was addressed to the magazine that had sent Cris the brochure on the books. Next to it was a dictionary, which he must have consulted often. "Dear Sir," Cris had written, "I read your ad on remodeling old houses with very distinct pleasure. The set costs $15, unfortunately I have only $5. Would you sell me 1 (one) of the books for $5, you can pick the one that is best. It is for a friend of mine."

The signature—"John Crispin" followed by the family name—was large and, I thought, defiant; and it struck me all at once as strange, as unfamiliar to a frightening degree. "Why, look," I exclaimed, "he's a *person*." I saw him, that stubborn little entity, that product of my wife and me, setting out into a world of mistakes and conflict and fear. I said to my wife, "Obstinate, but growing up without any personal choice even in his name. Do you remember how we named him?"

She nodded. It had seemed a great joke at the time. Just before his birth, we had debated possible names. I had recently seen the motion picture *Henry V* with Laurence Olivier, and had been intrigued by the sound of "Crispin." My wife preferred a less unusual name. We had just bought a puppy for Larry, and my wife said to me, "You can name the baby if I can name the dog first." "All right," I said; and she replied promptly, "I name the dog Crispin." Though my wife, having outsmarted me, was willing to be generous and allow me to name the baby Crispin after all, I compromised, using it for the middle name; but we soon began to call him Cris.

"John Crispin," I said aloud.

"You're not angry with him, are you?" my wife asked.

"Oh no," I replied. "How could I be? During the commercial, do you know what he said to me? That if I would loan him ten dollars he would tear down his village. He knows I think he dreams too much."

"His village and his carnivals have been a help to him," my wife said. "Remember when you and Larry argued about the bonds and bombs? He pretended not to notice, but he had nightmares that night. I hadn't wanted to tell you."

"Why did you *now*, then?" I cried.

"I had to rock him the way I do Jimmy."

"That's enough," I said. "I'm going upstairs this very minute and put ten dollars under his pillow."

"No," she said. "Ten dollars buys groceries for two days. And wouldn't it be better for him to take care of it his way? Let him send his letter." She reached for my hand. "I'll tell you what," she said. "Stewart Park's open again. Why don't we take the boys tomorrow? Jimmy can ride the merry-go-round and Cris can feed the ducks and Larry can go swimming."

"*If*," I said, "Jimmy doesn't cry and Cris still wants to feed the ducks and Larry agrees to come."

"Yes," she said. She turned off the kitchen light and we started up the steps, guided by the faint glow of the night lamp in the bathroom. "If I had my choice all over again," I said loudly, "do you know what I would like to be?"

"You'll wake Jimmy and Cris."

"I'd like to be the operator of that merry-go-round, the one who comes every summer in his trailer. I'd like it to play 'The Tennessee Waltz' the way it did last year. But I'd have to remodel it into some new kind of merry-go-round that satisfies *everybody*. You would be riding a horse and smiling, and Cris and Larry and Jimmy too; and there would be Ingrid without her volcano, and both my parents and your mother before she had her stroke and your father."

"When you've had too much to drink you talk like a child," my wife said tolerantly. "You sound just like Cris."

We entered the bathroom. "There are, however, a couple of things I like about that merry-go-round just as it is," I said. "One, you can hear the music from it all over the park; and two, from the merry-go-round you can see the lake all the way to Portland Point and the grain elevators. Did you ever notice how much those white buildings look like a monastery or a hotel on the Mediterranean?"

"The voice of the narrator," my wife said.

"All right," I said. "I guess any movie I would make would be crummy too. Let's clean the teeth we have left and go to bed."

And brushing with vigor in that pale glow of the night lamp, we made faces at each other in the mirror like hilarious children.

1962

Of Brotherhood
and a Dehorned Calf

4 AS A CHILD OF NINE OR TEN, SLEEPING restlessly on a humid Arkansas night, I dreamed I saw on the ceiling two round eyes, those of Christ, shining down on me. Waking at once, I realized the eyes were the ones which had gazed back at me from the bathroom mirror as I had cleaned my teeth an hour earlier. And I remember thinking then, But how do you know you aren't Christ? He is to be born again, isn't He? The thought so terrified me with a sense of my strangeness and isolation that to prove it wrong I whispered all the profanity of which I was capable; and I groped for one of my shoes on the rug and threw it as hard as I could through the glass of a raised window. When my startled parents came to the door, I told them I had dreamed of a thief at that window. The shattered glass, the profanity, and the lie made me *their* child once again; and, as secure in my mortality as I was in my errors, I slept.

Whatever the disadvantages of growing up, an adult doesn't need to engage in games or pretense to know, now and again with an intensity that startles him, the human connection. In the past few years, I have been aware as never before of all such moments of contact, both in the present and past. Three of these moments—the first from the past summer, the other two from earlier periods—have formed a pattern in my mind. Dissimilar though they are, they have become variations of the same experience. That experience, which ought perhaps to be a comforting one, has aspects which are disquieting in a way that—as a child in Arkansas—I would never have expected.

One quiet moonlit night this past summer, I suffered from that kind of sleeplessness which seems to thrive on all the remedies designed to end it: pills, hot milk, a close reading of the classified section of the old newspaper wrapped around the pork-chop bones and coffee grounds on the kitchen counter. When these remedies provided no cure, I opened the door to the liquor cabinet. Since it was near the end of the month, the whiskey was gone; but I finished off the gin and the last of a dusty bottle of crème de cacao. The moon brightened the window pane in the kitchen where I sat waiting without hope for drowsiness; an occasional truck roaring through the night shook the house and was gone.

I suppose I should have expected a good case of insomnia: after the children had been placed and replaced in their beds, after the eleven o'clock news, my wife and I had been discussing the world situation. While we talked, the radio, on low, moved from commercials to the *Archduke Trio;* but Beethoven's spiritual noises rang hollow, as if he had composed his tunes beneath a fallout umbrella amid the litter of toys in my backyard. Lying in bed a few minutes later, I raised myself to look out the window at the cemetery across the street: the mausoleums, the tombstones, marched in pale rows up the slope.

Then, from my kitchen stool, I heard the slam of a car door and the rise and fall of indistinct voices. Peering through the window toward the street, I saw the white bulb on top of a taxi moving slowly past, above the front hedge. In the night, one always awaits the expected noises; and so I listened for the thud of a house door. After a long interval, I heard instead a crash as if wood had splintered, followed by a subdued cry.

Of course I had to investigate; unsolved mysteries in the full of the moon only add to the worries of the insomniac. I saw old Mr. Yeager, who had moved from the neighborhood the previous year, seated on the walk before his former house; the moonlight gleamed in his white hair. He was the husband of the woman who had daily walked up the graveyard hill in pursuit of her health.

"Who fastened the gate?" he asked crossly as I approached. "The children are grown and gone, there is no need for the gate now. Don't you know—" and he looked at me as if I were the culprit who had fastened the gate, now collapsed, across the porch steps—"don't you know that an *insignificant* gate like that is a danger, not a help? Marie is married, and Tom is in England."

"Hello, Mr. Yeager," I said. And I felt myself a foolish intruder, standing before him in my bathrobe and slippers; for he was a man of such dignity and reserve that it seemed quite proper for him to be seated wherever he might want to be seated. Until his retirement, he had worked in some professional field: this I knew, for other neighbors had spoken vaguely of the important research he had directed several decades ago, before his drinking had become a problem. I had never spoken to him before. He and his wife had bought a smaller house elsewhere in town. I had seen him only infrequently in the years we had lived near each other, and only one occasion had seemed of much importance. That was the time an empty automobile had come careering down the street and over the curb, demolishing one of the pillars of the dilapidated porch and moving the whole front wall back eighteen inches. I remember the number of inches for he had come out the basement door—the car was jammed against the front one—with a ruler in his hand, crying in delight, "The wall's pushed back eighteen inches! Imagine that!" And his thin little wife had joined him, exclaiming over the damage. Both of them had taken such enjoyment in the splintered wood that their reserve—her illness had given her a queer detachment of her own—was gone; they had embraced each other. They were so devoid of cares, so fond of each other at that moment, that I admired them both on the spot. When the poor lady who had forgotten to fasten her brake finally found her car she could not apologize to them, they were far too pleased by the novelty to pay any attention to her stumbling excuses; and so she burst into tears.

This one moment in which I had seen him excited had always seemed to me the explanation of that self-containment which normally marked him, even on those occasions after he had sold the house when he would return to it—as he had this night—forgetting in his intoxication that he had ever left. He was simply a man of such generous nature that nothing could ever long vex or demean him.

As I expected, his crossness quickly vanished on that moonlit night this past summer; he gave me a charming smile. "I've done it again, haven't I?" he said. And he looked with approval upon the house that once had been his. "They've fixed it up wonderfully these new people, wouldn't you say?"

"Yes," I said; for the "new people" had altered the house and grounds considerably in the year of their ownership. When I had moved to the neighborhood, the Yeager yard had been a pleasant sea of tangled grapevines and tasseled grass; squirrels played upon the roof of the house, scrambling in and out of holes in the shingles. In every heavy rain the faint rumble that echoed down the block was but another slab of stucco tumbling from the exterior walls.

"We used to have a parrot," Mr. Yeager said. He tried without success to rise from the sidewalk. "The children named the parrot Ninotchka. Ninotchka is dead, Marie is married, and Tom is in England: or have I told you all that already?"

"I didn't know about the parrot," I said. As I was speaking, the porch light came on. "It's the new people," said Mr. Yeager, "the fixer-upper people. Hello, there," he cried. "I'm afraid I did in your nice little gate." A face peered out the door window, and then the light snapped off again. "Do you suppose they're angry?" Mr. Yeager said. "It's possible, I suppose it's barely possible, that they put the gate there to stop *me*." And he laughed.

I said: "I'll get my car. You wait here."

"It would be a pleasure," said Mr. Yeager.

And so I drove him home that night. He was a large man, well over six feet tall, and drinking had added to his proportions; I had difficulty in raising him to his feet and supporting him as we walked to the car. Within, however, he sat erect. "I had a bit too much to drink," he said. "This is extremely kind of you." He gave me lucid directions to his house. He'd had the lack of forethought, he told me, to buy a place on the steepest hill and the narrowest road in town: he imagined it would be best if we stopped the car at the foot of the hill and walked up.

Once he was out of the car, I took each of his great hands in mine. I walked backwards, shuffling along in my slippers (I had, however, put a pair of trousers over my pajamas when I'd gone into my house for the car keys: a gesture toward propriety that I assumed would have been foreign to him), pulling him up the hill after me. The little town was silent and the moon, now directly overhead, blazed in cold serenity upon us. The steepness of the slope put our eyes at the same level; we seemed to be peering desperately at each other with every awkward step.

"We must be more quiet," he whispered suddenly, though the only sound was the soft scuffling of our feet. "My wife is very ill." His eyes filled with tears. "My wife is dying and I am dying," he said. "We're dying everywhere and the children are gone." And he said: "I am so ashamed of myself."

"Hush," I said. "Hush, Mr. Yeager," still holding his hands; he could not brush away the little trails glistening on his cheeks.

"Yes," he said, "I am so ashamed of myself," and he lurched to the side with such force that we both nearly toppled into the gutter. "Why do I drink like this? Why?"

It was not until then that I felt lightheaded, giddy at last from the sleeping pills and the gin and the crème de cacao and the crisp air and the need for sleep. "If I thought it would protect them, if I thought it *right*, I would build them a shelter," I said, thinking of my children. "How am I to feel, Mr. Yeager? Should I ever have married?"

"I am so ashamed," he said again. "I should be a man of some dignity."

Looking into his glittering, moon-struck eyes, I knew him for what he at that moment was, my brother.

My memory, oblivious to calendars and clocks, rearranges the past for its own ends. One of the few specific dates I recall is that of my jeep accident: Friday, April 13, 1945. Franklin Roosevelt had died the day before; shortly the war in Europe would be over. Three of us—in addition to myself, a public relations officer and an artist were in the jeep—had been driving all day, this way and that, looking for an ingredient German printers referred to as *Fischleim.* We needed *Fischleim* in order to have pictures in the forthcoming issue of the divisional newspaper I edited.

On that Friday, our troops were advancing so rapidly they left pockets of German soldiers far to the rear. The roads we chose were frequently blocked. On one occasion, as we turned around before some recently felled trees, bullets whined past our heads: a group of Germans lay at the top of a ridge overlooking the barricade. We laughed, for our lives were charmed; we had taken on some strange exaltation from the inexorable forward movement of our troops. We were victors in search of *Fischleim.* In several towns German soldiers—squads of them—ran toward us, their arms upraised. They knew surrendering to be dangerous business, and so they wanted us to see them as harmless; smiling, they climbed like puppies onto the bumpers and hood. But *Fischleim,* not their future, was our concern. I couldn't see to drive, and gestured for them to get off.

Fischleim was obviously a rare commodity in Germany in the last days of the war. In our search, we spoke to a number of frightened municipal authorities. In one town, we were directed to the house of an influential citizen, a Nazi who had controlled the local printing establishments. The public relations officer—he was a captain, and Jewish—and I went to the door and rapped. The man immediately answered, as if he had been waiting for us. Although he wore a conservative business suit, his bearing was much more military than the captain's or mine. A tenseness in his manner, as if he were approaching his moment of truth and had rehearsed his role a hundred times, surprised us into silence. He looked long and contemptuously at the captain before raising his hand in the Nazi salute. *"Heil Hitler!"* he cried. And then, arms crossed and chin up, he waited for the sacred bullet.

Never had there stood before me such a willing victim, nor one whom I had more reason to despise: he was the walking and talking cliché, the inspiration for dozens of wartime movies. Yet for a terrible instant I saw the little captain in all his Jewishness, against which the Nazi and I—both of us blond, both of us blue-eyed—were defined.

Such a response comes, I think, from some compulsive desire in which the nay-saying is inextricably bound up with its opposite: we wish to deny the values we trust most strongly at the same instant we wish to reinforce them through guilt. Whatever its cause, my momentary betrayal infuriated me against that Nazi. And the fact that he could be *my* victim, as helpless as the millions of Jews herded into boxcars and gas chambers—this now made me wish to kill him as his sort had killed the Jews, as if he were a chicken or some other absurd fowl. But this feeling born out of revulsion, served only to intensify the identification with him. I was conscious of the loaded revolver at my hip and of the beating of my heart; and I was horrified at my confusions.

"God!" the captain said. We were both too embarrassed to look at each other; and we turned back to the jeep.

Ultimately we found the *Fischleim,* but our exultation had left; neither *Fischleim* nor newspaper mattered. We were at least a hundred miles from our divisional headquarters which, when we had left that morning, had been located at Sonneberg, but which by now might have been moved further onward, toward Bayreuth. Already it was late in the day, and we wished to drive as far as possible before dark. Rounding a curve in the narrow road, I came upon what might have been a child's trap—it was no more than a large and ancient pistol, its barrel sharpened to a point and its butt held firmly between a space in the bricks—too quickly to avert it. The front left wheel hit the spike, which punctured the tire as it lifted the vehicle. We spun off the road, and the other two occupants were thrown clear as the jeep began to roll. Neither of them was injured. The steering wheel, bearing the weight of the vehicle, pressed across my midsection before the jeep righted itself; something within me had broken, and I was flat on the ground and unable to move.

The captain must have stopped another vehicle, to request an ambulance; I know, at all events, that an ambulance eventually came. I felt no pain, and talked with the captain and the artist as we waited. The latter had managed to remove the pistol from the road, and he brought it for my inspection.

"Now, who would make a nasty toy like that?" the captain asked.

"Some German boy, some Nazi child," the artist said, "maybe the baby of that mother *there*," and he pointed toward a woman who was walking slowly across the pasture toward us. Behind her, the sun was setting; I saw her only as a dark shape until her shadow fell across my face. She wore a frayed and colorless smock, that great-breasted *Frau;* she was old enough—her hair was gray—to have given several sons to the Fatherland, yet possibly she was young enough to be bearing another. As she knelt heavily by my side, I saw that this fat German wife was crying. I thought her immensely fatigued: the burden of my injuries was but a small addition to those she already carried. Still, she made the effort to remember the school English she had learned years before. "Where," she asked, "where are you hurted?"

While I am a reliable reporter of her words, it is quite likely I am distorting her appearance and her emotions. A victim sees the sky above his head and a constellation of faces. From his still point he interprets his universe in accordance with his nature and the degree of his shock. As for my own view of myself, I saw my injuries as at least a partial consequence of my flawed self: I was guilty of more than reckless driving and a monomaniacal quest for an ingredient that would enable me to reproduce on pulpy paper a photograph of a woman's gartered thigh. And when the woman said to me, "Where are you hurted?" I saw in her eyes my own fallen state and I answered, *"Meine Beine"*—not because my legs *were* hurt (they weren't) but because I knew that phrase in German and wanted to reply in her native language. The captain was kneeling then too, trying to make her see and acknowledge that antique pistol: she averted her gaze, she would not look at it. I cannot of course speak for her, but for me we were mother and son, husband and wife, sister and brother.

Six years ago, when I lived in a Kentucky town tucked away in the hills of the Cumberland National Forest, I came to Ithaca—it was my first acquaintance with the region I now think of as mine—for a job interview. The "interview" turned out to be a two-day series of talks and parties. Though I enjoyed myself, I was exhausted by the visit. And the notion of leaving a little town in a Kentucky valley was disturbing, even though I had resolved upon escape. My wife and I, in search of permanence after years of attic apartments and house trailers and barracks in Ohio and Iowa, had bought a home in Kentucky, a small frame dwelling on a blind alley, a pair of paved tracks that served only three families. My hands—painting, repairing, building—had reached nearly every exposed part of that house. In the yard were two young fruit trees—one cherry and the other peach—that we had planted for our children. Upon my return by bus, as I listened to the crippled ballad singer who always sat in a wheelchair outside the depot, I felt I understood for the first time the people who stubbornly held to such an impoverished and remote region for generation after generation.

Kentucky, in that period between my acceptance of the new job and our departure for upstate New York, had never been so beautiful. Wild roses bloomed against every ancient fence that June, and the brown and confining hills moved back across the valley to become green and distant mountains breathing out mist at sunset. I suppose such a tidelike movement of the hills in spring is typical enough of the region; but I had never been so aware of it before. Nighthawks fell from the sky at dusk: I saw each tiny body and heard every rasping cry. A neighbor angered me by felling a hundred-year-old oak for the sake of his lawn and tulips.

Beyond the limits of that town, off the state route to Maysville, there is—or was then—a dirt road, not much more than a cart path; it is the kind of road that always attracts one because of an initial dip toward a creek followed by a gentle curving climb into the woods that makes wherever it leads a mystery from the start. Although we had taken many walks, my wife and I had never taken that one; early on an exceptionally bright Sunday, we decided to explore the road immediately, since another chance might not come before we moved. Larry was six, Cris only three; so the walk was quite leisurely, with many reversals in direction. But we finally managed the curve. Before us, at the edge of the wood, was an overgrown pasture, an orchard of gnarled apple trees much too old for bearing, and a small and sagging barn. We investigated the barn: cubes of hay and odds and ends of equipment told us it was still in use. My wife and I were so occupied with the children—Larry was attracted by a well-honed scythe and Cris by a rickety ladder leading to the loft—that the man was upon us before we were aware of his presence.

"Well, you're on time," he said, startling us.

"For what?" I cried, turning around; and I recognized Mike Caudill, the handyman employed, among other places, at the hardware store in town. I knew that the year before he had rented a long-neglected farm, hoping to augment his income with his own produce. Behind him I saw one of his sons, a boy of ten or so, holding the end of a rope and smiling shyly. At the other end of the rope, outside the barn, stood a calf, its feet widespread; its thin and milky horns gave it the look of a goat. My boys came running up, their eyes wide.

"Did you ever see a *dee*-horning?" Mike asked. Clearly his response to us was in part a result of his hospitality—he didn't wish us to feel ourselves as trespassers—and in part a result of his pride in the calf. Dressed alike in faded and torn overalls, he and his son were gaunt; the calf, however, was plump and glossy in the sunshine.

"No," I said.

"Well, then, you folks stand back and watch," he said, motioning us out of the barn. As we moved into the sunlight, he refastened the rope, looping it around the calf's makeshift halter and tying the ends to hooks at each side of the doorway. The immobile head of the calf gleamed in the sun, but the body was dark within the barn.

"Charley, you get the shears," Mike directed, and his boy obediently ducked under the rope and disappeared into the barn. "It's *his* calf, so he's to help," Mike explained to us; and then he smiled at our older boy, who must have been frowning. "Oh, you needn't worry," he said. "It don't hurt much."

But Larry protested: "It's a nice calf with the horns *on*."

"Charley feels the same way, but he plans to show the calf at Louisville," Mike said. The state fair, I knew, was held every September in Louisville. On Mike's lips, "Louisville" was an enchanted and faraway place, and I wondered if he had ever been there. "They won't judge a calf unless he's *dee*-horned," he went on patiently, "and Charley, he wants a ribbon. Charley," he asked, as his boy returned with the long-handled shears, "Charley, you want for him to have that ribbon bad, don't you?"

"Yes," his boy answered in a low voice. "He ought to have a ribbon."

I held Cris in my arms, and my wife put her hand on Larry's shoulder. I don't know what I expected: though I imagined dehorning a calf to be little different from, say, cutting my own toenails, I was still perturbed. Mike directed his son to hold the shears at a midpoint on the handles, and placed his own hands farther down; together, they slashed at the first horn several times—perhaps the edges of the shears were dull—before they could sever it, but the other one toppled more easily. Then they stepped back, though not in time to avoid the blood. A fine stream rose from each stump in a high and pulsing arc, staining their arms and overalls as it fell.

"There," Mike said tenderly to the calf, "there"; and the blood, gleaming in the sunlight, continued to rise like two fountains. Forced earlier into that position by the pressure of the shears, the calf's head remained tipped at a slight angle so that one stream arced away; but the other stream dropped back on the skull, trickling down between the eyes and matting the soft fur. Large flies floated from the old orchard to swarm around the two wounds. If I use such words as "forgiving" and "loving" to describe the eyes of that securely fastened animal, I am imparting to them, I know, qualities derived only from my own guilty response and the childhood memory of mildewed paintings in basement Arkansas Sunday-school rooms of a crucified Christ, head bowed and slightly askew. Still, it seemed to me as if those eyes so mildly regarding us all—Mike and his son, who had made the wounds; my wife and children and me, who had idly stood by—had joined us all beyond our will in a pact none of us could break; that though I was soon to be leaving Kentucky, I could never, in some sense, ever leave him, this man I barely knew, nor his son, nor their calf.

My children, of course, were fascinated by the spouting blood; my wife was watching them in apprehension. Mike was wiping the stains on his son's arm with a soiled handkerchief. "There, there," he said to his boy, who, while as motionless and silent as the calf, seemed dazed.

Then Mike said sharply, "It's bled clean, Charley. Get the grease." As we left, the two of them were daubing the stumps to stem the flow while the flies circled above all three.

Possibly brotherhood can be found in nobility of action and the virtuous cause; but I have discovered it—as these episodes suggest—chiefly in feelings of shared helplessness, impurity, and guilt. Caught in periods of depression by the sense not only of my own unsatisfactory nature but of the equally unsatisfactory nature of the world of men about me, I have thought brotherhood—that ostensible touching of wings—a circling flight from and back to the dark box of my ego. Angered with myself for crying Brother! whenever I meet up with my own flaws, I have on occasion thought, The blue-eyed puppet Nazi in your guts wants a comrade; and the game I play in consequence is quite different from the one I played as a child in Arkansas when I still needed to prove myself human. Lying sleepless in bed on warm summer nights in the north, I have tried to forget not only my own breathing self but all other living persons: I wish to remember neither old Mr. Yeager nor the German farm wife, neither Mike Caudill and his son nor even my wife and children. Perhaps—given the desire to escape the human contact—it is paradoxical and irrational that I should concentrate on the calf, the little animal that brought such contact. Still, in the struggle to separate the calf from mankind, to see him without his tormentors: in such a struggle lies the whole point of the game. If I am successful in my concentration, my two shut eyelids become one dark heaven into which that dehorned Kentucky calf slowly swims like a constellation, and from whose milky stumps the thin streams rise like fountains; he grows in size until he floods the farthest limits of my mind with his blood. But such a victory for unity is a cold and frightening one, and I am immediately brought from it by the deep breathing of my wife or the cry of a child as he dreams.

The Crossroads
Near Frenchburg

5 AT A CROSSROADS NOT FAR FROM FRENCH-
burg, in eastern Kentucky, there is (or was for the
years I lived nearby) a signpost inscribed NADA
and pointing up a little-used gravel road. For the first mile or two of
that road there is a scattering of unpainted farmhouses on the slopes
of the hills, but the road soon reaches a ridge and plummets into a
forested valley. The trees, mostly pine and oak, are second or third
growth; the road, in fact, is built on the bed of a narrow-gauge railroad
used to haul out the virgin timber in the days when this part of
Kentucky was continuous forest.

The community of Nada is not to be found, despite the signpost;
but eventually the road burrows for about half a mile through a hillside.
Wide enough for one-way traffic only, the tunnel is as damp as it is
dark; water drops from the ledges and rough roof and collects in
puddles on the rock floor. Its horn blaring, a car now and again bounces
through the long hole, headlights transforming the section immediately ahead into a tube of shimmering beads. In my occasional jour-
neys through this tunnel, bats always fluttered over the windshield;
and though both cars I owned when I lived in Kentucky were sedans,
I have dreamed of driving through the tunnel in a convertible, feeling
leathery wings and small protruding eyes hard as pearls touch my
forehead and back.

Beyond the tunnel, the gravel road connects with a narrow asphalt
road that parallels a shallow river; on the far side of the river, limestone

bluffs rise straight up for two hundred feet, perhaps more. The eroded tops of the bluffs are turreted and from the distance resemble a castle wall; odd needle-shaped forms, some standing out from the central bluffs, have been carved through the centuries by water and wind. The asphalt road soon merges with a highway. If the motorist turns to the left, he enters a state park where the major attraction is a high spine of limestone, a natural bridge. Here there are housekeeping cabins, a dining lodge, and a small lake for swimming where one can also paddle about in the little foot-propelled stern-wheelers that Kentucky park officials refer to as "dreamboats." It is a popular park, and the picnic tables are often filled on a summer's afternoon with vacationers from nearby Winchester and Lexington seeking relief from the heat of their offices and kitchens. One hears in the park the clang of horseshoes against stakes, the cries of children, the laughter of both children and adults; and the smell of burning charcoal is everywhere.

Six years after leaving Kentucky, lying in a familiar bed in an old New York farmhouse whose lovely strangeness slowly but daily dissipated like perfume spilled in the drawer of a seldom-used chest, I sat up morning after morning to recall that queer little signpost floating in summer heat; and then the whole journey, soaring bridge as well as confining tunnel, would recur. In its insistence and ambiguity, the memory disturbed: I had expected greater clarity and peace in a rural environment.

Each morning the memory vanished to be replaced by the static view I had purchased with the house and which I saw through a window of wavering and many-paned glass: a red barn with a gambrel roof and a rusted weather vane that forever pointed east; the straight rows of a cornfield, the tassels brown and dry in the sun of late October; a deserted asphalt road that disappeared beyond a gentle rise; along the rise, a line of nearly bare elm and maple trees; and in the distance the long blue spine of Connecticut Hill, the highest elevation in the county, the central section of its base hidden by mist. And each morning my wife—already out of bed, dressing silently as she planned what to do that day to exorcise the ghosts of the previous inhabitants—

saw me as I continued to look through that old window that nearly reached from floor to ceiling; and she smiled. "Isn't it lovely out there?" she said. "It's so lovely it doesn't seem *real.*"

"That row of trees," I replied. "It's like a cardboard cutout against the hill. I mean, it's all so three-dimensional you think it might be a trick."

So we had spoken to each other every morning since we had moved—the one time in our marriage that the act of leaving house for house had been determined wholly by personal choice, since I had made no change in employment—from the small stucco house in Ithaca; and so we would probably continue to speak until custom altered the vista into simply another aspect of the "real," of the comfortable commonplace. I had discovered that to sense the expected pleasure in a long-anticipated thing, one apparently has to question its authenticity over and over, has to imagine it as belonging more to the dreams from which it came than to the tangible world in which it exists. I was wary of thinking of my apple orchard or the pegged and hand-hewn beams in the basement and barn as anything other than fantasy, for fear that whatever I valued in them would vanish.

Yet I needed to *possess* my property. And I wanted to look at the house and fields and know, beyond the knowledge of ownership, the serenity I had felt just once before in my life, in 1944, and then only for two weeks. My infantry division was newly arrived in Normandy from the United States and I had not yet seen bodies stacked like hay or even the corpse of an animal. It was September, and the fighting was already in eastern France, near Nancy. Encamped in the garden of a château that, though it was no more than a mile or two from Utah Beach, had been untouched by the invasion, I had daily walked the little roads of an impossibly green Normandy. Cows grazed in pastures reclaimed from mine fields; cocks peered at me from dung heaps that, in the cool hours of the day, had already commenced to steam. Over the apple orchards and hedgerows, the motionless blimps, tethered above unseen ships on unseen water, gleamed in the sun. Once, with a friend, I walked to a seaside village. We stopped in a freshly scrubbed and deserted café where the girl who came from a back room to serve us

Calvados reminded me of my wife—I had been married three months then—when she tossed her long black hair and smiled and said, "Hello, *Américains.*" On the way back to the château at sundown, we met at a crossroads shrine a toothless crone resting from her burden, a large wooden bucket of milk. While two distant church bells began to toll the hour, she filled each of our canteen cups with milk still warm from the cow.

Though the rolling Finger Lakes countryside is, despite the corn-fields, nearly as parklike as Normandy, I could not recapture the peace of those first two weeks in France. As Larry and Cris boarded the yellow school bus in the morning—it stopped with a great squealing of brakes beside the mailbox at precisely 8:09—I would sometimes run after them with something they had forgotten, glasses or books or lunch money, and then I would continue across the road to the red barn. Its loft was a museum of found objects. There were clay jars filled with a sweet-smelling oil, rolls of barbed wire, a keg of nails with square heads, three sets of plow harness, rotting burlap bags stuffed with beans the color of mahogany, a cabinet containing nothing but a dozen yellowed sheets of paper. On each sheet was a name and a date, such as "Peggy, 6 Fbry. 1848." The handwriting was meticulous, the ink faded. I wondered what the dates meant. And were the names those of children who had once lived in the house or neighborhood? Or were they possibly the names of cows or other livestock? It bothered me that I did not know, that I could never know. Another name had been scratched deeply into a beam: "John D. Jonson." Each *J* was reversed, so that it looked like an *L*. On a workbench lay boxes of rusted eyebolts, plow points, hinges, and pieces of chain. A homemade carpenter's plane—the blade was missing—carved from a heavy block of walnut unexpectedly filled my eyes with tears.

Encased in its bubbling submarine of bone, the mind—drowning through layers of shimmering frond and coral, falling past metallic fish with whiskers and smiling lips—must construct new and startling combinations. My paralysis seemed a kind of drowning. I thought myself at times to be ill (I was superstitious enough to believe that the purchase of any lovely vision could easily lead to lingering illness or death); and whatever I saw or remembered became touched with a feverish significance. The pattern of moles on Larry's thin chest: I had of course seen these moles countless times, but to see them now, as the boy lay sleeping in the little room he himself had chosen for its bright wallpaper and its view of the pond, was to see the whole terrifying extent of a thirteen-year-old's vulnerability. They were tokens of mortal life and, as marks shared with me, of a heritage over which the child had no control; and they made me wish to stand above him the whole night, listening to his every breath.

And I remembered, quite without reason, a streetcar storage barn in White City, a suburban area of Little Rock; as a child, I had crawled beneath the large locked doors on a number of occasions to look at the trolleys—there must have been fifteen or twenty of them, little streetcars of such ancient vintage that the barn was like a museum—lined up in parallel rows within the dark building. The barn was situated next to a municipal swimming pool; and, as I moved from one dusty car to the next, I could hear the cries and laughter from the pool. Each car had a raised and open platform both in the front and in the rear, each contained twin rows of six or seven straw seats. Yellowing advertising cards with pictures of visiting concert singers and outmoded shoes and hats dangled on strings from the ceilings. I would climb to the platform where the motorman had once stood, by the great wheel that looked as if it belonged on a ship. I would look back at the straw seats, at the reds and yellows and blues of the tiny stained-glass ventilator windows in the raised section of the roof, at the advertising cards; and I would look forward and down until I could see the muted sparkle of the brass of the large lamp in front of the car. And then I would imagine that I was clanging the bell—there was a foot pedal that operated it—as I moved the car out of the barn and down the curving right-of-way that led from these suburban heights above the Arkansas River to the busy city itself. What a pleasurable feeling it had given me to imagine such a journey! There was enough fear—for the signs outside the barn clearly warned that, as a trespasser, I would be prosecuted—to thrill me deep in the belly; but I knew the barn to be neglected and that nobody would find me there, that I was really quite safe so long as I only stood silently in the gloom and *thought* of myself as a motorman speeding with my carload of startled passengers past stop after scheduled stop, clanging the bell furiously as the trolley floated down and down.

Now on the first long vacation of my life—for I could at last afford some leisure, even as I could at last afford, though not without scrimping, the kind of house I had always desired—I could think of no proper way to use my time. The previous owners of the house had renovated it; there was not a single room whose wide plank floors were not sanded and shining, whose walls were not smoothly plastered and papered with fresh colonial prints. The two bathrooms, upstairs and down, gleamed with tile and not a faucet leaked. So I filled box after box with apples, half of which would spoil before my family could munch their way to them, and aided my wife with her domestic chores.

While my sons were away at school, I missed them; but when, triumphant from their tussles on the wild ride home, they charged off the bus, I became alert and nervous, guarding the ancient house and barns against their mindless onslaughts. One afternoon Larry rolled a great multicolored stone from the corner of the red barn into the front yard. Upon discovering the change, I cupped my hands and called, "Larry, Larry," the name echoing and re-echoing among all the deserted barns; and when the boy emerged from the woods, breathing hard and his jeans full of burs, I pointed to the stone and asked coldly: "Why?"

He was bewildered. "It's *pretty*," he said. "I *like* it in the yard."

"Do you really?" I said. "How long do you suppose it lay there, where you found it?"

"I don't know," he replied. "Do you?"

"A century," I said, the sense of all those years lending a weary exasperation to my voice. "At least a century, for God's sake."

"Well, well," Larry said. "Now it's got a new place for another century." He put his hands in his rear pockets and swaggered. "For God's sake," he said.

"I'm sorry, I *really* am, if I've hurt your pride, Larry, but you should have asked before you—"

"You want me to put it back?"

"I'll help," I said.

"You needn't." And he tugged angrily at the stone. Crouched down, he looked small, a frail child with an unfair task; but I felt powerless to intervene.

Later that same day, just at dusk, my ten-year-old son burst into the house. "He loves me, he let me pick him up on the road," Cris screamed from the hallway. "Everybody *look*."

We ran to him: I from the living room, my wife from the kitchen. Larry, nursing his sense of rejection in some far corner of the house, clumped down the stairs trailing old comic pages.

"Who loves you?" my wife asked.

"My ph-ph-*pheasant*." Cris's eyes were dilated and his face flushed. He shrugged off the unbuttoned jacket he had been wearing like a cape. The bird, a young male, was pinioned under his arm so that its long and pointed tail jutted out behind the child while its head was pressed against Cris's chest. "He saw me coming," Cris said, "and he just *stood* there."

"It's not because he loves you," Larry said, being spiteful. "I know why he didn't fly away."

"Why?" Cris asked; he had become suddenly grave. "Why, Larry?" Cris had always trusted his older brother implicitly. I was afraid of what Larry might say, and so warned him: "Be careful, Larry."

"He ought to know the way the world is," Larry said. "He ought to be *told*."

"Told what, Larry?" my wife asked. At the time, her question, asked so calmly, seemed to me a rejection of my own responses, a betrayal of my desire to shield and protect. "Oh, now—" I began; but Larry was already speaking, enunciating his words with that unusual precision children use when they are attempting to control a growing rage: "The 4-H mem-bers at school get paid to raise the ba-by pheas-ants. They feed them. They make them in-to pets. Then the day be-fore the hunt-ing season starts, they turn them loose in the corn-fields.

When the birds see the hunt-ers, they sit still and wait, because they think the hunt-ers are their friends. So the hunt-ers bag their lim-it with-out e-ven *try*-ing. Bang! Bang! It makes the world hap-py."

"Is that true, Larry?" Cris asked.

"Ask *anybody*," Larry said. His nose twitched and his eyes blinked. Cris, horrified, clutched the bird even more tightly. The pheasant, glorious in its colors, peered out from the dark diamond of the eye not pressed against Cris's chest. Life to me at that moment was a speck of flame, a fragile and self-consuming thing; and I cried, "Oh, not so hard, Cris. You'll break his neck," and Cris in sudden fright released his hold altogether. The bird fell fluttering to the floor. Both of the boys dived for it, as did my wife, but I was the quickest. I held the bird, that little wild thing with the soft feathers and the brittle bones. "So," I cried, "so": I was beside myself with a senseless anger. "Stand back, all of you idiots," I cried to the wife and children that I loved; and they backed away in surprise. "I will hold him," I said, my voice as precise as Larry's had just been. "I will hold him safe un-til the two of you, Larry and Cris, find him a strong card-board box with a lid. You will put holes in the lid for air, and find some straw in the big barn for a bed. And your mother will find some ker-nels of corn for his sup-per. He will live in spite of you all."

And the three of them, very quietly, did as I commanded. The pheasant watched them depart; I knew that my eyes held the same beady intensity.

Without its black or dark-green shutters a white colonial farmhouse would be bare and austere; but in the country, where fields offer no impediment to the winds, each louver in each shutter whines and vibrates on all but the stillest of nights. One hears the sound of the shutters, the occasional rustle of what might be rodents behind the walls, the caterwauling of wild barn cats never seen in daylight, the cry of an owl in the nearest patch of woods and a more distant answering cry. And, after midnight in a house by a country crossroads, a car can be heard—the soft whir of tires on asphalt, even the sound of tappets—while it is still a mile away. Whether one lives on a busy city street or ten miles out on a country lane, one hears an equal intensity of sound; for the mind, which tunes out excess noise in the city, amplifies the sound of every stealthy movement in the country.

One night—less than a week after the young pheasant had been brought into the household—I lay awake, unable to sleep because of the incredible noise, watching the red lights blink on the Connecticut Hill radio tower six miles away. My wife turned restlessly at my side. I whispered to her: "I think I hear a rat somewhere."

"I hear nothing," she said.

I said, "There are rat holes in the storage room. I have put the poison in the plastic dishes. Is there anything more that I can do? Rats carry disease, they destroy."

She did not answer.

"I could have used traps instead of poison," I said. "The poison eats at their bellies, they go mad for water; they get outside by themselves if they possibly can. Their necks are broken by the traps, perhaps it is less cruel that way, but you have to carry the bodies outside. And if you have many rats, you may never be able to trap them all. I suppose the poison is better. Even though a rat may die behind the wall or under the floor."

"We are far out in the country," my wife said, "but I would be happy here—I could be very happy here—if you were. Why are you so afraid?"

"Afraid?" I echoed. "Am I afraid then?"

Again she did not answer. She turned on her side and almost instantly fell asleep, as if purged by her question. Later I too slept. I did not wait until morning to recall that signpost at the crossroads near Frenchburg. In my dream, though, the gravel road was gone; the old narrow-gauge track of the logging railroad had been returned to its proper bed. But in place of the locomotive and cars there stood on the track at the crossroads one of the little trolleys from my Arkansas childhood. And how attractive it was, how it appealed to me in my dream! The brass lamp gleamed in the sun; within the trolley, the glowing stained-glass ventilator windows made of the car a tiny portable shrine; and the track, sparkling in the pure sun and curving up the gentle hill and into the quiet woods, was an invitation, a promise that gladdened me. "Well, why not go then?" my wife said, at that moment standing beside me on the motorman's platform, a young woman who tossed her long black hair and smiled at me radiantly. "I understand there are boats ahead, as well as a soaring bridge." "But there is a tunnel," I said coldly. "Don't you understand about the tunnel? There are bats in the tunnel, and who knows how many deaths? How many children, how many birds?" My wife refused to understand. Smiling still, she nodded in agreement, as if what I had said were simply a confirmation of her innocent desire to make me happy, to give me the children I would love, to float with me in a boat and to stand by my side upon a bridge. "No," I said, for the trolley had commenced to move with a dismaying and reckless speed. "No," I cried aloud, and my voice awakened me. My wife, in a heavy sleep, breathed deeply in monotonous rhythm with the blinking of the distant red lights on Connecticut Hill. A breeze played briefly with the shutters. The darkness of the room was the darkness of the tunnel, the darkness of the universe; I felt suffocated and threw off the covers. The memories that came to me then were quite beyond my control, stinging images, until now hidden deep inside myself, of all the violent and meaningless accidents and deaths I had known: the wheels of a cement mixer on a flattened body, one finger of the victim's hand encircled with a plain wedding band and the nails of all the fingers carefully shaped and scarlet with polish; in a ditch a decapitated German soldier, the first corpse I had seen after my division left Normandy, the still-helmeted head cradled like a bloody child in his arms. And another memory, a different sort, of an impoverished Kentucky hill family—father, mother, and child—whom I had picked up on a country drive after their Model-A farm truck had broken down. My wife and I and Larry—a baby then—had sat in the front seat, the unwashed but gentle strangers in the rear, admiring the plaid seat covers and the softness of the ride and the smooth-cheeked smiling child in my wife's lap. "How old is the youngun?" the hill woman had asked; and my wife answered, "Two. How old is your boy?" "Why, four," the woman said, marveling. "But ain't he the bony and puny one, next to yours?"

These memories became my obsessions, parading before me again and again in the stifling dark. If one could only remain in the timelessness of some stasis, standing on the platform of an antique trolley or holding out a canteen cup for milk at a wayside shrine! At forty, at the traditional age of maturity and fulfillment, lying at last in the country dark, in a room of that ancient house for which my whole life had been the search, my mind swept restlessly like a broom into the very crannies of the past my house should resist, and I could remember nothing but disorder—injustices, brutality, and deaths not even given the meaning to be found in malice. In the clarity of my despair, I saw that I had husbanded and cherished whatever was precious to me until my embraces had choked it.

"Oh, Jean," I said in alarm, "oh, Jean, wake up, it wasn't the rat, the scratching noise."

"What?" she said, barely awake but startled. "What? What?"

"The poison," I said incoherently. "The pheasant." For I knew at that instant that the pheasant had escaped from its box in the storage room and somehow managed to find the glittering grains of poison I had hidden so carefully behind the immovable steamer trunk; the claws of the pheasant had scratched the floor as the brilliant bird with its burning belly ran in panic from one corner of the room to the other.

"Bird," she said. "Fear. Sleep," and she reached for my hand; and ultimately I too slept again.

I woke at dawn that morning, strangely relaxed and purged. My dreaming, my obsessive memories, had become part of my response to the house; it no longer existed as an ancient and incorruptible structure apart from myself. My paralysis had vanished. It was as if the terrors of the night had become embedded in the ceiling and the walls: I saw cracks in the plaster I had never noticed before, little curlings in the paper at the corners of the room. I felt a solemn tenderness toward my wife, and gently kissed her. I eased myself from the bed and walked down the long hall, past the open doors of the bedrooms where my children slept, and into the storage room. The pheasant lay safely in the deep straw of its pen, its head tucked into its body feathers for warmth.

"Thank God!" I said, and laughed at my own foolishness. And still in my pajamas and with my feet bare, I pattered downstairs, rummaging about and peering into every room. Some of the floorboards over the furnace had shrunk, there were narrow gaps here and there into the basement. The floor had settled at one end of the living room, causing the door frame to tilt crazily. I thought, I'll have to get at those things. I walked outside into the wet grass. The sun was shining on the red barn and the brown cornfields. Reaching above the billowing mists, the long blue spine of Connecticut Hill was at one moment an enormous and lovely bridge and at the next an enormous and all-consuming tunnel; and it seemed to me that it could not be one thing without becoming the other.

1963

A Report to the Trustees

6 WHAT FREEDOM A LONG TRIP SEEMS TO give! The exaltation that seizes us as the whistle roars and the dock with its clusters of well-wishers glides back and then swings away, a waving arm; or as the grass-lined runway suddenly falls and the whole busy earth shrinks and the horizon becomes a slope—what is this exaltation but the awareness of our immense possibilities of love toward the mankind left behind or below, of our infinite and unique potentialities? Travel takes us away from the compromises and passionate disorders of daily living and infuses us with hope and idealism.

Such a feeling of promise—of my ability to partake of the greatness, so often thwarted or crippled, of the human soul—remained with me throughout the first months of the half-year I spent in Europe with my family. I suppose the elation was a consequence not only of the trip abroad but of the writing fellowship I had been awarded that helped pay its expenses. And, too, I believed I had achieved, in the struggle to gain spiritual possession of that old country house we had bought the preceding fall, a maturity that could bring fulfillment to my middle and late years. Our house had the grace of unpremeditated wings, one of which was built as a court chamber in the days when judges rode their circuits on horseback. I had dreamed of such a house, rising like a white island from a sea of corn and wheat, for as long as I had dreamed of houses; and the image of it, as a secured object, lay comfortably in my mind even as a photograph of it was tucked away in a corner of my billfold.

In our suburban Paris apartment near the Porte d'Orléans—we spent five months there, before journeying by car through Switzerland and Italy—the cement wall forbade the hanging of pictures. The patterned tile floors of kitchen and bath and toilet were a cold geometry. In the kitchen was a sink, a toy enamel box of a stove, and a giant Westinghouse refrigerator, our only link with home but as efficient and sterile in one land as the next; in the bath another sink, a *bidet* (for Americans, a receptacle for rinsing hand laundry), and a huge white tub with the gleaming coils—useless, there being no hot water—of a shower attachment. The furnishings elsewhere were nondescript modern. In winter, with the windows closed, no sound from outside could permeate the series of tight little cubes in which we lived. The only sense of a former human presence in our rooms came from a brown stain on the living room rug: the owner of the apartment, in hanging the curtains before our arrival, had slipped from a chair and, falling, had thrust her arm through the glass of the window. My study was the bedroom, my desk the table for breakfasting the French always keep near the beds; I placed it by the window overlooking the courtyard. Here, in February, I could look down upon the bare limbs of the clipped trees, at the desolate sandbox; I could look up and down and to right and left at the countless curtained windows of all my faceless neighbors. As I scribbled at my desk, I knew that words had mystic meanings, that puns were profound. Put a cross before error and you have terror. I could look down into the empty courtyard and feel my pity enfolding the world.

The neighborhood school was but a few blocks away. For a brief period each morning a procession of children and mothers, emerging from the tunnel beneath our apartment and vanishing through the tunnel in the building opposite, would pass through the courtyard. First came the older children, trudging along with their heavy satchels; then the younger children, their hands clasped by the mothers who, in earnest conversation with one another, swept them briskly along. One crisp

February morning we joined the procession: our two older sons were to enroll that day. My wife held Jimmy's hand; the older boys stayed close to each other and to us. The children who had arrived early were already in the schoolyard, separated from us by a high fence with iron pickets; they darted in groups like birds, shouting and kicking one another on the shins with their heavy shoes. Our older boys glanced furtively into the yard but said nothing.

In the school building, we sat in a row on a bench in a dimly lit corridor to await the director. Both of the older boys had brought books; now they opened them self-consciously. Larry had a blue French-English pocket dictionary; he had studied French in his school at home in preparation for our trip. Cris's book was large and glossy, *The Golden Book of Chemistry Experiments*. His mother is a chemist; soon after we had moved into the farmhouse, he had asked for one of her discarded laboratory coats and, although it brushed his ankles, he had worn it with a swagger. He had swept out a corner of the dark basement for a laboratory and arranged his bottles of chemicals on a shelf that had once contained jar after dusty jar of dried-out elderberry jam.

The director of the school was most polite. For our sake he talked slowly, patting the children on the shoulders as he spoke. Our thirteen-year-old perhaps should attend the *lycée*, he was of the age for that; but since he was to attend French schools only for a semester, since he might find some difficulty in adjusting to another language as well as another curriculum, since he had as yet no training in Latin, it perhaps would be better if he remained here, in the director's school. He, the director, would be happy to have two boys from America in his school. In the classes devoted to English, our boys could learn French while the French children learned our native tongue. . . .

"*Monsieur, vous êtes très gentil,*" I said; my wife, being more proficient in French, had been doing most of the talking for us. Larry, embarrassed at my accent, looked away, but the director smiled. There is, I suppose, a kind of contact between people to which the barriers of language and tradition are, in some odd way, a help rather than a hindrance. I thought that the director understood my boys and why they clutched their books so. *Monsieur, vous êtes très gentil:* it gave me a simple joy to say that phrase, the same joy I was to feel a month or six weeks later when, on a midnight walk along a narrow street, I was able to give a Parisian lost in our darkened suburb the directions to the nearest bus stop. To know nothing about another person; to sense that, whatever your wishes may be, the twin worlds of Self and Other are equally impervious; and yet to arrive at some common understanding, however trivial—there is in such encounters a pleasure, an awakening to the hope of some ultimate kinship. Isolation and unity are the two faces of the same coin. My wife and I shook hands with the director before he led our older boys down the corridor. Then my wife and I and Jimmy escaped to the street.

In our farmhouse my study is the former parlor. The white-painted wood that frames the windows and doors in this room is fluted in the manner of classical columns; the windows—for it is late December—have a veneer of white frost upon which is superimposed the blurred outline of the apple orchard. The sun is shining; on certain panes the frost has become rippled ice, each ripple a spectrum.

I was attracted, in a recent issue of *Paris Match*—that *Life*-type magazine which, because of its simple prose, gives Americans the illusion of mastery of a foreign tongue—by an underlined injunction to imitate *"les vitraux de cathédrales."* There was an article on *les mystères du Zen* in the same issue. Though the injunction, being only a suggestion to householders for decorating windows at Christmastime, had nothing to do with Zen, I thought, What a fine phrase! What do we do in Europe—at least we Americans who have no religious affiliation, nothing to make us cross ourselves and pray or to confess our sins in the little boxes—but go from cathedral to cathedral, in Paris and Chartres and Bourges, gazing upon statues and statuettes, upon arches within and spires and buttresses without, feeling ourselves interlopers in sacred places until we concentrate upon the stained glass? Here we can melt as well as any adept into the mysteries of the Virgin or simply into some dim and undefinable pattern of twelfth- or thirteenth-century colors. I have sat for hours on a bench in the Sainte-Chapelle in Paris waiting for those brief moments in winter when the sun burns at the windows. Though I didn't think of it then, I suppose that what I felt in the Sainte-Chapelle in those moments was similar to what I felt, first as a child and later in dreams, when I looked at the stained-glass ventilator windows that transformed antique trolleys into silent shrines. But all this is prelude to a more recent event, one that—at least for my part in the dialogue—probably would not have taken place had I not, for nearly seven months, been so far from home.

Not long ago, in the campus lodge where—since it provides both a view of the lake and innumerable cups of hot coffee—I hold most of my conferences with students and perhaps too many of my classes, I talked with a boy who was in danger of expulsion because of his propensity for sleep. He was an engaging, if drowsy-eyed, young man. In his freshman year, he had made the Dean's List. Then one day in his sophomore year, on a sudden impulse he had slipped out of the classroom in the middle of the lecture and returned to bed. Lying beneath blankets in the moment before sleep, he would think all tasks to be possible, he would have grand ideas as to what he would do in the world—join the Peace Corps and go to Africa, where he could help the natives, studying tribal rhythms in his spare hours and composing the kind of vital music he felt imprisoned in himself; maybe finally he would become a poet or an astrophysicist, marry a goddess and have a dozen beautiful children. . . .

He sighed as he recounted these thoughts. "Then I go to sleep," he said, "and when I wake up I think, 'What's the use? What's the use of getting out of bed, where I can dream all these things before I go to sleep?' When I wake up the world is disgusting, I am disgusting, nothing has meaning except those moments before I fall asleep. Listen, I had a job in a grocery downtown that paid for my room and meals but last month they fired me for not showing up on time, and now I'm so far in debt that soon I won't be able to get credit. At first I slept ten hours at a time, then fourteen, and now—can you believe it?—I'm asleep twenty hours out of the twenty-four. Wouldn't you despise yourself if you did that?"

"Do you think there might be a physical cause?"

He shrugged. "Maybe it's because there was a girl who decided I wasn't the one. Maybe it's because I used to read the newspapers too much. Maybe—oh God!—because my parents were divorced before I finished high school."

"What do you do in the hours when you are awake? Obviously you don't go to class."

"I eat," he said. "Sometimes I write. Here," he said, reaching into the breast pocket of his jacket, "here's something I've written." And he handed me a crumpled two-page manuscript.

Sipping my coffee, I read it slowly. It was the account of a young man who, while eating oysters in a seafood house, is horrified at the thought of his body—his intestines and sexual organs. The style was graceful, the sentences suggested a beauty at war with the content.

"What do you think you are, you and your sleeping and writing?" I asked. "A goddam refugee from a Russian novel?" I don't know why I spoke in such a manner; but looking across at him, over that manuscript of his, I was struck by the thought that I was looking into a mirror that gave me back the image of my youth. "We all like to believe our little pains are unique," I said. "For Christ's sake, I talk with somebody like you—some young idealist hurt during adolescence by his parents' mistakes—at least once a year. You and I—you know what we are? *Everybody.* Look at me and see yourself in twenty or twenty-five years."

He was smiling. "Your parents were divorced too?"

It is odd how we help each other by speaking of our past confusions and failures, not of our victories. I wanted to help myself—this younger version of myself. And I told him how, in the middle of the Depression, my parents had been divorced, how my father had remarried and been divorced again; but how finally he had remarried my mother. I told him about my fourteenth year, when I had lived with my father and his second wife in Chicago, first in a skyscraper apartment overlooking the lake and then—when we couldn't pay the rent—

in a dingy one-bedroom flat on a streetcar line in a suburb called Bryn Mawr.

All three of us had felt trapped and unhappy. Once, when I was walking in Jackson Park, a pervert made advances to me, and though I ran from him I felt from that moment on that perverts recognized me as one of their number; I found it impossible to think clearly in school, I could not finish a book. So I took innumerable walks, almost running to protect myself from strangers; and sometimes—for I had a used portable typewriter, a gift from my father to which I was so attached that I can still recall its smell of oil, its little carriage return lever, the way the name CORONA was inscribed on the plate before the keys—I would write stories. My head would be emptied of fatigue only when I sat before that typewriter.

One day while I was at school, my father—he must have been between jobs then—and his wife read one of my manuscripts; when I came home they praised my efforts, but something else was on their minds. "You try to get your stories published, don't you?" my father asked. I said that I had thought of sending the one they'd read to the *Daily News*. My father's wife smiled and said, "Since you want to be a professional writer, shouldn't you have a pseudonym? Professionals always have pen names. Your father and I would be glad to help you find a name." "We thought of an English name like William Somerset," my father said. "What do you think of William Somerset?"

I didn't want them to see how disturbed I was, how ashamed I was they *they* were so ashamed of what I had written. "Thank you," I said. "Maybe we can talk about it later," and I went into the bedroom and locked the door. I could think of nothing but a phrase from my school composition text, "The style is the man," and of the inner corruption that must have stained every sentence I had taken such pride in composing. "Oh God, help me," I said. Oddly, one of my legs began to throb. Sensing the approach of terror and panic, of the whole battery of those dark forces we normally keep in abeyance, I willed for the fatigue, the blessed fatigue, to reach me first; and it did.

The boy in the lodge said, "So in my forties I'm to be you. What's it like to be forty?"

"Nothing is resolved, at least not in the early forties," I said. "In the forties, you're married and have three children. You love your wife and children so much you're in danger of smothering them with your protection and words of caution. You fear you're psychotic at times in your hatred of disorder and irrationality. You aren't so fatigued, but you think of other ways of dying to peace: you go to Europe, you look at the Virgin in the stained glass at Chartres and fall in love with her crossed eyes and those of her Child; at home you buy a farmhouse ten miles out in the country. Every once in a while you get a pain in your left leg that you recognize as psychological because it has something to do with fear and self-incrimination. But you're glad—I think you're terribly glad—to be alive. It's a question of balance. When you're full of self-hatred and shout at your kids to shut the door, it comes out '*Je t'adore*,' and of course they leave it open and everything's as good as can be expected."

"I think I'll try the library," the boy said, retrieving his manuscript. "I feel like doing some work."

"This coffee is no good, it's weak," I said, yawning: I *did* feel sleepy. "I think I'll go to my office and take a nap."

In Paris, of course, this conversation was still far in the future; but I was gaining there the detachment from self that enabled me to remember what once I had to bury or distort. How can I say what I feel, as I peer through a hole in the frost at the white and desolate fields, at the apple orchard and woods beyond? Though I think I understand their dangers, I wish to make some sort of defense of all escapes, of the dreams before sleeping, of the exultation at the beginning of a long journey, of the sense of mystical affinity found in stained-glass windows, of the sense of kinship provided by the very impersonality of life in a huge apartment complex in a Paris suburb. Hysterical liberals often have messy private lives and aching bones. Mankind is ugly when I know I am ugly, all Germans are brutal when I am brutal, the world is petty when I am small, my fear of chaos and disorder without reflects my fear of disorder within. In separation, in the contemplation of some crystal or tinted world, we leave, if we are lucky, our dank egos to feel the passing touch of some harmonious order. We know it to be beautiful, this order: and whether or not it is true, whether or not it ultimately could carry us to a cold detachment and death, it ought at times to be courted; for its memory will remain to haunt all our days, to give us, after we have lost our sense of its nearness, the faith and courage and tenderness to pursue it through all muddledom.

From the vantage point of a country crossroads in upstate New York, Paris is, as it is from any point in America, a spiritual essence, a good feeling in the belly and bones. On Thursdays and Sundays, the two days of the week when there was no school, we—all five of us—traveled by *métro* to some still-unvisited corner of the city. To come up out of the ground anywhere in Paris is to find some building, some vista, to delight the eye. My wife and I saw, sometimes with the children and sometimes without them, art exhibits and plays and operas and ballet. At night, under the single living room lamp of that sparsely furnished apartment, my older son and I often played chess together, something we'd never done at home; or I read books—those lengthy Victorian novels I'd always put off, borrowed now and renewed again and again from the American Library on the Champs Élysées; or I took long walks, often with my wife, through our suburb or the Latin Quarter or along the Seine. Since there were few Americans in our suburb—only one other family among the hundreds in that apartment complex—we received from the shopkeepers and the vendors in the nearby open market a kindness and courtesy that they seldom accorded to their fellow Frenchmen. The young husband and wife who ran the neighborhood Goulet-Turpin gradually coaxed, through candy and smiles, our three-year-old into saying *bonjour* and *merci* and *au revoir,* though he would never add *monsieur* or *madame;* the ten-year-old put up a notice on the apartment bulletin board that he would like to exchange American stamps for French ones, and a number of mothers brought their children with envelopes of stamps to our door. None of them would enter the apartment; but they would stand in the hall, glad to wish us welcome to their country and pleased to know that we liked it.

My own joy and confidence continued. I thought myself always on the verge of some grand truth. One morning, while shaving after rising late, I saw that my temples were graying, that my cheeks had fattened out—the meat and fish and vegetables and fruit of the *marché du plein air* were always fresh, always good—and that in general I was coming to resemble my father. I thought of him with the sympathy of sudden understanding, remembering how he stood before a mirror many years before and shaved off his mustache because it made him look too much like *his* father. Ah, the stories of his father that I had heard from my own! My grandfather had been an insurance salesman, and his wedding present to my parents had been the first installment of a policy upon which they had to continue to make payments, to him, each month. At the wedding dinner, my father, full of happiness, had begun to sing, and my grandfather had said: "Young man, you are at the table!" And then I thought of my mother, seeing her not as a young woman but white-haired and seventy; I remembered her, as I always will remember her, standing before an orchard in Ashtabula, Ohio, a branch of white blossoms in her hand, smiling a welcome to me, the traveler whose car had just entered the driveway. My parents had recently moved to Ashtabula, that locale for faded vaudeville jokes, and my father was about to make his final unsuccessful bid as a business-man; in six months they would have sold their furniture for debts, the house and orchard would be bulldozed to make room for another factory on the burgeoning lakefront, and my parents would be in a flat in Akron.

After I had washed the lather from my face in the cold water, I went to my desk in the bedroom. Spring had come to the courtyard, the trees that once had seemed clipped to death were filmed with a pale green. Jimmy and a Japanese child were sitting together in the sandbox, chanting *un, deux, quatre, merci, d'accord*. What would my child think of me when he reached my age? Remembering my memories while shaving, I felt in possession of some queer key, some unexpected insight into the relationship of a son to his father and mother. The son, I thought, identifies with his father, whose name he bears until his death and which he in turn must pass on to his children, only to the degree that he is willing to accept the past: not only the past of his own childhood but the past of his ancestors, the whole human heritage in which heroism and nobility, however undeniable, are blemished again and again by betrayal, by willful self-destruction and the destruction of others, by the egoism of passion. He identifies with his mother to the degree that he can respond to the future, to the generous promise, to the hope that the blemish ultimately will be redeemed. It struck me as odd: the father, the active principle, the one responsible for change, belongs in the son's memory to history; the mother, the passive principle, always to prophecy and the potential.

I thought, I am glad I look like my father; but I was saddened for him, saddened for that parade of generations regressing infinitely into the past; and when my two older boys, unburdened from their heavy satchels because it was noon, ran into the courtyard, swooping up the youngest boy from the sandbox to bear him laughing toward the tunnel and the apartment entrance, I ran to the door to welcome all three, crying to my wife, "They're home for lunch!"

Looking back upon those months in Europe, I see that I accomplished very little, that I wrote far less than I had hoped. Perhaps, in removing one's self from the daily tension and habitual entanglements, one really can't accomplish much that is tangible. And, as Paris became familiar and the speech of the Parisians more than an elusive succession of nasal tonalities, my sense of freedom—so wild and triumphant at first—lessened. The great apartment complex, which once had seemed so sturdy and tight, turned out to be jerry-built; at least the rumor was that the contractor had been imprisoned for his deceptions. The roof was faulty and already required a new surface: little elevators with buckets of asphalt and sand bounced up past my window, workmen swarmed on the rooftops of the individual buildings. The boilers for the steam heat had been too small, and gave out one by one in our months in the apartment even as the hot-water boilers had given out before our arrival. The boiler room was on the ground floor, beneath the apartment to our immediate left; little workmen from Italy arrived with their drills and pneumatic hammers, removing the old boilers, demolishing the concrete floor and ceiling slabs to make room for the new and bigger boilers. The racket above and below was distracting, a combination of heavy thuds that shook the building, metallic whines and Neapolitan songs. I tried to write in a café but felt myself a poseur; I tried to write on a bench beneath the poplars by the grand canal of the château at Sceaux, but either it would rain or I would be surrounded by dogs and by children who thought I was an artist and wanted me to draw their pictures; if there were no other distractions, the beauty of the grounds—the flower gardens, the vistas of clipped grass, the woods, the pools—held my attention.

And there were problems with the boys: Larry broke the plate glass of one of the apartment building's entrance doors, bringing an indignant management upon us, with a bill; Cris became unruly at school, having been made angry, he told us, not only because he had been kicked too hard in play but because a playground teacher had crossed the mouth of one of his more garrulous French supporters with Scotch tape and threatened him with the same treatment. My wife was called to see the director at 4:30, the school dismissal hour. No longer *gentil*, now vibrating with fury, he met her in the corridor while children swarmed past them. "The big boy," he cried, grabbing Larry out of the throng and putting his arm around him, "he is a good boy, he is an angel, but the little boy—" and here he spied Cris and pointed a trembling finger at him—"the little boy, he is *méchant*, no, no, he is *mauvais*." Cris shouted at the top of his lungs, *"Vous êtes fou!"* and darted out the door while the other children laughed. *"Voilà!"* cried the director triumphantly to my wife. "Ah, so you hear with your own ears. *Mauvais!*"

After I heard this tale from my still-shaken wife and my still-rebellious ten-year-old, I said to Cris, "You certainly played into his hands," and he said, "Everybody calls him that, but behind his back. I said it to his face. Isn't that more honest?" "But you were impolite, whatever you feel to be your justification; you were rude to an adult, to the director of your school. You had the nerve to insult him not because you were brave—after all, you ran away—but because you could hide behind the fact that you are a foreigner. If you were French, he might really punish you."

"In one way or another," my wife said, "I suppose we've all been hiding behind such a fact ever since we arrived, it's impossible not to. Whatever *my* feelings about the director—and I can't say, as an American, I want to excuse *that* kind of Frenchness, that calling of one child an angel and the other bad, evil—I *do* think there ought to be a note of apology to him." "I'm sorry," Cris said, breaking at last into tears of repentance upon discovering sufficient sympathy for his cause; and he, his older brother, my wife, and I worked patiently at the dining room table to compose as courteous and elegant a note in French as we could manage. The next day, Cris handed it to the director, who smiled and embraced him, saying, "Now we are good friends again, yes?" At the end of the school year, both boys—along with most of their classmates—marched to the auditorium of the *mairie* to sing the "Marseillaise" and receive prizes from the mayor.

One day I ceased to work at my desk altogether, I lost completely my sense of well-being in remove. My total loss of freedom is not what is important about that day, but that is the whole point. The Italians continued their racket of renovation in the boiler room; the French continued to raise their little elevators to the roof. Our particular building was eight stories high, but a four-story wing jutted out to the left of our bedroom window to form a corner of the courtyard. While I was typing, I could see a man on the roof at the far end of that wing, standing next to one of the portable elevators. He was tinkering with the apparatus and talking with a fellow workman, who, standing farther back on the roof, was invisible to me except for his head. The workman at the edge I judged to be young, at least his outline against the sky was a thin one; I could see that the heels of his shoes extended beyond the edge, that he must be balancing himself on the balls of his feet. I called to my wife to look with me. "Isn't he crazy?" I said. "If we were home, if that were an American workman, I would shout at him, I would cry, 'Stand back, you fool.'" "You *could* call to him in French," my wife said doubtfully. I said, "He must know what he's doing, don't you think? The other man doesn't seem alarmed. If I called to him, '*Attention!*' he might turn to see what fool was shouting and fall because of *my* alarm. I scare too easily. French workmen aren't Americans. Oh my God," I said, "I can't look," for the workman had raised his arms in some expansive gesture: teetering there, oblivious to mortality, he *had* to be a young god making a cosmic joke. "These French," I said; "I've got to get some coffee," and we both left the window. A moment later we heard a single scream followed by a crash. I ran back to the window. "Oh Jesus," I said, "it's *happened.*" He had fallen with the elevator, he was a hump of white coveralls between the building and the walk. For a moment I couldn't move, I felt that old guilty pain in my left leg. Like an elderly cripple in a panic, I jumped down the stairs, out the door and through the tunnel into the courtyard.

Already the form on the ground was surrounded by workers, by shouting Italians and Frenchmen. "He's alive," someone said; a sweater was thrust under the victim's head, a coat placed over his body. I wished they had been my clothes. I was a spectator at the rear of a crowd, a foreigner more foreign than the Italians, for there was nobody for me to speak to. Then I heard a chorus of the three kinds of French emergency vehicle sirens. The police, the firemen, the ambulance drivers—they arrived at the same time, the police and firemen with gleaming helmets and pencil-thin mustaches, those tokens, with their uniforms, of their status as public officials. Glad for the arrival of Authority, I returned to the apartment, an American thinking of home.

There is a last episode from France to relate. A few days after the accident, my family was invited to a christening party for the baby born to the fellow Americans—they were Catholics from Indiana—in that apartment complex. They lived on the top floor of a tall and narrow structure raised precariously from the ground on pillars: modern architecture. From their opened French windows one had a vista of all Paris—the Tour Eiffel, bits of the Seine, the Sacré Coeur, Notre Dame, and every other familiar landmark. Off in the distance, the factories of St. Denis lay covered in their own smoke. Far beneath us was the roof from which the workman had fallen: and of course we were clustered near the protective bars of the window, speaking of the accident. The host, who was an engineer, had invited some French associates of the firm for which he was working; by chance, one of them was a friend of the victim. "He is still alive?" I asked. "He will live," the Frenchman said. "He will always be a cripple. It is very bad." "I saw him before he fell," I said. "I could see his heels over the edge. He was taking chances, he wasn't careful enough." I suppose I was exonerating myself with such a statement: the criticism was unnecessary. But, oddly, I felt some sort of identification with the man who had fallen, as if both of us somehow had been reckless with our lives, with our responsibilities. Perhaps it was my Puritan conscience, chiding me for my lack of produced work, for my past sense of exultation and liberty. I looked out of that window, frightened by the distance to the ground: I could fall, if pushed; my youngest child might slip through the bars. I cried to the Frenchman, "Why was he so foolish, your friend?" He shrugged. "It is simple," he said. "He was married, you see, just the week before—so young, so full of life, so full of passion!" His eyes filled with tears; nodding my understanding, I left him to search for our youngest boy.

In Naples the heat of August comes not only from the brilliant Mediterranean sun but from the body warmth of a million people in constant physical and emotional agitation, people confined within narrow streets beneath dripping laundry: the clotheslines, three or four deep, one for each floor, stretch from building to building as far as the eye can see. Once out on the streets, our little car, which had been parked overnight in the basement garage of the hotel, became instantly suffocating. We were packed in with all the debris of a three-week trip: candy wrappers from Switzerland, tourist folders from Venice, bits of a plaster "David" bought in Florence and broken in Spoleto, watermelon seeds from Rome.

Smiling vendors walked beside us, showing their merchandise at the windows: silk scarves, pocket knives with decorated handles, postcards, ashtrays and other trinkets made from mother of pearl, black-market Swiss watches; a child smaller than our ten-year-old begged a cigarette. The air was thick with the smell of hot manure and urine. Past the desperate rubble of slums built from the ruins of a battle fought a year or a century ago and where naked babies sat in the shade of a crumbling wall I drove our new car, glad for the dust that hid its shine. Young men on Vespas scooted up beside us, shouting, "You go to Pompeii? I am your guide, follow me," and invariably they would try to wave us up a little side road to some community the main highway had bypassed. "But don't you want to see the factory where I am the worker?" one of them cried reproachfully from a crossroad. "We are in a hurry, we leave tomorrow by ship," I shouted, driving on.

Perhaps our lives move in cycles beyond our control, from periods of detachment to those of involvement and then back again; I had thought myself—at least for the rest of this year of my life—through with the need for stained-glass windows, through with the desire to escape in all of its manifestations, but now I wanted to forget all the myriad appeals of poverty even as I wanted to forget my crumpled clothes, the trickles of perspiration running down my arms from my armpits, and a crying three-year-old bewildered by the lack of a home other than a crowded car. Italy, on this last day, was to provide the coda—however unsatisfactory and lacking in triumph—for our visit to Europe.

There is no need to say much about Pompeii. Despite—or perhaps because of—the merciless sun, I felt a richness, the sense of all the pleasures the body can offer, to be in the air: this atmosphere touched and drew me, but in the end proved too heavy. Perhaps if I had been D. H. Lawrence, touring Italy with only my wife, spirit and body might have seemed at peace, as if one. Our three-year-old, though, had rejected his toilet training as long ago, as far away, as Zurich; his pants had to be changed behind a steaming wall of what once had been a wine shop, and the redeeming moment—when he stood in wonder and held out his living hand to a frozen one, to the two-thousand-year-old statue of a beautiful child his own age—was insufficient. Larry had to be sharply told by the guide to leave the scattered mosaic tiles alone. The old guide had boils on his arms and scabs on his hands. As he pointed out the phalli and political slogans on the buildings, as he winked his eye at me, his theme was, "Things never change, man is always the same." Of my family, only I was allowed to enter with him what he called "the excitation room, the one which prepares the man for love," in which we were surrounded by pictures demonstrating that fairly extensive variety in sexual positions. "Things never change," my guide said, and he put his festering old arm around my shoulder as we walked out. Only I was permitted to watch, in another building, as the lock was removed from a hinged door which, when opened, revealed an enormous phallus and a painted bunch of grapes. It is the secrecy, not the image (in the room, behind the door, in the child's mind), that is indecent, that corrupts. From the Forum, Vesuvius, cold and remote and as mysterious as death, loomed up; we bought a copy of a little slave bell—our acquiescence that we had been, in spite of all, stroked by some long-dead richness—paid the guide, and departed for the mountain.

We wanted the shorter toll road up Vesuvius, but became lost and took the longer one from Boscotrecase. It winds up through barren lands of solidified lava, up and up that mountain of gorse and ashes, of finally nothing but ashes. The heat vanished; we put on sweaters, but still were shivering as we came to the end of the road. Here a hiking party of about twenty persons was assembling for the rest of the ascent. I asked the new guide, "How long for the trip?" "Fifteen minutes," he lied cheerfully: it was three hours later and nearly dark before we returned to the car. Now, in single file, bearing walking sticks, we slowly ascended a sharply twisting path. My wife, Larry, and I took turns in carrying Jimmy. Our immediate goal was a glittering peak that—an hour later—turned out to be a slope of empty Coca-Cola bottles, thrown from the refreshment platform at the summit. Obediently drinking Coca-Cola on that platform, we could see the Bay of Naples stretching out to Sorrento and beyond; and we could see the old gash on the slopes beneath us, a wound that reached to Pompeii. In bored tones, sounding like a phonograph record as he spoke first in Italian, then in English, then in French, our guide outlined the remainder of the trip: we were to walk along the lip of the cone for less than half a kilometer and then descend a short distance into it, where we could stir our sticks into little holes and see the smoke spurt out.

We had barely started when I made a fool of myself. The path was perfectly safe, wide enough in most places for two to walk abreast. I was holding the hand of my three-year-old when the fear—the absolute fear of all that nothingness—overwhelmed me. I do not suffer, normally, from fright of high places; but I did relive that moment during the christening party when I had looked out the window, down upon the roof from which the young workman had fallen, and from that roof to the ground; and I had the queerest sense that my child and I, lost in all those ashes, had no recourse but to fall—not outward, toward Pompeii, but inward, into that mammoth but ever-constricting cone. I think—to explain it now—I had so much, when I stood below in Pompeii, *wanted* to be on top of Vesuvius that the actual effect of *being* there, and of sensing nothing but desolation and waste, was nearly annihilating. Between the full assumption of guilt and the full assumption of emptiness there is little to choose; in my forties, on the summit of Vesuvius, I was as close to panic as I had been as a boy in Chicago.

My wife took my son, raising him in her arms. Though I hadn't realized it until his screams ceased, I had been holding his hand so tightly and crying with such intensity, "Don't be scared, don't be scared," that I had sent him into a terror of his own. My wife said to me: "Are you all right? Are you ill?" "I'll be all right," I said. "I think, though, that we mustn't go a step further, any of us. We'll wait here until they come back." For the rest of the party, after a moment's hesitation, had gone on. *They* apparently had felt no fear, and there was at least one grandmother in their number. We watched them, my older sons angry with me and perhaps embarrassed for my sake. The party descended a dozen or so yards into the cone of the crater, someone stirred a stick, and a puff of smoke emerged from the ashes. On the way back down the path, we heard that one curious lady had put her arm down a hole just large enough to accommodate it, and had in consequence blistered her skin; but the guide had been provided for such an emergency with a jar of petroleum jelly.

The next day we sailed for home.

These experiences in Europe suggest to me—I was to say some such thing to the boy in the lodge, and I can't imagine a view more conventional—that a balance is required of us, an equilibrium between opposing forces. And yet my impulse is toward one rather than the other. Though I am fearful of winter driving, I enjoy—usually—the ten-mile trip from our house to Ithaca, and the trip back. There is a long and steady slope near the town, followed by several bends and a further slope. As I approach Ithaca in the gray of an early winter morning or in the dark of a winter night, the automobile seems far above the countryside, a throbbing airplane slowly descending, banking, and descending again upon some twinkling center of life. Returning home by night or day, I can see my house while I am still a mile distant: its immaculate whiteness or its gleam of lights appears, vanishes, and appears again. And, late at night and long after my children are in bed, I enter—it is for *my* sake—the cubicles in which they sleep. Jimmy has a favorite blanket pulled up to his nose, and I look into his room first. Then I enter Larry's room. On his wall is a large French Tourist Office poster of the Place de la Concorde at night. On his desk is the radio-operated, gasoline-engine model airplane upon which he has been working ever since our return from France. He has a transistor radio, a special fancy for station WBZ in Boston and for a disc jockey named Bruce Bradley. Why does he choose, out of all the numbers on his kilocycle dial, a station so hard to find with a tiny radio, a station that fades and returns, fades and returns? The other night, in his room, I found him asleep, the radio on his pillow by his cheek and still playing, the music some pop tune; as I reached down to turn it off, a faint voice, a miracle beyond believing, said "Bruce Bradley and WBZ, Boston."

I enter Cris's room last. On his wall is another French Tourist Office poster, a grand picture of the cathedral at Chartres. Cris always falls asleep with his lamp burning and his glasses on, for he looks at his collection of postcards from Europe in the last moments before slumber; often one is still clutched in his hand. Propped upright on his desk is a snapshot in color of his grade in France, sent to him by his French teacher and taken while he was still a student in her class; all the boys are wearing tight short pants, and each is nearly indistinguishable from his neighbor. Also on his desk is a battered Smith-Corona portable typewriter, one that I purchased in the early days of my marriage and that, after I bought an office machine for my own use, I loaned to him to write up the results of his chemistry experiments. The winter wind rattles the shutters, there is the momentary blur of snow upon the dark window panes. How far we all are from France, how far even from Ithaca! And how infinitely separated my sleeping children from each other, and from me! Gently I remove my son's glasses, click off the buzzing fluorescent tube, and return to my study with some vague and elusive memory of order in my head and a desire to do a few more pages of the manuscript that I did not complete before I vacated an apartment near the Porte d'Orléans.

1964

Every Day Requires
an Atlas and More

7 THOUGH IT CAME LATER THIS YEAR THAN usual, Labor Day was one of the finest days of the summer in upstate New York. The temperature rose to the mid-eighties; the sky until sunset remained a rich blue. Each nearby bush and tree, each contour of the distant hills to the west and the south, was sharply defined. In the morning, Larry (now almost fifteen) and I worked on ladders to complete—before the sun blinded us—the caulking and painting on the west side of the house. Cris (now eleven) was bent on his knees in the garden, picking tomatoes half hidden in the weeds and clearing the weeds away from his patch of pumpkins. My wife washed and scraped blistered paint from several pairs of shutters we had discovered in the loft of one of the barns. Our four-year-old, Jimmy, found a broken paintbrush and pretended to paint the foundation stones near my ladder. On this singular morning, there were no arguments, no screams; even the dogs and cats—this year we have two of each—were at peace, the cats basking on the picnic table, the dogs sleeping in its shadow.

After lunch, my wife drove the children to Ithaca to see the Levins; Larry was to spent the night with their son. In the afternoon, wanting to feel the sun on my back, I took off my shirt as I painted the shutters my wife had prepared for the black enamel. It was slow and mindless work, which I enjoyed. Four silver aircraft flew high above—two tankers refueling two bombers. When the maneuver was completed, the tankers veered off, one climbing to the left and the other to the right; the bombers continued to follow their invisible, parallel lines. When I had finished with the shutters, I put on my trunks for a swim in our pond. Earlier in the summer, we had made a beach, covering the mud with bank-run gravel and then with sand. The warmth of the sand felt good beneath my feet and between my toes; the cold water—the pond is fed by a spring—was at first painful and then a delight. Floating on my back, I looked at that lovely late-summer sky. Turning my head one way, I could see outlined against it the green leaves of the willow we had planted by the pond's edge soon after we had moved to the country; turning my head the other way, I could see our old house, its new paint gleaming in the afternoon sun.

I was sprawled on the sand in the sun when my wife returned. She and the two younger children put on their suits to join me at the pond. "Did you know that today is Jewish New Year as well as Labor Day?" my wife asked.

"I could believe anything about this day," I said.

"Florence Levin is so funny!" she said, wading into the water. "She kept saying, 'We ought to be *doing* something today, this wonderful day.' They don't belong to the synagogue, and if you don't belong you have to pay a hundred dollars to take your family to a holiday service. She had her girls in their best clothes—nice tailored suits. The girls were walking up and down the gravel path—you know how well kept their garden is—and Florence sat on the bench nearly in tears and saying, 'I know I shouldn't be upset. I don't hold to traditions, but we ought to be doing something. My parents would have taken *me* to the synagogue.'"

I said, "Isn't it queer how you think about your childhood—everything that made you feel good—on a day like this?" My words surprised me, for until that moment I had not been conscious of any such thing. But I felt as if I understood Florence Levin, which meant, I suppose, that I, too, was saddened by I didn't know what.

That night, just after we had finished supper, a red Oldsmobile convertible came to a stop at our crossroads and inexplicably burst into flames. I called the nearest fire department and then squirted upon the engine the contents of the two-dollar extinguisher that, carried in the glove compartment of my station wagon, had given me a sense of security over the years; the fire hissed in malice, the red and yellow tongues leaping at my face and that of the nervous young owner of the car. A neighboring farmer, a man who some years earlier had lost an arm in a corn picker, came running with a dry-chemical extinguisher, an intricate, gleaming affair with valves and dials; though he'd purchased it within the month, it wouldn't work. "That's how it is with the equipment you buy today," he said matter-of-factly, tossing it into the ditch. With his gleaming hook he pulled the blistered and smoking hood back down over the engine. The fire licked through the instrument panel to the front cushion and then up through the canvas roof. Cris walked around the car snapping pictures to send to the newspaper. Jimmy ran into the road carrying a red book made in the shape of a fire engine. "Whee, whee, out of my way!" he cried. I grabbed a boy with each hand. "Stand back, it could explode. It could even burn down our house," I said. I was irritated that they should feel so free. We could hear the siren at Enfield Center blowing again and again.

"How long will it take them to get here?" I asked my wife.

"I've always wondered," she replied.

It took fifteen minutes and thirty-five seconds from the time I phoned. The fire truck led a line of twenty or more cars belonging to volunteers, or simply the curious; each car contained a family. Our front yard became a carnival, lighted by the burning car. The front wheels were twin circles of flame. While the firemen busied themselves with extinguishers and the fire hose, Cris carried our telescope into the yard; he was immediately surrounded by children and parents who wished to see the rings around Saturn and other marvels. The owner of the car wandered over for a look and then returned to his soaked and smoking wreck. "I've always wanted to see Saturn through a telescope," he said, as if to see it would have consoled him, "but the tires make too much of a smudge."

After the excitement was over, after the crossroads was deserted again—even the burned-out car gone—I walked into the country dark to retrieve the telescope. A bit of cosmic debris shimmered into a momentary arc. I looked at Jupiter through the telescope. A bloated mass with a throbbing pimple, it wavered across the lens, a row of trembling little moons accompanying it like starved chickens. My grief was far out of proportion to the disorder of the evening, even as my joy that morning had been in excess of my mindless tasks. What are we, that we are moved at a touch between serenity and desolation?

Perhaps in our middle years we would make order of our past because of the very anarchy of our feelings. We would say of our forties that they constitute a watershed, a high point from which we can examine the topography behind us; in that landscape vanishing toward our earliest memories, we would find separate squares of land, each with its fences and each representing a stage in our development from innocence and illusion. Such an implied compliment to our present rationality and wisdom!

Late on Labor Day night, after my wife and I had looked through the wholesale catalogues for fire extinguishers, after we had gone to bed, I lay awake, thinking of certain tales, of little squares of land in my past.

Soon after my father moved us to Little Rock in the early years of the Depression, my brother and I discovered the swimming pool at White City. It was a long distance, much of it uphill, from our house on South Cedar Street to the pool. Though there was a streetcar, we could not afford both the fare and the swimming fee; usually we could afford neither and sat on a bench outside the wire fence. My brother, who was fourteen, watched the girls sunning or diving. I was ten, and liked to look at the fat man. Late each afternoon, he waddled out of the bathhouse, smoking a long cigar and holding a newspaper. "Pardon me, pardon me," he would say as he approached the lithe girls lying on the boards by the pool's edge; they would shriek with mock alarm, some of them tumbling into the pool and others rolling out of harm's way. His huge rear swaying, he would descend the ladder at the deep end. But what a transformation once he commenced to float! His blubber buoyed him; water was his element. Lying on his back, his body a ship and his cigar its funnel, he would give a kick now and then to keep him on course as he glided beneath the diving boards and around the perimeter of the pool, serenely reading the *Arkansas Democrat*. It pleases me still to think of this man, this shy bear daily turned whale or ship: how many of us have been able to fashion our indignities into such enjoyments, to find such recourse from the penalties of our appetites?

My father also was fat and smoked cigars, but he seldom swam. Nothing ever satisfied him long. He had owned a Marmon agency when he was barely of voting age and had built upon its roof what the newspapers called the largest advertising sign in the Western Hemisphere. But when he had heard of three freighters at Baltimore loaded with fine German steel that nobody else knew what to do with . . . His restlessness made my childhood a course in the geography and grammar schools of the East, Midwest, and South. In Oklahoma City, before the Depression, he bought twelve planes—Spads or Nieuports, relics of the war—in order to keep one aloft. I remember my mother's crying with pride, "There's your father!" as I looked up with her into a blue sky at the tiny wings circling our neighborhood. And I remember, from the year before we moved to Little Rock, a touring car moving slowly through the Ohio countryside at night, in a fog so thick that the headlights had been switched off. I sat on the rear seat with my mother and brother, the three of us huddled beneath a blanket; my father's head loomed before us. He was peering forward as he drove, following a bobbing yellow lantern. We were on a bluff high above an unseen river. Then rows of blurred lights appeared before and beneath us; we were curving down the hill toward a town. "East Liverpool," my father said, laughing. "We've made it to East Liverpool. What ever would we have done without Dr. Szabo and his lantern?" Dr. Szabo, our guide that night, had invented the lantern he carried. He was accompanying us on a trip to Pittsburgh to see to the details—they never materialized—for the manufacturing, by my father, of several of his inventions.

Years later, soon after I had been discharged from the Army, I left my wife in Cleveland to look for a magazine or newspaper job in New York. I wanted I didn't know what—certainly not the few jobs offered me—and so I drove back, alone, to Ohio. In East Liverpool, I stopped for a cup of coffee in a nondescript café and knew I had been there before. I said to the man who served me, "But the counter belongs on the *other* side of the room," and he said, "We moved it ten years ago." Immediately, I saw my father and Dr. Szabo smoking and sipping coffee and talking with excitement while the rest of us drowsily waited in that little oasis for the midnight fog to lift, and I had the sudden wish to be a child of eight or nine again, wholly dependent upon a father to carry me to comfort and dreams.

Of all the years of my childhood, I remember with greatest pleasure that year of the Depression when we lived on South Cedar Street in Little Rock in a tiny house in a dubious neighborhood. The grounds of the state asylum adjoined our back yard. On the day that the van with our furniture arrived—we had come from Toledo—the neighborhood boys gathered in a line on the sidewalk to watch. Proud of my miniature golf course, I set it up around the crates and chairs in the front yard and played a game by myself. My brother put on his skis and grasped his poles, making elaborate motions.

"I know what them things are," one of the watching boys said in a low voice. "They're shees, from the north."

"They are called skis," my brother replied promptly.

"What language do they speak where you come from?" the same boy asked.

"English," my brother said.

The boy said in disbelief, "That's what *we* speak."

My brother and I were inexcusable Yankee braggarts that day. "We speak it as it ought to be spoken," I said, lying on the grass to get the proper line for my ball, and my brother bent forward to speed down an imaginary slope. The boys on the sidewalk waited until our parents and the movers were all in the house, and then, with a fierce yell, they attacked. My brother fled in one direction and I in another, and when we returned his skis were gone and so were all the metal parts of my golf course.

But within a week my brother and I were attempting a drawl. I saw a boy in the next block playing miniature golf with my equipment and aping my showoff antics. We cursed each other and swung our fists viciously through the air. Then he helped me return the parts to my yard, and together we stole some new lumber from the garage of a house down the street. My brother's skis appeared mysteriously on our porch one morning, the day after he had walked downtown with several other boys to steal a bicycle pump at the Walgreen store. To acquaint me further with the neighborhood boys, my mother invited them all to an afternoon party of cookies and pop; they came, bearing toys as if it were a birthday. "Why did you do that?" my mother asked in astonishment. "Why, Ma'am, it wasn't no bother," the oldest one said. "We just went down to the dime store and *took* them."

What a grand year that was! We set fire to the dry grass of the asylum grounds and watched from a thicket while three fire trucks sped up and the inmates cheered from their windows. For a week, we hid an escaped inmate in the abandoned shack of a neighborhood alley, bringing him each night bread and half-eaten candy bars and foul cigarettes we made from tobacco taken from the asylum's own crop and cured for a few days in the sun. He never spoke a word to any of us, though we were a semicircle of reverent disciples in the darkness while he ate our food and coughed on our cigarettes; when he vanished, we felt a betrayal and looked for a message in the dust of the window and floor. In the evenings, we stalked each other through the high grass, the younger boys with harmless guns that shot loops cut from inner tubes and the older boys with air rifles cached during the day (with moldy copies of *The Shadow* and *Thrilling Stories*) in a cave we had dug in the pursuit of sassafras roots. One boy would fire at us from the branches of a persimmon tree; we liked to ping our returning fire against the German helmet he always wore.

My father, then a tire salesman, was away on lengthy trips. I missed him with a lonely passion. On the nights when he was expected home—perhaps once or twice a month—I would refuse to play the evening games, but would listen to the shouts and cries from the field as I sat on the porch step, smoking a piece of grapevine I kept in one of his discarded cigar boxes and watching the headlights of every passing car. My father's Packard rarely appeared before I went to bed, but waking in the morning I would smell the aroma of coffee and cigars and hear his deep voice as he spoke in the kitchen with my mother. I would fall back, smiling, into a final quarter hour's sleep.

On the Sunday afternoons that my father was home, we had large meals, regardless of our debts; surfeited with beef or ham, we would sit at the table for hours while he reminisced and spoke of his hopes. That large table, once an expensive piece of mahogany, had been battered in countless vans; sturdy yet, with round legs ending in brass claws, it so filled the small room that we had to squeeze into our chairs on all sides but one. My father's talk awed me with a sense of immense possibilities; I became, like the table, an extension of his personality. His face would be radiant as he beat his fists upon the table.

His major dream that year in Little Rock was of Normandy, a subdivision not far from the pool at White City. Sometimes my brother and I, after we had looked through the fence at the girls and the fat man, would pass through the gate with the Normandy sign and wander up the curving streets of the subdivision. All of them were named for American presidents. Only one street had houses. They were large houses in French Provincial, English half-timber, and American Colonial styles, all of them too costly for those Depression days. The developers had gone bankrupt. At first, it seemed incredible to my brother and me that we might live in one of those houses, but my father thought that South Cedar Street *demanded* Normandy. "Do we want our children growing up ruffians? Do we?" he said sternly to my mother, as if her doubts were consigning my brother and me to a life of crime. I remember saying to my brother, "Daddy can do it," and seeing him nod impatiently, as if I had spoken some obvious truth. And somehow, though we had no money, he achieved for us the largest house on the street. It had three bathrooms, and in my first-day delirium I wandered from one to the next, flushing toilets, my father following after me and laughing like a boy.

But in that fine house we were more destitute than ever. My mother, who had always been self-effacing, became worried and irritable. Now without friends, I managed to persuade my closest crony from South Cedar Street, the boy who had stolen my miniature golf course, to spend a night with me. Cowed by our new house, he gave me a respect that forbade friendship. The sparsity of furniture made the rooms echo, but the echo impressed him. We slept together in my bed, and during the night he thrashed about in a dream, scratching my leg. "You scratched me. Your toenails are too long," I said. He said quickly, "I'm sorry," and sat up in the dark. I heard a nibbling sound. "What are you doing?" I said. "Don't do that." But he held first one foot to his mouth and then the other, nibbling and tearing at his nails; and as I heard those soft sounds I knew, as I had not on the day we moved to Normandy, that one area of my life was behind me.

Once, my brother killed with a footstool a pancake-sized tarantula in the luggage room; a day or two later, a brilliantly colored centipede rustled up the outside of my bedroom screen. When my father, home for one of his weekends, heard of these invasions, both brought about by the nearness of the house to the pine forests, he spoke of building a stone wall or a moat. Where were his imaginings taking him, to what world would he go? Frightening though they were, a hairy spider and a worm with poisonous claws seemed to me ignoble enemies against which to build a castle, and my father smiled at his own words, but the Normandy of his mind must have held pennants and embattled ramparts. He left on another trip, his discontent remaining in each of the many rooms of the house he had desired.

Normandy, at all events, was close to the swimming pool. In those days, I seldom missed an entrance by the fat man, who every day at the same hour emerged like a bear from the bathhouse to float on his back in the pool, smoking a cigar as he read the sports and comic pages of the afternoon newspaper. The hunger with which I looked for his waddling walk surprised me.

After a year—our second in Little Rock—my father, to keep ownership of that disenchanted house, had to rent it for the amount of the monthly payments. We moved to Paducah and to Fort Smith, and ultimately, when our tenant left and no other renter was forthcoming, back to Normandy. Daily, we expected foreclosure and eviction.

My father now was never home; the fat man was possibly dead, for I was never to see him at the pool again; my mother and brother and I were constantly low-spirited.

One hot August afternoon, my mother said to me, "Here's fifty cents. Go get a haircut."

I didn't wish to stir. "You know we can't afford a haircut," I said.

"But I want you to have one."

"No," I said sullenly.

"Get a *haircut*," she screamed, flinging the coin across the room, and then she fell to her knees.

"Mother, what's wrong?" I asked. "Mother, I'll get a haircut." And I began to search under a chair for the money.

She came on hands and knees to help me. "There's something you must know," she said quietly. "Your father has left for Texas, he has found somebody else he wants to marry. But you must see how *desperate* he has been. Remember what he has been to you; someday he may come back," she said, embracing me. "Remember and hope and wait."

This phrase has come down to me through the years, along with the memory of a year on South Cedar Street when I awaited simply the scheduled appearance of a father who could endow me so richly, on each faithful return, with a past and future that—whatever *his* trap—I was freed to live in the present.

In the fall of the last year of the war, my unit was briefly stationed outside Nancy. Our division had just entered combat. We worked in an abandoned insane asylum and slept in tents behind the buildings. The days were rainy and misty—I recall, in the mornings, low-hanging cloud banks and the pervasive scent of burning wood—but the nights were often cold and clear. The enlisted personnel served on sentry duty; our turns came every third night. Standing by the barred gate, we could hear the accordionist at Mon Dernier Sou, the nearest café, play over and over two songs, "The Beer Barrel Polka" and "La Chanson de la Sierre." At ten and eleven and twelve, the church clocks in Nancy would strike the hours to the ragged and tinkling accompaniment of the clocks in the nearby darkened houses. During the first nights of our stay at the asylum, there were sporadic flares on the eastern horizon, followed by the rumble of howitzers.

I was a corporal, a classification specialist in the Adjutant General's Office. The four enlisted men in the classification section were all recent college graduates. Our sergeant, George, who was from Maryland, wished to be a political scientist; John, a dour Irishman from Massachusetts, had barely begun, before being called into service, a high school teaching career in history; Stuffy, the son of a New Jersey newspaper publisher, planned, as did I, to go into journalism after the war. On the nights when we were not on guard duty, we remained in our office to read books and write letters and to listen to the classical music the German radio stations played almost continuously, or we walked down the road to Mon Dernier Sou for a game of chess or checkers. But it is the music—the distant accordionist and the Beethoven and Mozart on the battery radio—that I remember best.

Captain Oliver, the officer in charge of our section, had been chief psychologist for a California public-school system. He was the sort of person whose advancement depends upon impulsive—perhaps even willfully irrational—acts so endangering that a quick and brazen counteraction, one taking full advantage of the initial error and of his own professional expertise, is required. Our section had the most luxurious room in the asylum as a result of one of his impulses. While the last Germans were being routed from Nancy, our company was bivouacked on a hillside field fifteen kilometers to the west. One day, the captain learned that our troops had taken the city and that hot showers were available at the University of Nancy. "Come on, we'll all get a good bath," he said in excitement. "Corporal"—he looked at me—"you will drive the jeep."

"But if Nancy is occupied, Headquarters Company will be moving," George said.

"Precisely," the captain said. "So time is of the essence."

While the rest of the company was having lunch, we slipped away. The captain was pleased with himself after we had showered. "Didn't that feel *fine?*" he cried. "We're the cleanest group in the A.G.O. Of course, we missed lunch. *They* are one up on us there." For a moment, he was dejected; then he smiled. "French cooking," he said. "Some bistro. Soup, fish, a good white wine."

"But, Captain—" George protested.

"Time is still of the essence."

Two hours later, not only clean but well fed, we returned to an empty hillside. Our clothing, our pup tents, our typewriters and heavy office files had all been packed and moved. From the top of the hill, we could see the dust billowing up from the slow-moving line of trucks on a road arching toward the southeast. "None of you will be blamed," Captain Oliver said. "Oh, no. That is the freedom of the enlisted man. But I may be court-martialed. The more slow-witted the colonels, the more they insist on the regulations." Then he turned to me. "If you have any gratitude," he said, "if you have any appreciation for the risks I've taken to give you a bath and a French meal, you will take that little road"—and he pointed to a lane that roughly paralleled the one chosen by the convoy—"and beat the colonel to our new area. There will be the usual convoy signs to lead us in."

With some fairly antic driving, we arrived at the new quarters in advance of the company. "All right," said the captain. "Fan out and find the plushiest room. Take charge of it. Don't budge." We were seated around the table of the large staff dining hall—a room with chandeliers and French doors overlooking a formal garden—when the convoy arrived. "Where the *hell*—" began the colonel, the fat National Guardsman who was in charge of our A.G.O. But Captain Oliver broke in with brisk authority. "I have a complaint, Colonel. My group, as you know, works longer hours than any of the others. The discrimination in quarters shown against them in the past has disturbed me. I don't intend to burden you with our small problems, but I do want you to know that I take seriously my responsibility to my men. As you can see, I've brought them here early to stake out their claim. I judge *this* room to be sufficient for their needs." The colonel lost his anger in his confusion. "Why, yes," he said. "All right, if you think so, Captain."

Actually, the classification group had little work to do. John, who was in charge of the pink cards of all the officers in the division, kept busier than the rest of us, but only because he worked at a slow pace, savoring the information contained on each card. Cynical about the qualifications and intelligence of commissioned officers, he would memorize the histories of the officers in our company whom he most disliked. "Major Musselman is worried that the war may end," he said one day. "I heard him tell Major Sullivan that he was going to investigate the possibilities of becoming Regular Army after the war and keeping his commission. 'Say, that's not a bad idea,' Major Sullivan said. 'Let me know what comes of it, will you, Charlie?'" John chuckled. In recent months, he had cultivated his low chuckles into an irony we all enjoyed. "Before the war, Musselman was a mimeograph operator and Sullivan a custodian at the Boston Armory."

After every engagement, our group made contact by telephone with each of the three infantry regiments and both of the field-artillery battalions, to determine the extent of the casualties. To get these statistics, we cranked the phone and asked for such code names as Black Owl or Fire Tower. There would be static and a hum, and then a distant voice would identify itself as, say, Black Owl and furnish us with a series of further codes, which we would translate into figures for the dead, the wounded, and the missing. We kept a chart of the operational strengths of the regiments and the battalions; our captain, to impress the colonel, instructed us to make the chart a huge one, with striking colors and a carefully printed legend in India ink. Protected by a glassine envelope, it was hung on the wall opposite the French doors.

In our few weeks at the asylum, we made three trips to the replacement depot at Toul, primarily to obtain riflemen and platoon leaders. As their names were called, the soldiers, all of them recently arrived from training camps in the United States, would climb with their equipment into open trucks. The trucks would be loaded to capacity and beyond; the replacements would give a halfhearted cheer as the last man struggled aboard. On all three occasions, it rained, and the men were drenched before they got under way, but each time they were singing as they left. Once, as the trucks bounced out of the depot in a downpour, they sang "Old MacDonald Had a Farm," their moo-moo and bow-wow and oink-oink sounds a forlorn appeal to some lost country of the mind. The riflemen would be taken directly to their units, the officers to our headquarters company to spend the night and to be picked up the following morning by their company commanders.

On the return in the jeep from our first trip to Toul, Stuffy said, "We've got all the luck," and George said in a gentle voice, "Do you feel guilty?" and Stuffy, who was barely five feet tall, said, "No. What German could ever hit *me*, even if I *were* a rifleman?" But I thought him close to tears, and he stayed up all that night, while the distant artillery rumbled, to talk with a new second lieutenant, a replacement too frightened to sleep. "What did you talk about?" George asked Stuffy the next morning, after the lieutenant had left. "*Crime and Punishment*, for Christ's sake," Stuffy said. "Jazz—he plays the clarinet—and the little Hegel we both knew. And, oh God, he hates military life, he hates the thought of killing. . . . When I first saw him, I could tell he was one of us."

"Except that he has to do the killing," John said.

"Yes," Stuffy said. "Except for that."

George, John, Stuffy, and I were banded together—at least, in part—by our awareness of the ignobility of our work. And we were joined by our common dislike of the military organization and mind. Whatever his concern for our cleanliness, our erratic captain was not of our number. Like many another Army opportunist, he would wear on his shoulders by the war's end a maple leaf, or perhaps even an eagle. How much the four of us felt ourselves one upon hearing a report that the four-star general who was the commander of our Third Army had slapped the face of a shell-shocked soldier in our division—he had been criticized for a similar act earlier in the war—calling him a coward and ordering him back into combat! Our private code for this general was Tamburlaine, and we intentionally confused the deeds of the two. "Tell us of some famous warrior, John," we would ask our historian as he deliberated before his pink cards, and he would say, "Tamburlaine— known also as Tamerlane or Timur—was a great commander, but one known for his pride and a certain lack of compassion. He killed eighty thousand at Delhi and in his vainglory built pyramids of their skulls."

Perhaps the new Tamburlaines with their shining boots and riding crops were the sort of men it took to vanquish the Nazis, but George, Stuffy, and I, ten or fifteen or twenty kilometers behind the fighting, simply felt pity for a suffering mankind and a hatred of all violence. George, our soft-spoken sergeant, was the son of a farmer, and in his drawl I could sense a heritage of labor and warm soil. Like all of us—like the whole generation now in uniform—George had grown up in the Depression years; he had been touched then by some notion of a social order in which all men would be brothers. As for myself, when I received my induction notice, my response—I was a senior in college and editor of the newspaper—had been an editorial in which I spoke of the universal language of Beethoven and Brahms, a language that someday would join all men. Someday! A visionary gleam of order, nurtured by books and music and vague political ideas, lay behind all our chartmaking days in those gray buildings near Nancy, with their background of tunes—those of the distant café accordionist, or, on the radio, that lovely evening prayer in "Hänsel und Gretel," which, in translation, begins, "When at night I go to sleep, fourteen angels watch do keep." And, of course, bits of Beethoven and Mozart.

One night, while I was on sentry duty, the rest of my group, their arms over each other's shoulders, went singing out the gate and down the road to Mon Dernier Sou. I had thought to join them, but by the time the new sentry arrived I felt no desire for cognac and talk. So I walked to the office to tune the radio to our favorite German station. A recording had just begun, and I wanted to identify it. One could imagine, in the drumbeats and insistent grandeur of the developing theme, a procession for the soul, a ceremony in which humanity, divested of its grosser elements, acted out its destiny. Resignation—perhaps even tranquillity—was possible, but at an inexpressible cost. A violin repeated the theme, making it delicate and nearly gay. Outside, there was a continuous drum roll. Slipping around one of the blankets tacked over the French door, I stepped into the garden. In the light of a half-moon, I could see high above me formation after formation of bombers, exquisite Vs of Flying Fortresses. "Why, it's Beethoven. Of course," I said aloud, for the music had followed me. "The violin concerto," and the bombers, now part of the musical statement, headed inexorably toward Germany. Their thunder diminished; just as the violin began the cadenza, the radio went dead.

Disturbed, I returned to the office to write a letter to my wife. We had been married on my last furlough, before the division was shipped to Europe. In the few weeks we had been together, we had spoken of what we might do after the war; perhaps we would travel around the country until we found a town to our liking, a community with tall elms and friendly old houses, with a good public library and museum, and with a weekly newspaper we could buy for a song. I suppose such clichés of the imagination are plausible only to very young couples, and to them only in periods that for one reason or another prevent the search. But, as always, I spoke of our plans in my letter. I had nearly finished writing it when, without warning, the violinist returned to complete his phrase. It was as if he had stood with bow suspended while the bombers roared toward their target. Now the cadenza enabled him to display his craftsmanship, to make sounds that climbed and quivered and tumbled. The virtuosity excited me. After that portentous lapse, how brave these acrobatics! Yet the violinist's noise was a recorded one, the station represented an enemy driven by fanaticism and madness to the slaughter of a race, the bombers were *mine*. My brother, like my father before him, had been attracted to flying; an instructor of military pilots, perhaps he had trained some of the men on this mission, perhaps they were his friends.

The slow opening measures of the second movement were accompanied by the distant roll. While the larghetto played, those graceful winged shapes from my country thundered overhead, returning to their base, their formations beneath the moon as exact as ever. I stood again in the garden until all the bombers had vanished and the concerto came to a close that perhaps was intended to be triumphant—but the soul of Beethoven, as well as my notions of harmony and order, had lost the power to shelter.

The next day, George asked me to do some trivial task. I snapped at him, "Why don't you do it yourself?" Our captain said, "What's that? Are you refusing an order from your noncom?" "It wasn't an order,"

George said. "It was a request." "George," I said, "I'm sorry." Headquarters Company left the asylum that week to take over the old Gestapo buildings in Metz, where I managed to transfer out of the A.G.O. to edit the divisional newspaper. I was pleased to have the infantrymen crowd around the newspaper-laden jeep, grabbing copies. In the winter, Stuffy wrote that he and George and John envied me my new job and that the captain, as the consequence of some near-fiasco, had become a major. After my discharge from the Army and for some years thereafter, I never consciously thought of my brief stay at Nancy, and if for one reason or another it did come to my mind I ridiculed myself for having cloaked, like any adolescent, a faithless and brutal present with the robes of a future grace.

In the forested hollows of eastern Kentucky, there still are people who, regardless of the antennas on the cabin roofs, will die without leaving the county of their birth. Mostly, they are of Scotch descent; their names, like the hills, gradually erode, and the Caldwalls are now the Caudills and the Caudles. The frontiersmen, the hunters, the seekers of a land as verdurous as their dreams, have become small-town merchants, miners on relief, revivalists, salesmen of burial insurance and old Fords, bootleggers who are jailed only during election week, farmers of land tilting to the valley floors.

The only non-natives of the region (or so it seemed to me while I lived there) belong to the service professions; they are librarians, social workers, teachers, nurses, a few doctors. In summertime, bookmobiles driven by Smith and Vassar girls bounce wildly over the dirt roads and dry creek beds. I have heard of an Eastern college girl who came to Kentucky to drive a bookmobile and stayed to marry a local boy—one with the charm of a gay and irresponsible nature. Disowned by her wealthy family, distrusted by the women of her new community, she gave birth to a son in a hillside cabin. Her husband was caught in some theft and imprisoned in the county jail. Marriage to her had given him a pride and a fastidiousness that made him reject the jail fare; he demanded that she cook and bring his meals to his cell. She would put her baby and her husband's supper in a toy wagon, which she would pull down the town's chief street to the jail, her eyes cast upon nothing but her own bare feet.

And I have heard the story of a Jewish refugee, a professor of history, who had been a brilliant scholar in Berlin. After escaping to London, he received an offer of a teaching position in an institution so far back in the Kentucky hills that muleback was the most feasible means of arriving there. The faculty lived in cabins, they ate from tin plates and drank from painted Campbell-soup cans. There was a community outhouse, and a pump for washing faces and cleaning teeth. The professor from Berlin accepted the offer; perhaps he thought—after all, the school had invited *him*—the institution a place like Harvard. The day after his arrival, he slit his throat with his razor.

I had just completed my graduate studies and was in Kentucky on my first teaching assignment. Five years had passed since my discharge from the Army. The town was hardly the one my wife and I had dreamed of finding while we were separated by the war; still, wanting to like it, I felt the appeal of its poverty and isolation. The main street followed a creek that flooded each spring; residential streets the width of alleys either came to a dead end before a bluff or, finding a gap in the encircling hills, wandered into the countryside to become wagon trails and then footpaths. The old men gathered together in the summer evenings on the benches of the courthouse lawn while their children and grandchildren attended either the movies or a vigorous prayer-and-hymn session at one of the many small churches. On Saturday nights the jukeboxes in the cafés competed with the loud-speaker of the store that displayed used appliances—old refrigerators and stoves and fans—on the sidewalk. The owner of that store, a graduate of the college where I taught, would try to sell, with comic pantomime and great bursts of laughter, jiffy can openers to motorists stopped before the town's single traffic light. I remember seeing, soon after I arrived in town and the week before the public schools were open for the year, a hill father and his junior-high-school daughter in one of the clothing stores. He was dressed in clean overalls, she in one of the cotton prints that I was to learn were made from flour sacks.

"Wouldn't you like something like this?" he said, pointing to a pair of sturdy brown shoes, but she looking wistfully at a pair of bright-colored pumps. They studied the shoes she wanted. "Will they wear?" he asked the clerk, who answered with regret, "Not so well as the regular school ones." "I reckon we'll buy them anyway," the father said, and he and his daughter smiled at each other while he took some crumpled bills from his pocket.

The instructor of French at the college was a granddaughter of an Italian princess. She lived frugally in a garage apartment, most of her pay going for the support of destitute aristocrats in Italy. I liked her for her vivacity and intelligence and the pride with which she carried herself, but the dream of the past was upon her; she raged at the ignorance and sloth of her students, at the lack of culture in that Kentucky hollow into which she had been driven.

Another of the instructors, an elderly archeologist, had discovered in his twenties the remains of an Inca community in a remote Peruvian plateau. There was a fragile, even a nebulous, quality to him. My office was in a basement, and the cement slab of my window ledge made a bench for people outside who wished to talk with me. The archeologist sat on the slab late one afternoon. I had just been reading a book on Hinduism and had been fascinated by the notion of a deity of whom, since he possessed no attributes, nothing could be said. I mentioned to the archeologist that Brahma was impervious to all conceivable advances in science. "Yes, there is certainly much of value in Hinduism," he replied mildly. "Do I really exist? Is not the world, everything that we see, an illusion?" He peered through the screen at me, his blue eyes pale and enormous.

Partly, I suppose, for some quality he shared with the archeologist, I was intrigued from my first meeting with him by one of the middle-aged instructors in the English department. He was a slender man, with a shy smile and a drawl that emphasized his gentleness; he had appeared at my house one day while my wife was busy with Larry, a baby then. I sat on the grass while he sprawled out in the autumn sun. That evening, I walked around town with him, watching as the nighthawks dropped from the sky and the mist rose from the valley.

We said nothing to each other. At the movie theater, he stopped to look at a Western from the open door until the manager asked us to buy tickets. I accompanied him to his apartment to meet his wife (she wasn't home) and to drink wine and listen to a recording of a "Brandenburg" Concerto. But our lack of conversation was beginning to make me uncomfortable.

"What do you teach in your Victorian literature course?" I asked.

He thought about the question for a painfully long period. "If it's a poor-to-average class, I'm afraid I stick pretty much with Tennyson and Arnold and that crowd," he finally said, making an apologetic sweep with his hand. "I can't see that they could really *harm* anybody."

"No," I agreed.

"If I have a good class, I like to think they can read 'In Memoriam' and 'Dover Beach' without much help. I don't believe in courses limited by dates, anyway. I teach my good classes Augustine and Aquinas." He looked away from me, embarrassed. "Sometimes—it's what I do with a really *fine* Victorian class—we read a bit in Latin and maybe even a bit in Italian. I like to end the year with the 'Fioretti di San Francesco'— you know, 'The Little Flowers of St. Francis.' Tell me, have you ever been to Assisi?"

I considered myself capable of meeting the world without dream or self-deception; I believed in those useful actions that make us feel more at home in the human world. My wife and I had bought our first home in Kentucky. What I wanted was to be a good teacher at the college and an accepted member of the community. I thought that the instructor who had best achieved these goals was Albert Fischman, the plump and nearly bald biologist who had come, a refugee, from Vienna. I admired him for his love of his sturdy wife, for the affection he displayed toward nearly everybody. On warm days when the classroom windows were open, his shrill lecturing voice, colored by his Austrian accent, could be heard everywhere on campus. He belonged to the local bridge club and the men's civic organization. At Christmastime, he sold cut evergreens for the latter group on Main Street, outvying in his good humor the merchant who tried to sell can openers. He derived as much pleasure from such activities as he did from arguments with his colleagues about Dostoevski, Camus, and Existential philosophy, the paintings of the Impressionists, or the destiny of Russia (he could speak Russian fluently).

Only in his overriding love for music did he remain a Viennese. Once, my wife and I drove with him and his wife to Cincinnati to attend an outdoor performance, at the zoo, of "Aïda." Leaving the stands after the final curtain, he began humming, as another member of the faculty had told me he would, a waltz from "Der Rosenkavalier." Any opera put him in good spirits and reminded him of "Der Rosenkavalier." With its mockery and gaiety and enchanting tunes, Strauss's opera was to Albert a memento of his youth and of prewar Vienna.

He and his wife had escaped Hitler, but nearly all the other members of both their families had died in concentration camps. In New York, Albert, despite his training and experience (the holder of a doctorate in biology, he had taught for some years in a Viennese institute), had been a middle-aged copyist for a sheet-music publisher. When he had asked if he might go to Kentucky to see about a job in his own field, his employer had said, "If that's how you feel, you're fired." In recounting to me his employer's response, Albert said, "You can see what kind of copyist I was." And he added—for he was addicted to the obvious—"A lousy copyist." He said, "So I borrowed the money to come here by train. You know what Railroad Street looks like when you first see it? A set for a cowboy movie. O.K. I was so glad they took me I cried. I knew it was for life—you can't do research in a little college, and with such an accent, no research, who else would take you? But what does it matter where you are? And who should weight himself with the past?"

Albert found eastern Kentucky a green and lovely place; he delighted in the names of its towns—Dwarf and Pippa Passes (called for years Pippapass until somebody reread Browning), Pomp and Salt Lick. He was touched even more than I by the innocence of some of the students (when I told him that as a result of my misspelling of a student's name she had begun to misspell it, too, thinking that I should know better than she, he smiled and said, "Of course she would! Of course!"). He was a friend of farmers as well as townspeople. That exile from Vienna was more at home in that hollow than I, for all my wishes, was ever to be.

I had some remarkable students in that little hill college, and one group of them—they met for weekly discussions before the fireplace in my house—was among the best I've known. When my classes exceeded my expectations, I was delighted, but my expectations, raised higher by each student superior to his predecessors, were bound to be defeated. And I found it difficult to accept with any equanimity one of the causes—the semi-literacy of some public-school teachers—for the showing of my poorer students. In my first summer, I taught a small group of elementary-school teachers from rural areas who, because of state requirements, had to attend college to keep their certificates. They were to read aloud, for analysis, selected prose passages. Daily, when it came her turn to read, one white-haired woman would look about in consternation, throw up her arms, and exclaim helplessly, "Oh, I've forgotten my glasses *again!*" Finally, I told her she was not to enter the room without them; and the next day, wearing her glasses, she struggled to read, waiting for somebody else to pronounce for her all words of any difficulty. "But I teach just the early grades!" she cried, breaking into tears.

When I spoke of her to Albert, he said simply, "In Germany, of course, you would find nothing like that. But what does a rigorous educational system produce?"

"You condone near-illiteracy here because of the Nazis there?"

"No, I don't condone it," he said. "I don't suppose, though, that it matters."

"Of course it matters!" I said.

He looked at me kindly, and then patted my shoulder. "Reading poor examinations makes me sick to the stomach," he said. "But I have no solution to the ills of mankind. You have to take what comes."

The semester that brought me the gifted students who met in my house also brought me a class of inept sophomores. The sophomores took their final examination on an overcast afternoon. Earnest and frightened, they stared at the ceiling for answers. One boy and girl, very much in love, looked openly at each other's papers. I watched them, thinking—with equal amounts of pity and cynicism—that neither could help the other very much. At one point, the girl leaned over and nipped the boy's ear; his eyes became glazed. How alien I felt to that lovesick couple, how divorced from all those bewildered and ignorant hill children! The classroom was on the top floor of the building; I wandered to the open window to look out upon the town. I could see the frame stores, the movie theater, the series of tiny house roofs that included my own. By the depot, a freight train whistled and began to back its empty livestock cars toward the little stockyard. Strands of mist drifted before the moist, green hills, sealing us all in that hollow. And it seemed to me then that the greater world was a honeycomb, an endless series of these sealed worlds, each inhabitant of each town or neighborhood a microcosm within a microcosm and yet each inhabitant my brother. It is a common enough feeling, this double sense of loneliness and unity, of a human connection made known to us by our awareness of isolation: I was to have the same feeling in Paris a decade later. But it left me dissatisfied with myself and my achievements.

Several years before I left Kentucky, the Fischmans bought a house. To my knowledge, it was the only material thing they had ever wished for, and when their savings approximated the price of a modest white cottage with a second bedroom that Albert could use for a study, they bought it outright. Albert, stout and clumsy though he was, spaded a garden. He puffed behind a lawnmower, he dug out dandelions, he planted a tree. He painted siding, in the process dripping paint on his clothes and bald head. In the dry season, he set fire to a weed patch, nearly burning down his house as well as a portion of the Cumberland National Forest; after that day, he would not light a match outdoors. In a sense, their cottage was the Fischmans' child. In Vienna, they had barely reached the stability that would have enabled them to have a family when Hitler became a threat.

My wife and I frequently visited them in the summer evenings. The house was immaculate and brilliantly illuminated. Albert played operas for us on an elderly phonograph; he would stand before the little machine, conducting and joining in even on the soprano arias until his wife would say, "Albert!" The evening would end with coffee and hot Austrian pastries that Mrs. Fischman had baked while we were listening, the aroma from the kitchen counteracting even the pathos of the ending of "La Bohème."

After the music, I could speak to Albert of personal and perhaps even evanescent feelings, knowing that he would understand before I began the attempt to explain them. But once when I spoke of the feeling I had experienced during the examination of my inept sophomores, he replied almost curtly, "I do not believe in vague desires. They lead to headaches and heartaches and worse. Yearnings I leave to Wagner. Will you have another piece of pastry?"

One evening in the fall term of what was to be my last year at the college, I took a walk, alone, through the few streets of the town. It was still relatively early. I had become, of course, thoroughly familiar with the community and knew what to expect: in the new cement-block church, occupied by the radical splinter group of a sedate congregation, a preacher, aided by occasional rhythmic hymns and a rapt audience, would be grasping toward that moment in which he could speak in unknown tongues; at the bus station, the blind ballad singer would be in his wheelchair, sleeping until the eleven o'clock bus from Lexington arrived; behind the ferns of a dusty store window on an alley that led to the railroad depot, certain farmers stealthily would be drinking illegal whiskey they could not afford. Walking past the crumbling, whitewashed brick courthouse and the benches for old men, I thought, with a passion that surprised me, I don't want to grow old here; I don't want to be buried in this town. And I saw that the construction I had recently completed on my house—an addition to the living room and a new bathroom, two improvements that I had thought would make my house as important to me as Albert Fischman's to him—was only a sign of my discontent. That spring I applied for my present position in Ithaca.

Our farewell visit with Albert and his wife was little different from our other visits with them. To me, it was such an important farewell that I wanted tears to be in his eyes; I was upset by his smiles. I wanted to shake him and to say in anger, "Why aren't you as lonely this moment as I? Why is it that you can accept and I cannot? Tell me, what is the secret of happiness?" But the evening passed like any other.

As Albert and his wife stood by our car, though, he said, "I hear you haven't been able to sell your house."

"No," I said.

"And you can't buy a house in New York until you sell it?"

I said, "It doesn't matter."

"Well," he said, putting his arm around his wife, "we have decided to buy it. O.K.?"

"No," I said.

His voice, as he tried to persuade us of the rationality of the proposal, was that of the high-pitched lecturer I had so often heard as I wandered across the campus. They would put a small mortgage on their house for the down payment, he said; they would rent ours to somebody until they could sell it.

"You would take such a chance?" I cried. "Oh, Albert!"

"It is not much to do for a friend," Albert said.

Of course, my wife and I refused. As we drove away, Albert Fischman's arm was still around his wife; behind them I could see through a chintz-curtained window into their bright living room, with its pictures hung high upon the walls at regular intervals. And I knew with appalling clarity that after I had left this miserable and poverty-stricken hamlet with its human and educational problems as insurmountable as its limestone-topped hills, I would pity it and love it and think that if I had but stayed I might have been like Albert Fischman after all. I said to my wife, "I hate it here. It's suffocating. I'm glad we're going."

Last year, while I was in Paris, a friend from America asked me to accompany him and his wife on a motor trip to Aachen, where he had some business to transact. I had no idea of the route one takes to get from Paris to that corner of Germany; everything I saw was a surprise. Our road paralleled for a time the Marne and the course of some of the fiercest fighting of the First World War. We passed the inevitable series of military graveyards, each with a flag by the gate to identify the nation of those buried beneath its acres of crosses; we saw the signpost to Armentières; we drove through the streets of Château-Thierry. The historical perspective we had—the knowledge that all the destruction of that war was without purpose—gave, of course, a melancholy and unreal quality to the landscape. Our car was a cozy and efficient German vehicle that my friend had just purchased. Coming down a long hill, we saw below us and across the flat countryside of Champagne the spires of the cathedral at Reims.

Though the spires at Reims are too similar to give the distant profile of the cathedral the queer sense of an antithesis that somehow makes a unity of the profile at Chartres, I felt as we approached the town and the cathedral the same pleasure that my first view of Chartres had given me: those twin spires seemed an enduring answer to the route we had just traveled. The month was April, the day overcast and cool. The cathedral, as well as the little square before it and the surrounding souvenir shops, was deserted. The air within the cathedral remained that of winter; except for the rose window, the interior at first struck me as austere and colorless. The building was in surprisingly good repair. Joan of Arc had stood next to Charles VII during his coronation in Reims, but one did not feel in that echoing nave the presence of a past which lurks in the shadows and soot and colored glass of so many Gothic structures.

And yet this interior had an atmosphere of its own—a poignant serenity—and I whispered to my friend, "What is its secret?" not yet thinking that I had asked myself the same question about the same quality in a man I had admired in eastern Kentucky, or that the interior held something for which I had been searching since my childhood. Pointing to the myriad of little statues rising in the wall, my friend said, "They've been damaged and repaired. Look, this whole building has been destroyed and put back together." And, of course, it was true. Many of the statues were missing; a number of those that seemed intact had been cunningly cemented together from fragments. Stones were pitted, apparently by exploding shrapnel. Perhaps if I had known in advance of the shelling of Reims in the Franco-Prussian War and then much more extensively in the First World War I, would have been less moved; but in looking from statue to statue, from stone to stone, in perceiving separately each of the many acts of restoration, I had the sense of a fragile peace that existed only as the consequence of outrage and violence. It took such violence to gain the sweet tranquillity of Reims. It was then that I remembered Albert Fischman, who had known how to live in the present. I believed I understood his secret at last.

One must be cautious about making pronouncements occasioned by cathedrals. Before great monuments, even great minds have been known to express some pretty foolish sentiments. Still, to glimpse in a cathedral, *any* cathedral, the meaningless of a past that is also the meaninglessness of what is to come is not so perverse as it might appear. Such an insight is, I suppose, as encompassing as the vision of a God who participates in every action, every object, of the universe. Perhaps some such acceptance of purposelessness in past and future is our only means of recapturing whatever it is that has haunted and deluded us since childhood. In that cathedral, for the moment that I believed I shared Albert Fischman's secret, I might with propriety have made a votary offering to some fat and happy little saint floating toes up on the lid of his stone casket.

At a souvenir shop, I saw a postcard photograph of the burning cathedral, the orange and red flames leaping from the shattered roof as high as the spires; it was the image I half expected to see in the rearview mirror—for I was taking my turn as a driver—as we left Reims on that overcast afternoon.

On the night of this September's full moon, my wife and I waited until the children were asleep to pick one of the pumpkins Cris had been refusing to harvest. My wife made pumpkin pie; furtive as thieves, we ate the first warm pieces on the porch step at midnight. The new paint on the house glistened in the moonlight. From the dark woods to the east, we heard the sweet notes of a bird we had never heard before, perhaps a fall warbler heading south. The call was answered by an identical call from the woods to the west. Singing as they went, those two invisible birds flew toward each other, to meet in the maple in our yard. Their songs made eyes of our ears; the world held a promise that blindness can see.

A few nights later, I lay in bed remembering Reims. I could not sleep. I came downstairs to take two aspirins with a slug of whiskey. Then I wandered into the music room, for in this room is a large reproduction of Utrillo's painting of the cathedral. The light from the next room poured through the doorway, touching the colors and making them shimmer. For a hallucinatory moment, I thought the painting and the wall behind it to be on fire; the chirruping of crickets in every corner of every dark first-floor room was the crackling of the spreading flames.

The following Sunday, I went to the town dump with the weekly garbage and debris. My family accompanied me, at my request, and the two dogs—one a mongrel and the other Black Judy—jumped into the car with us. I sometimes think the town dumps of America have usurped the church's role as Sunday meeting place, for on Sunday morning, at least at our dump, one finds families like my own. One also finds young lovers embracing in their cars, boys shooting rats with .22s, elderly people dressed up in their best clothes and talking from car windows to each other.

Larry was tossing some worn-out clothing onto a smoldering rubbish heap when a rumple-haired, bare-chested man in his middle years came running over. "Don't burn up my bread and butter!" he cried, retrieving the clothes. On his left arm was the tattoo of a naked girl; her breasts moved with each swelling of his biceps. Both dogs were barking at him from the rear of the station wagon.

"What a fine dog!" he said, and his eyes became watery.

"The German shepherd?" I asked.

"No, the curly-hair," he said. "When I was a boy, I had a dog just like that, but I shot him. By God, the smartest dog that ever was! I was offered five hundred dollars for him, but would I take it? No sir, not for my old Curly."

"Why did you shoot him?"

"I should have shot my uncle—that bastard! My neighbors said my Curly was stealing their chickens and they'd have the law on my old man. It was my uncle that stole them—I seen every last one of those chickens in his coop and me with the burying shovel still in my hand. Bam! Bam! I gave that shovel to those chickens, I tell you! God, I wish I still had my Curly! Money can't fetch that kind of friend!"

Like that scavenger my age at the dump, I suppose I exploit my past the better to know my longings. A curly-haired mongrel or a fat man in a pool become ludicrous childhood images of peace and wholeness to be pursued until the ending of desire. Yet neither he nor I nor anyone is quite so simple as this suggests. For we are the totality of our pasts; we lose nothing, and each day is the summation of everything that has preceded it. I look back at myself as I was on Labor Day and say with patience to myself as if I were a child, Look. Look at this house. The mindless joy you felt as you splashed paint upon it and later as you swam in your pond is the joy of a period in your childhood that you have never lost. It is the peace that music gave you in the Army; it is what you once saw in Albert Fischman; it is part of what you felt in a cathedral. God knows everything it is. The desolation you felt as you looked at Jupiter after the fire is every desolation you have known. It is your father leaving you; it is truckloads of soldiers going into battle in the rain and singing "Old MacDonald Had a Farm"; it is bombers over your head while you listen to Beethoven; it is a wall of mended statues and a postcard in which Reims burns with Kodak colors. For we grow by accretion—a pile of joy here and a pile of desolation there. The irrational intensity of our feelings in middle age comes from the awful size of the piles, and we're lucky if we can find in our minds some cathedral grand enough to hold them both.

On windless mornings in late September, the ground is covered with frost, the leaves fall in sunlight like colored rain and the pond steams like a kettle. Though I can't be sure that what I've said is as true as it should be, I know at least of Labor Day that it has had a clear consequence: we have a household fire extinguisher hanging on the wall by the kitchen stairs. It has a chromium dial and a gleaming red tank. It cost thirty-three dollars, and is guaranteed effective against all types of fire.

1965

Standing on the Public Square

8   THE PRESENT TENSE IS INCAPABLE OF conclusion. The moments we relive in the present tense are not moments of a whole action; they catch the wave on the verge of breaking, not the breaking and foaming wave that will dissolve in a hiss upon the beach. There is one moment of my life, a few days after my eighteenth birthday, that I think of as presently occurring. I am standing by the Soldiers and Sailors Monument on the Public Square in downtown Cleveland. It is dusk. The pigeons have already found—on the sooty ledges of the Public Library, the Society for Savings Bank, Cleveland College, and the Old Stone Church—their resting places for the night. A brightly lighted but empty streetcar, its motor throbbing like a heart, waits nearby. I am looking at the college; I will soon enter it as a freshman, and under my arms are the books I will study, their stiff bindings still holding inviolate that promise found in the scent of fresh ink and glue and paper. The building (it has since been destroyed, to make room for a parking lot) is seven stories high, its architecture vaguely Romanesque. It has an intricate series of arched windows and several narrow balconies supported by stout Roman goddesses. At the top of the structure, the words CHAMBER OF COMMERCE can be seen in daylight hours, for the building has not always been a college; a red neon sign attached to the concrete ankles of the goddesses advertises its present use as an institution of higher learning.

The year is 1939, the month is September; a war has just commenced in Europe. But with what fascination I am looking at that sign! The building itself—a plump and pinkish silhouette behind the glowing letters—is to me friendly and warm, a stout receptacle for spiritual coinage and a fitting companion to the neighboring Society for Savings. I will ignore the war as best I can, for the education of boys my age has not prepared me to accept it.

In grammar school in New York and Arkansas and Kentucky as well as Ohio, I was made aware of my good fortune, despite the difficulties of the times, in being an American. London had fogs and the canals of Venice carried sewage; in India, Mahatma Gandhi and his people were starving, although cows were allowed to wander at will through the gardens, trampling the vegetables they didn't eat. In Japan women slept on wooden pillows to protect their lacquered hair styles, and the feet of infant girls were tightly bound to keep them tiny. Likely as not, a Russian groom would throw his bride to the pursuing wolves as they returned in their droshky from the wedding. If the brides didn't die from the wolves, they died in childbirth; their husbands, meanwhile, languished in chains in some Siberian salt mine. In my high school civics classes in Ohio and Illinois and Michigan, I drew maps of Utopian cities of a future America, cities without slums in which the curving streets were named for presidents and spring flowers. In my history classes I learned of the folly of war. I looked at battle photographs, at the men lying dead in the trenches or stretched out against barbed wire like tattered and fire-blackened Christs whose sacrifices have been in vain. And I was taught, as part of the enlightened idealism in the air, to be wary of that patriotism that had been inculcated within me. An examination of my country's history would show its role as exploiter as well as defender of human rights.

As I gaze upon those unblinking red letters of my future Alma Mater, how good I feel! In that quiet and dusky interval between rush hour and evening night club and theater traffic, I am perhaps safer and more complete than I ever will be again. I know how to select what is valuable from all the nationalistic and religious muck of the past; I know what to ignore in the present. My belief is, people are brothers and should learn how to trust each other. Whatever the truth about

Christ's parentage, the Golden Rule is O.K. I would place love and friendship above national interest. I would never kill another man. It is very simple. My devout mother agrees with most of my convictions. My father, a businessman, takes only minor exceptions. My friends and past teachers are in agreement, and so too, I am sure, are the textbooks under my arm. I haven't as yet read it; nevertheless, the ending of my modern European history text, published in May—and now, a quarter of a century later, lying open, battered and yellowing, upon my desk on a day in late summer, a season of serenity here but of continuing ambush and terror in Vietnam—is part of that present moment as I relive it. The writer speaks of the contemporary period as one of "war, dictatorship, and chaotic art and science." But then there are these two sentences, magnificent in their rhetorical rhythms: "The lamentations of Jeremiah were followed by the rise of Greek civilization; the lucubrations of Salvian, by the emergence of European civilization. It may well be that Spengler is but the darkness preceding the dawn of a still more glorious day in human civilization." Those rhythms beat out into the gathering night, to merge with the bells of the Old Stone Church as they sound the hour.

With the help of my older sons and that of college students who on occasion come out into the Finger Lakes countryside to visit us, I have spent the summer working on barns and fences. We tore down a large barn weakened, years before we bought our property, by a hurricane and neglect; we saved a few of its sound hand-hewn timbers to reinforce rotting ones in another barn. Around this barn we built a wooden fence and within it stalls for the two-year-old gelding and the six-year-old mare I bought in midsummer. The mare is stubborn but gentle, a family horse that had belonged to our plumber. The gelding is pony-size; he follows the children about like a dog, and likes to rest his head on their shoulders. Earlier in the year, so that we could have a crop of hay and at least the beginnings of a pasture when the horses arrived, my wife and I spread clover and timothy seed in one field, and timothy and bird's-foot trefoil in another. From a neighbor I had borrowed a couple of old Cyclone seeders, the kind that are carried over the shoulder and shower out seed into pants and shoes as well as the ground when the crank is turned. Revolving the cranks furiously, my wife and I raced each other down the fields as a light rain was falling; we laughed and sang, having a fine time playacting as farmers, and some of our seed actually managed to germinate and grow. In August Larry and I put a metal roof on the red barn we use as a garage. Sitting on the peak of that high barn, I put down my hammer to look at my world—the white-painted house, the other barns, all of them turned silver by the sun and wind and snow; the fields and the woods. Jimmy played in his sandbox. My wife was in the garden, picking corn. Cris sat on the fence rail, stroking the horses; they, hoping to get the corn husks, were pressed against the fence, intently watching my wife. I could imagine at that moment no place I would rather be than this farm, and I knew myself the most fortunate of men. I was sure *my* gooseberries were not sour; and yet, looking at the activity beneath me and the altering cloud patterns on the distant ridge, I felt an insubstantial and deceiving quality in my environment, and thought there was something absurd about me, a college professor in his forties, sitting blissfully in farmer's jeans on the top of a barn roof.

I returned to my hammering. But mechanical labor simply abets the unreality of the present time and place. The solitary mind becomes the only reality. Like a child making rock candy, one drops a string into the liquid of the past and observes, as if the process contained no further act of volition, the developing crystals. On that barn roof— heated and blinded by the reflection of the sun on each sheet of metal my fifteen-year-old son and I nailed down—I remembered myself standing on the Public Square in Cleveland, and felt again the old idealism. But the string I dropped into the past was more tangible than that. I was thinking of my curious youthful commitment to journalism. As a boy and young man I had made of newspapers the repository for, and the guardian of, the human good; and for a time during the second war I had thought of myself, in my editorial work, as the last supporter of that good. Even now the names of newspapers—*Beacon-Journal, Star,* and all the rest—have a vestigial magic for me, as if they were part of some lost ritual or rite; and I sometimes say them over to myself in bed on nights when I cannot sleep, much as my old friend Albert Fischman would counter insomnia by thinking of the wallpaper design in each of the rooms of each apartment in which he had lived before he bought his house in eastern Kentucky.

I finished high school in a small consolidated school fifteen miles from downtown Cleveland; I was editor of the mimeographed school newspaper and village correspondent for a Cleveland daily. The stories I mailed to the city newspaper were altered by unknown professional hands. My account that children were being given a spoonful of cod liver oil at the school lunch counter became a story of their "reluctant spooning." The local blacksmith, thought to be the last survivor of his trade in the county, supported himself by engaging in light machine work; months later, the story I wrote about him came back to me, strangely altered, in the weekly news magazine for high school seniors. His name had been garbled, a "ski" added to the end; his duties were now the pristine ones of primordial blacksmiths. His forge a metaphor for the melting pot, he had become an immigrant taken into the American mainstream, a Pole turned into the stalwart hero of the Longfellow poem. A musty account book that I found on a shelf in the old school on the village green told me that Raymond Moley—an area youth who later became a member of President Roosevelt's Brain Trust—had been paid, as a schoolboy, a small sum for cleaning the outhouse. This story appeared, meticulously accurate, in a number of newspapers and magazines. In posting my news items, I had the sense that they were being channeled to a mysterious center, the secret heart, of America, to be ignored or transformed or used verbatim in accordance with their relevance to some benign social truth that, like a Platonic absolute, I could perceive but the shadow of.

In college, I wrote for the school newspaper. I still lived in the village, and for a time commuted to classes by train. As American participation in the war became more likely, I scribbled away, not only as a college reporter; for, out of some compulsion, I founded and edited a weekly newspaper in the village. My father, then in the automobile business, gave me an old Ford to help me in *my* enterprise. I printed in red paint the name of the newspaper on both doors and parked with impunity in no-parking zones. I proofread material while driving from city to village and back, the galleys on a piece of cardboard held against the steering wheel. According to the gossip column in the first issue after Pearl Harbor, "the village was quiet on Sunday and Monday, as residents stayed in their houses, listening to the radio." It was the new weekly's only acknowledgment of our entrance into war. Soon after my appointment as editor of the college paper, I took on a third job in journalism, that of nightside copyboy for the afternoon newspaper that once had paid me for my news stories. Actually, I suppose, it was my fourth, for I was on a working scholarship at the college, paying for my tuition by serving on the janitorial staff and writing items for the college news bureau. Between and after classes I slept on a cot in the darkroom of one newspaper or another; never very heavy, I lost ten pounds my last year in college.

As nightside copyboy, I was often the only person on duty in the large city room. After the Public Library closed its telephone answering service for the night, I was the source of information for high school students working belatedly on assignments; from eleven o'clock on, I resolved poker disputes. My word was never questioned. How do I say what I felt during those long nights? I felt a love for I-didn't-know-what—for the sleeping city, for a whole nation sleeping from ocean to ocean beneath the same stars and moon. Listening to the clacking and bell-jangling of the United Press teletypes to which I fed each midnight fresh rolls of yellow paper for their new alarms, I imagined a wild ringing and sudden bulletins—the war has ended, Hitler and Hirohito have acknowledged in a joint communiqué their sins; weeping from their respective bunkers in Europe and Asia, they wave the white flags of surrender. Single-handedly I put out an extra edition. The joy my newspaper brings a waking public!

As my induction into the Army approached, I became more and more conscious of alterations in the people and institutions about me. When I told my mother I hoped I would fail my Army physical examination, she said with a tremble in her voice, "I hope you pass." My gentle mother! The dean of students, an elderly woman whom I considered my friend—in my freshman year, believing I might become a scholar, she had encouraged my interest in political structures and had asked me to give an hour's lecture on Marxist theory in her European history class—told me coldly, "I am ashamed of you," after I quoted to her, in defense of my wish to stay out of war as long as I could, one of her remarks about human brotherhood.

The change in my father was of a different sort. In one miraculous transformation, he left expensive automobiles, the Republican party, and the quest of a private dream of success that had kept him unstable in his personal loyalties and made him, throughout my childhood, renounce job for job and city for city; for the duration he became the operator of a turret lathe who worked from eight to twelve hours a day, an official in his local labor union, and a Democrat. In a moment of fatigue, he lost part of a thumb to his machine, but was back at work the following day wearing a blood-stained bandage. At a time when I was becoming increasingly peevish, he turned selfless and kind; he was able to understand my predicament, and compassionate enough to withhold judgment. After my village newspaper failed for lack of funds, he asked for my old Ford as his contribution to the motor pool. Dressed in baggy coveralls, he would drive that rattling and garishly painted car off into the early morning mists that in the spring and fall often covered the Lake Erie shoreline. Once, seeing him leave the driveway as I returned from my night job at the newspaper, I thought, "My God, Dad, you've got guts"; but I never told him of the pride I felt for him at that moment, and I soon enough accepted his behavior as another odd example of the American psychic metamorphosis.

The daily newspaper for which I worked had become shrill and declamatory and—or so I thought—hypocritical in its patriotism. One of my last acts as copyboy was to roll up one night more than a hundred feet of rubber matting newly installed on the city room floor, load it—it was so heavy that later, when I admitted to the act, nobody would believe I had done it alone; but I had been full of noble glow—on a handcart and place it before the editor's office door. I taped to it his editorial from the previous day's paper asking Clevelanders to sacrifice, for the sake of the boys overseas, whatever items of rubber they could possibly do without. I heard the editor was furious, but the mat vanished, the bare floor a testimony to the efficacy of editorials. A week or so later, I became a soldier.

The divisional newspaper I worked on in Europe was my own idea. Restless, aware that some other overseas divisions had them, I suggested to the captain in charge of public relations that we start one. He spoke to the general's aide who spoke to the general; the general decided we could put out a trial issue. I was appointed editor. The captain and I were the staff. By this time our division was fighting in Luxembourg. We were given the kitchen of a bombed-out farmhouse, one near the Belgian border, as an office for that first issue. It was snowing on the fields and within the kitchen. We wore gloves as we typed. Occasionally we had to warm our typewriters on the lid of the kitchen stove.

An itinerant pair of American civilians engaged in propaganda work for the government had managed to confiscate all the newsprint in the area. They offered us some for the first issue, but said that if our newspaper continued we would have to furnish them with two bottles of Scotch for the newsprint of each succeeding issue. They were a dubious pair, ostensibly experienced in journalism; one of them told me he had left an editorial position on a Cleveland daily to do his bit for the war effort, and when I asked him for the name of the newspaper he mentioned the one I had worked for. His own name was unknown to me. The two of them were looking for balloons to send messages of some sort into Germany, but their main concern was to publicize, with the invasion of Germany imminent, the ruling against fraternization with the enemy. One of them boasted that he already had as mistress a German girl, a member of the former royal family who had remained in Luxembourg City after the German army had retreated. I thought of them as petty racketeers and knew that my newspaper would be beyond corruption, whatever the bribes we had to pay.

The editorial in the first issue said we intended our weekly to be like a small-town newspaper that considers its chief task one of getting the names and activities of its readers into print. The second issue—for the general not only permitted us to continue but provided the required Scotch from his personal allowance and saw to it that we would have a driver for our jeep, a private with an artistic bent who could draw cartoons for the paper—spoke of our pride in our division, for we were "the kind of outfit that doesn't romanticize war." We had published three or four issues when the general sent his aide to tell the captain to see him. The general was completely in accord with our presentation of the news, the captain told me after the interview; he had congratulated us for the success of the paper—it had raised the morale of the enlisted men—and said that henceforth he would be one of our contributors. He planned to write a column, a weekly message from the general to his troops, for the front page. Immediately I became indignant. I said, "The front page is for *news,* not opinions." "But he's the *general,*" the captain said, and I replied, "You can tell him he can have his column on the second page, along with our editorials. Either that, or I quit." "You'll be busted to rifleman," the captain said. I said, "O.K., if that's the way he wants it. If I can't run a good newspaper, I don't want to run a newspaper at all." But the general, more flexible than I on such a matter, agreed to appear on the editorial page.

The captain had stolen our jeep from another unit on the day the division landed in Europe, for the Army had made no provision for public relations vehicles in its Table of Equipment. Since we would have had to list the serial number of the jeep to obtain anything for it other than gas or oil, we could not get tires. Our spare had long since been put into service. One day our artist-driver, a dreamy young man, drove to the printer in Luxembourg City for the latest issue; though he came back by the same route, the return trip had been, he said, inexplicably bumpy, and he thought that something was wrong with the jeep. The captain and I investigated. "Well, we're done for," the captain said mournfully, looking at a rear wheel. All that remained of the tire were a few ribbons of rubber. That night the artist and I located the motor pool of a neighboring division. We had brought along a jack and a lug wrench. Hiding in a ditch, we watched the two sentries until we had timed their movements; then we dashed under a jeep. We had thirty seconds or so in which to remove each lug and to hide again under the jeep, and of course we had only the same length of time to escape into the ditch with the wheel. It is odd that the enemy should have been the United States on the one occasion that I behaved like a soldier on a patrol mission; but I would have been willing to take on any risk for that newspaper. The success of our mission gave me such a sense of elation I couldn't sleep for the remainder of the night.

Late that winter I drove to a rest area where an infantry company had been sent after a particularly severe period of combat. I had been asked to interview a rifleman whose exploits had made him, I had been told, a soldier's soldier. He had killed more of the enemy than anyone else in his regiment. Earlier in the war he had been wounded in the arm, and his platoon officer had persuaded him to go to the field hospital only by holding a pistol at his head. The other soldiers of his unit were playing poker in a farmhouse; I found the man I was looking for in the field behind the house. He was practicing his marksmanship by shooting at a line of cans on a fence rail. He wore a wool cap turned backward. His build was much like mine. We sat on the ground—the day was sunny—for the interview. He embraced his knees as he talked, frowning at his feet or at the sky; occasionally he would look quickly at me with a shy smile. Back home in southern Ohio he was a coal miner and he knew he would return there and to that kind of work. For there was a girl back home he planned to marry. He loved her, and though his squad kidded him about it, he was determined to stay faithful to her. Around his neck was a little gold chain that held the cross he wore against his chest; his girl had given it to him and he believed— at least so long as he kept the vow he had made to her—that God would keep him from serious harm. He unbuttoned his shirt, that coal miner turned Arthurian knight, to show me the glittering talisman before his heart.

He became confidential as he spoke of his military exploits. He had always been something of a hunter, and was embarrassed by the praise he had received for the Germans he had killed. "If you shot that many deer or even squirrels, the sheriff and game warden both would be down on you, wouldn't you think?" he said, marveling. "Why should

I get credit for what I did? Fifteen of them had their hands up, coming out of a basement. As if *that* could save their hides! A couple of BAR bursts is all it was, and who even needs to aim?" He pointed to an expensive German watch on his wrist. "Just last week I was taking a prisoner back to the cage; I told him, 'Give me your watch.' It's a pretty thing, and I suppose he thought so too. That dumb Kraut tried to hit me when I reached for it, and if I hadn't of shot him, what then?" He looked at me earnestly. "But I didn't think it was right when the lieutenant added *that* to my score. It just don't seem right to credit a man for something so easy, and over a watch! The lieutenant said it was for the sake of the platoon, that no other platoon had a guy shot so many Krauts."

I wrote the story of this soldier quickly, emphasizing, as I did in all the stories I wrote for that incorruptible Army newspaper of mine, only the parts of the interview I had found compatible with my own experiences and the values nurtured in my past; in the pages of that weekly I was preserving, like a dried spring flower, the old and generous heart of a pre-war America. There was a hotel in Luxembourg City that served as headquarters for many of the civilian newspapermen covering our sector of the war; the captain and I always left several copies of each of our issues in a lobby that had been converted to a pressroom. A week or so after the issue containing my interview was published, I was driving the jeep—we didn't trust it to the artist anymore—down a small road that led to the Saar River when I met another jeep driven by an Associated Press correspondent I had once played gin rummy with at the hotel.

He stopped his jeep and waved at me to stop. "Congratulations, Corporal," he called. "For what?" I asked in surprise. He said, "For that story about the boy who stayed virtuous, even though he had to kill so many of the enemy. It's bound to be in all the papers back home; you gave them just what they wanted, the perfect war story. A poor boy who becomes a hero. A new Daniel Boone or Davy Crockett, a new legend. A boy who's religious, pure in heart, and as brave as he is loyal. All that crap. Marvelous, Corporal, simply marvelous! I wish I had written it."

Driving on, I felt my skin prickling with the knowledge of my folly.

I was, after all, the perfect publicist for war; there was little wonder that the general had supported my efforts, giving up each week two bottles of Scotch for the newspaper and agreeing to have his own comments on an inside page. Whatever the aberrations of war, the beliefs for which I had felt myself the sole custodian were the continuing beliefs of the majority of my countrymen.

At first my awareness made me cynical about my work on the newspaper. Not many nights later, the captain, the company commander, and I sat at a table of a deserted and recently captured German café contemplating—for the week had been a quiet one—the lack of news from our division. The company commander had been a Hollywood scenario writer; the captain wished to become a playwright; I was beginning to think of some sort of career for myself as a writer, though not necessarily in journalism. "We ought to be able to make up a story," I said. "I mean, something funny, something good for laughs in the middle of war." The commander brightened. "Fine. We'll make up a story about Lem." Lem was the mail orderly for the company and a favorite of the commander; not very bright but remarkably good-natured, he had blundered in Europe from one mishap to another. "I don't know that we should *invent* a story about Lem," the captain said. "Wouldn't he object?" He thought for a moment about his own question before saying, "I guess not," and we all laughed. "All right," said the commander. "Lem is driving down the road in his mail truck—what happens next? Some untoward circumstance, that's what we need." I said, "A German comes out of the woods. He has a rifle aimed at Lem. 'I'm done for,' Lem thinks, for of course his carbine is so rusted it would blow up if he fired it. What then?" "I know," the captain said. "The German says, '*Bitte*, I see you are a mailman. Would you please mail this letter from me to my cousin in New York?'" The three of us were so delighted with our ingenuity that we tried to do a Russian dance around the table, though we had been drinking nothing stronger than captured wine. And then I scribbled down our story for the newspaper.

My jeep hit the trap in the road a couple of weeks later. I

underwent an operation in a field hospital in Germany and was flown to another hospital in England. On a morning that I was free of drugs and aware that my body was beginning to heal and that life itself was a matter for celebration, I heard, from the loudspeakers in my ward, a B.B.C. news broadcast. After the combat news, which was most satisfactory, the announcer said, "And now for a lighter moment," and he proceeded to read the account of Lem, the mail orderly. I listened in fascination to my own words, spoken in B.B.C. accents; and then I began to laugh at myself, and at my pretensions; and in such a fashion I acknowledged my American citizenship and rejoined the human race. The war ended soon thereafter.

Soon after my son and I finished our work on the barn roof, a former student of mine, one now doing graduate work in aeronautical engineering, took me and all of my sons for an airplane ride above our house and land. From an altitude of two thousand feet, I saw the gleaming barn roof, the new fence, the mare peering out of her barn, even the semicircle of small bushes my wife and I recently planted to give privacy in a decade to our picnic table. I was shocked at the smallness of the nearby woods. Years before they had been part of the farm I had bought, and from the day I purchased my property I had lusted after them, thinking them mine in spirit if not by deed. Jimmy— sitting on my lap in the airplane, he was pressed tightly to me by the seat belt—had become lost in those woods early in the summer; darkness had fallen to the accompaniment of hundreds of screeching birds by the time the rest of us found him, sitting on a log and sobbing. The height of the airplane flattened valleys and hills, making our property part of a continuous whole that included Lake Cayuga and the towns of Ithaca and Trumansburg. Undoubtedly in the farmhouses and towns beneath us were men with a military and family history not much different from my own, men who were destined, as Americans, for much the same future as I. If their worlds were occasionally as unreal as I had found mine from my barn roof, and if they too had moments in which they felt themselves absurd beings playacting at fulfillment, the reason, I thought, lay at least in part in that old antithesis between the secret wishes of a people and what mankind as a whole brings down upon itself. How hard it must have been for my mother to say so many years ago, "I hope you pass!" As for myself as parent, I didn't know if I were up to such a statement and hoped I never needed to find out. One of my sons—influenced no doubt by me, even as I had been influenced by an earlier generation—has protested vehemently against the contemporary violence; on several occasions he has awakened from nightmares of dark lit only by the torches of napalmed children. What, in the wisdom of my years, could I offer him? From my own past I had learned not much more than that newly transplanted sugar maples must be watered daily in those seasons when the well can least afford the depletion, that college professors know less than they profess, and that anybody who takes pride in the shining armor of a private idealism deserves to get his breastplate cracked, whatever the angels embossed upon it. Still, looking down the dipping wing of an airplane at my property, I found most strange the knowledge that those old and naïve convictions of mine, the ones I had felt as I had stared in fascination at the neon sign advertising the college I was soon to enter, were my continuing beliefs and all I had to give my life meaning; I found most strange the knowledge that, in some sense, I would always be standing on the Public Square at dusk, before a building yet to be demolished and a war yet to be fought.

Hector, Dick, and I

EIGHTEEN YEARS AGO I WAS A GRADU-
ate student living with my wife in a trailer on an
Iowa field. After a fruitless search for housing—
we had arrived in the university town at the last minute, our decision
to come a result, in those days before children and furniture and
property, simply of our Ohio landlady's anger at a party we had given
that she claimed had cracked the ceiling of the living room beneath
ours—we had bought the trailer and rented space for it at the edge of
town from Hector Bascomb and his wife, Rowena. She was a cook at
one of the fraternities; he was a retired, one-armed farmer. On succes-
sive Saturday afternoons of a sunny October, listening to vagrant bits
of band music from the distant stadium, we dug water and sewer lines.
Hector furnished us with advice, spades, pickaxes, and a flaring kit for
making connections in copper tubing. I admired my wife for the way
she lifted shovelfuls of dirt from the trench, and I imagined the pair of
us to be out of some Russian novel, a sturdy peasant couple preparing
our hovel against the Siberian blasts. Another student couple—the
husband, Dick, was younger than I, an undergraduate taking pre-
medical courses—bought a trailer exactly like ours, placing it between
our trailer and the street. I had already put a flush toilet in the
bedroom closet. Dick pushed back the overcoats to look at it and
immediately decided to install a toilet in the same place in his trailer.
He and his wife dug a ditch to meet ours so that the two trailers could
have common sewer and water lines running across the field and into

Hector's basement. Hector judged the frost line in that part of Iowa to be forty inches; we placed our copper tubing at forty-one inches, not wanting to do excess work on a project that, after all, would revert to Hector after we left. Dick and I already saw him as a shrewd old man, a farmer so obsessed with property that he was not distinguishable from what he owned; and we would give him no more than we had to.

An Army veteran studying for an advanced degree in English literature, I thought myself a writer preparing for his career under governmental patronage. Dick, also a veteran, was planning to be a surgeon. He had long and narrow fingers, and even then protected his hands with canvas gloves as he worked. His hands were capable of an agility and grace that mine were not; with my skull filled with arrogant notions of the supremacy and eternity of art, I thought it a pity he did not at the least give himself to the piano or violin. But he was a methodical and patient empiricist, most dubious of a spiritual reality or any subjective expression. Out of my imagination I would finally make something, I didn't know what, that would be beyond the corruption of my body; out of his training and skill he would bring diseased and mangled bodies back to health. Before each of us lay that mountain of time, that solid mass in which we would work out our pure and uncomplicated conceptions of what we were destined to be; it allowed us to enjoy the trembling of our trailers in the winter winds. A sense of transitoriness was our anchor, our rock, our bond.

Both of us were antithetical to old Hector, who, with his stump in a dirty sock, with his foul-smelling and nervous little rat terrier at his heels, puttered as if by habit in the debris of his field and barn. His field was a long, disorderly vista of his life. Beyond our trailers were chicken houses and dog kennels and a root beer stand, rotting remnants of enterprises he had taken up after the loss of his arm; beyond them a huge mound of dry and disintegrating manure. Beyond the manure lay rusted pieces of farm machinery from the days when harvesters were powered by steam, when plows and harrows were drawn by horses. Hector had given up only those possessions capable of bringing him better ones; in the year that I knew him, he managed, through an intricate series of barters, to exchange an old steam engine for a fairly new Ford tractor. Of course he had no use for it. He kept it locked in the barn, beside boxes of rags and bundles of paper and little kegs filled with bent nails and washers and screws; looking at it through a cobwebbed and grimy window, I thought it a perfect token of the meaninglessness of a life devoted to accumulation. He was inexorably placed by everything he had ever been or owned; placed by his dank stucco cottage and by the barn and the field to which, in his retirement, he had brought his past. Even his beliefs—time had turned most of them into superstitions—were possessions to be *used*. Professors of farming knew nothing, he told me one winter's day as he rocked his terrier in his lap by the kitchen fire, about the importance of phases of the moon in planting corn; and he had heard *with his own ears* one of them on the radio, disputing the indisputable fact that hairs from a horse's tail, dropped into a creek in early spring, will grow into worms by midsummer. He spat into the fire. "Do you believe me about the worms?"

"No," I said.

"I don't mind," he said, and looked at me shrewdly. "But if you ever write a book about me, I want a share out of your poke."

I was born only a few blocks away from Lake Erie, in a Cleveland suburb; as a child I connected the blue expanse of the lake with some still-to-be explored inner expanse, believing even then I would eventually be a writer. Lying in bed in spring and early fall, listening to the deep cry of the foghorn at the harbor entrance, I thought with pity of the suffocating multitudes who were landlocked and held to some mundane occupation. Of course, a field in Iowa is far from the Great Lakes; but I still had my dream of a destiny, and my trailer might well have been my boat, the vistas of rolling snow-covered fields the seas upon which I sailed to reach some harbor of the mind.

And what a comfortable little boat it was! Twenty-five feet from the tip of its hitch to the bulging red eye of its taillight, its generous center, its heart, was the galley. A cupboard door, hinged not at the side but at the bottom, dropped down to make a table. A recessed light above the stainless-steel sink illuminated the counter, the Coleman bottled-gas stove, the white Frigidaire. The living room was a sofa and an oil space heater. A plywood partition separated the bedroom from the rest of the trailer. One is aware of the trade names of all appliances in a trailer: the exhaust fan I installed in one of the ceiling hatches was a Homart, the little radio on the bookcase I built by the sofa was a Philco, borrowed for the year from my parents. While we ate dinner, my wife and I would listen to a sonorous-voiced professor reading his way in installments through *LaSalle and the Discovery of the Great West*. Late at night we would leave the galley light burning and walk in the snow, delighting in the graceful leaps over the high drifts of the raw-boned dog who in the fall of the year had leaped through our flimsy screen door in a reckless and happy demand for bed and board. We lived near the airport, and as we walked the beacon would briefly illuminate patches of the somber clouds beyond us. We liked to walk to the railroad station to see the arrival of the day's final passenger train, its headlight burrowing a brilliant cone through the thick flakes. Back home and under covers—we slept on the narrow sofa, having turned the bedroom into a study—I would tune the radio just beyond my pillow to station after station, trying to find, especially on those frigid and still nights when distant signals are carried without distortion or fading, all the cities in which I had ever lived and all the cities I hoped some day to visit. The dog would jump on top of us to escape the draft from the door. That winter I read myself to sleep with *A Week on the Concord and Merrimac Rivers;* when I got to the end I started over. I thought it impossible to have more congenial trailer partners than my wife, a stray dog, Parkman, and Thoreau.

In that tiny space my energy was infinite. I studied and I wrote; I picked up a hammer and saw and attacked the trailer's interior. It pleased me to think of the trailer as the discipline, the form, within which my imagination had to invent; and, whenever a new and ingenious possibility for a cabinet or a shelf occurred to me, I would build it as hastily as I typed. Dick, who was having trouble with his calculus, often visited us in the evenings to get help from my wife. Before he left he would look thoughtfully at each new alteration in our trailer. He would rub his long fingers against the wood to see how well I had sanded it (usually I hadn't sanded at all). And then he would say, "Do you mind awfully if I copy this? I think I might improve on it a bit."

Memory simplifies, for its impulse is order; in playing upon a given relationship, it can erode the irrelevant and ambiguous to leave the bones of allegory. If I remember myself as the maker, the little God of a portable world circumscribed by quarter-inch plywood, Dick has become simply the rebuilder, the patient craftsman who, with his kit of immaculate tools, remedies the imperfect original conception. His trailer was the duplicate world of mine; where I had built a bookcase, he built a bookcase, and where I had managed to squeeze in a narrow cupboard for cans of soup and bars of soap, he did likewise. But his latches worked, his little doors were neatly trimmed with molding, his nails were recessed and hidden by putty, his wood contained a warm and flawless sheen. I am sure he thought me as careless as I thought him dull, and had it not been for Hector peering through the early-morning frost of our windows to get proof with his own eyes that we had left our faucets dripping, perhaps not even the bond that we had as transients would have held us together.

Hector, of course, was the preserver, the hoarder; even then I had the sense that he was acting, however perversely, some traditional human role, though one which in my youthful assurance and egoism I felt far beneath my dreams. A part of his mundane task was to be guardian of the water meter, the reckonings of which he had to pay. When the frost line—its rate of descent was announced on the radio each day of that severe winter—reached forty inches, Dick and I tried to let the water drip all night; but Hector, who could hear the tick of the meter from his bed, would shut off the main valve in his basement. From our trailers we could see a dim glow in one of his casement windows as he descended the cellar steps in his nightshirt. Hector recouped any possible water loss by charging us fifty cents each to push our cars, which frequently would not start otherwise, in the mornings. He owned a 1924 Buick sedan; after each use of it, he would drain the contents of the radiator and crankcase into cans which he stored in the kitchen. A single flip of the hand crank—old Hector's one arm was still a mighty one—made the motor, warmed by its morning fluids, catch and purr. Dick and I, pressing fruitlessly on our frozen starter buttons, hated to look toward the house, that dismal cottage of the fairy tales; Hector would be waiting at the window between the tattered curtains, an expectant smile on his unshaven face.

The tenants' generous use of water plagued him even when spring came. In March he put up a sign on the basement shower stall he had built for the use of the trailer occupants. For Weekends Only, it said. All Families Will Shower Together.

Since Hector had contracted to supply us all the water we required in the trailer, I bought a huge second-hand tub. It was made of cast iron and had claw feet. I removed the feet and installed the tub in my study, beneath the sloping rear wall. I built a plywood enclosure for it, with a hinged and padded red plastic top. When the tub was not in use, the top became a window seat and a place for books and manuscripts. My wife or I, lolling in the luxury of hot water, looked disconcertingly like a corpse in an opened casket; but I had worked with care on the project, having become irritated with Dick's sense of superiority in his craftsmanship, and I was proud of it. One evening when Dick came over to get his usual help with an assignment, my wife and I lifted the lid to show him the tub. He stared at it bleakly. "I'd say it's too big for the hot water supply," he said; both our trailers had come equipped with three-gallon electric water heaters.

"We heat water for it on the stove, but we don't mind," I replied. "Personally, I like to use as much of Hector's water as I can."

"I see," he said. After my wife had helped him with his work, he came back to the study; I was working at my desk on a novel. "If you ever take your trailer off the blocks, be careful," he said. "That tub looks heavy enough to tilt your trailer on its hind end. Wouldn't it be a thing, though, if you were to fill it with water and then jumped in and the trailer—"

"Thanks," I said, interrupting him. "Thanks for all your advice and all your praises."

"That's all right," he said; he always took my remarks literally.

"You're a very serious person," I told him.

[127]

"Thank you," he said, looking at his hands. "I want to be a surgeon, you know."

Looking out of our window a few evenings later, my wife and I saw Dick and his wife carrying a small porcelain tub from a rented truck into their trailer. It was the kind of tub one takes sit-baths in, and was, he later told me, just the right size for the hot water heater. He built an enclosure for it that had a hinged and padded red plastic top.

My growing irritation with Dick was connected with my awareness that both of us soon would be leaving Hector's field. Both Dick's wife and mine had become pregnant, and as a consequence we were eligible for university housing in converted army barracks. Because of a surfeit of student trailers in town, neither Dick nor I was able to sell ours there; I contacted a firm in Davenport that sold used trailers, and they hauled off our home. I followed it in my car for a few miles out of town, for I found it painful to let that little world, whatever its flaws, vanish in a moment. The weighted rear end swayed dangerously. A week later Dick—he asked me first if I minded—phoned the same Davenport firm. The two trailers were displayed side by side on the lot. My wife and I drove to Davenport to have a look at them. Ours, of course, was the shoddier; the sight of it, gathering dust inside and out, was dispiriting. Dick's trailer sold almost immediately, and for nearly as much money as a new one; at the summer's end I had to retrieve mine and return it to Hector's field in the hope that I could find a renter for it.

Hector helped me re-connect the water and sewer lines. The day was humid, and both of us became hot and thirsty. His wife made iced tea; the three of us sat in old wicker chairs on their front porch. The rat terrier, of course, jumped into his lap. Rowena to me had been a shadow, for Hector conducted all business matters while she stood behind him; I had thought of her simply as his wife, a woman with thick legs and varicose veins who wore shapeless dresses and was really too old to be a fraternity cook. But it was she who now did most of the talking. "We've been proud to have a writer and a doctor with us for a year," she said.

I demurred. Dick and I had yet to prove ourselves, I said, and he was likelier than I to gain his goal. I said that I supposed Dick eventually would be a very successful surgeon.

"You both work hard!" Rowena cried. She had a high, expiring voice. "We could see your lights late at night! 'The doctor,' I would say to him"—and she nodded at Hector—"and he would say, 'And the writer.' *He* used to be the nicest whittler, carving little things out of wood! Toys I mean, for the children."

I expressed my surprise, for I hadn't known of their children. I had thought Hector and Rowena too ancient ever to have been parents.

Hector said that when children grow up, they leave. Both his boys lived to hell and gone, the other side of Cedar Rapids. His daughter had died so many years ago that he could no longer see her face. "Tell him," he said to his wife, "about my arm."

Trivial though it was, my misfortune with my trailer had made them sympathetic and friendly. It was apparent in the tone of Hector's voice that he was allowing me to enter, now that I was living elsewhere than his field, a part of his past that had previously been kept from me. Rowena's account was macabre. In his middle years Hector had caught his arm, as many farmers do, in a corn picker. The arm had been so mangled at the elbow that amputation was the only medical recourse possible. Hector demanded that the surgeon give him back the arm. He preserved it with formaldehyde in a glass container, which he kept on the kitchen table. When he regained some of his strength, he put a block of walnut between his legs and, looking at the embalmed arm, attempted to create it in wood. He wanted to capture precisely each wrinkle, vein line, and fingernail. He used three blocks of wood before fashioning an arm to his satisfaction; and then he built a harness of leather and steel to fasten the wood to his own stump. But of course he could not breathe life into it; it could never become the arm that lay uselessly in the formaldehyde.

Hector, Rowena went on in her high but gentle voice, had been unable to eat. He spent most of his waking hours in the kitchen simply staring at the container. She knew what she had to do! One night she had crept out of his bed and removed the arm from the fluid. She found a wooden box and stuffed it with cotton. She tied the fingers down, for she knew that one who has lost an arm feels pain from the missing member when the flesh shrivels and the little bones clench up to make a fist. Oh, she wouldn't have hurt Hector for the world! With a lantern perched on a fence post to help her see, she had buried the box in a far corner of the field. To herself she vowed never to tell him what she had done. But she hadn't realized how terrible he would be to live with that spring! In his anger at her he splintered the wooden arm against the coal stove! Finally she had to tell him. He dug up the box and opened it to see his own bones. Everything was all right after that. Habit and routine took over.

Rowena smiled at me. Hector, too, was smiling: he was glad that I had heard his story. We were friends. It had not been his intention to bring me down to my mortal size or to suggest any limitations in the areas of medicine or art. And though he had every opportunity before I left, he said nothing to me this time about a share out of my poke.

I saw Dick only once more before I moved from Iowa. We met by chance on a downtown street. He told me about his infant daughter, and I told him about my infant son. The novel upon which I had been working with such haste in the trailer had never managed to capture the purity of the idea behind it; I told him I had discarded it. He said he had been admitted to medical school. His last hurdle had been the personal interview. He frowned, as if hesitating to tell me about it; but then he spoke with frankness. I remember Dick as an exceptionally honest person. "I came into this room where the interviewer sat," he said. "I had bought a new suit, for I thought, you know, that this was an important thing. But he had only one question to ask." Dick took a breath. "He asked, 'Tell me, young man, what is *your* view about socialized medicine?'"

"What did you say?"

"God, I hadn't thought about it. It had never entered my mind that he would ask something like that. I've been thinking ever since that socialized medicine isn't so bad. You know, helping these poor people with their cataracts and cancers. But I knew what I had to say. 'Sir,' I said, 'I am firmly opposed to it.'" I had never seen Dick so agitated; he kept clenching his fists to make the knuckles crack. "Think of it," he said. "Even before you start, you've got to lie."

In the years since I left that trailer in an Iowa field, I have slowly and methodically become placed. I am as placed, as surrounded by my possessions, as Hector ever was. I now have three children, two horses, two dogs, two cats, two cars, a large field tractor and a small garden tractor and a Rototiller. I recently phoned my lawyer that I wish to buy the rest of the land—I particularly want the woods—that once belonged to my farmhouse; soon I will own nearly everything I can see from the front porch. Recently my wife and children and I ate our supper sitting on the living room floor before a log fire; and then, sprawled out on the wide pine planks, I drew a diagram for the fifteen-foot wall closet I will build some day in the large bedroom. My past is so littered with flaws in conception as well as execution that now, whenever I do anything, I go about it as carefully as I can.

Larry, the son born in Iowa, has practiced the piano ever since he was five, but he is not interested in music as a profession. His hands are just as agile as Dick's, and I wonder at times if he might not make a good surgeon. The thought pleases me.

Sometimes I have a dream. In this dream the morning is full of mist, the endless field covered with snow. I look into the opened grave, which is deep as a well, to see the dark gravedigger caressing an object that resembles a luminescent baseball. "Gravedigger," I call—and I can speak to him so peremptorily for he has but a bit part in an old play—"what are you handling?" "Alas," he says, "it is the skull of poor Jesus Christ." "It is too tiny and too perfectly round to be a skull, gravedigger," I say sternly. "Tiny and round it may be," he replies, "but do you know what this skull contains?" "What, gravedigger?" "In this little ball," he says, his every syllable twanging like a guitar string, "in this little ball lies all of Heaven and all of Hell. *Or so he thought.*"

It is one of those queer winter dreams that fill one both with foreboding and joy. Oh sweet Jesus! I say, waking, with my eyes in tears. You truly believed you could make and mend and hold! Carry on, you brave little baseball skull! And I love my wife and my children and my horses and my dogs and cats, and in my loneliness wish them all in bed with me. This is what it feels like, to be placed.

1966

In Praise of Chekhov

10   L<small>ONG AGO—IN GERMANY, NEAR THE</small> end of the war—two corpsmen came into the field and lifted me onto a litter. They were so careful and gentle that for their sake I gave a little groan, though I felt no pain. They strapped the litter to some metal bars above the back seat of their jeep. One of them sat beside me while the other drove. It was dark. Lying on my back, I could see nothing of the jeep. I floated slowly through the sweet air of a spring night, the head of the corpsman, with the cross outlined against the circle of white on the back of his helmet, bobbing and drifting along with me. On a hillside I saw a bonfire and heard some unfamiliar plaintive song.

"Drunk!" the corpsman said appreciatively.

"Who?" It was my voice.

"Happy! Drunk! They're supposed to stay put, them Russians from the slave camp, but whenever a freight goes east they rush at it. Some of them make it to the roofs. You should hear them laugh! We found a leg between the rails yesterday. The trains go slow through here—they never should have bivouacked them crazy homesick Russians near the tracks!"

The field hospital was a school or a church on top of a hill. Inside, the rough stone walls were whitewashed. I lay on a table looking at a pulsating overhead light; in the distance I could hear the rumble of a gasoline engine. One of the corpsmen unbuckled my boots and cut off my trousers and shirt and shorts with a pair of scissors. Snip, snip, snip:

I thought it wrong to ruin clothes like that. For a moment I fell asleep. When I awoke, the corpsman was still beside me. "Would you like some water?" he asked.

"That would be nice," I said, though I wasn't thirsty. He put a moist piece of cotton in my mouth. It was like a gag, and I didn't want it; but I waited for him to be called elsewhere before hiding it under the sheet. The table was on wheels, and a Wac nurse pushed me into an adjoining room where a young doctor was waiting. I said to the doctor, "I can't move my legs."

"That's the least of our worries," he said. He looked tired, but was friendly and cheerful. The nurse was shaving my pubic hair.

"How do you know what's wrong?" I asked. "You haven't even *looked*."

He smiled. "I make it a general rule to look before I operate, whenever I can."

"But I just got here."

"That's what you think."

"Just a moment ago I was driving a jeep that flipped," I said. "I was the booby who hit the trap."

"That's what lots of my patients tell me."

The nurse had finished with the razor. I looked directly into the doctor's eyes. "I want an honest answer," I said. "Am I going to live?"

"Such a question from a healthy young man! Such an insult to my handiwork!"

"I didn't mean to insult you," I said. "I'm sorry. Will I be sterile?" I thought such a question was probably the normal response of one whose pubic hair has been shaved.

"No," he said. "You'll have a dozen children."

"I have a Luger pistol," I said. "You make this a good operation, one that won't make me sterile, and I tell you what. You can have that Luger pistol."

"It's a deal," he said. "A Luger pistol is just what I need." He placed a mask over my face. "You're higher than a kite. Breathe deeply and you'll go higher yet," and I breathed in the ether that had made me sick when I had been a child in Arkansas and the doctor had lanced both my ears. I wanted to tell him to use something else to put me to sleep, that my ears were all right now and that I didn't want to be ashamed for throwing up all over the starched sheets and pillow cases. I started to struggle; but Dr. Buckley in Little Rock was holding my arms. "Breathe deep, breathe deep," he drawled, and I was a little boy in a racing car that roared off the road into a ditch.

The Russian was trilling sweetly from the roof of the freight car. "God bless you," I said. Blood dripped from his stump. I floated past him on a cloud. I knew it a trite thing to be doing, floating on that cloud, but there it was. I vomited all over the trite cloud. "I told you so," I said reproachfully. Hitler, all in red and with horns, rose up through the cloud and came at my belly with a pitchfork. "Trite! Trite!" I screamed at him. Held down by my thick umbilical cord, I could not get away from him. I tried to yank the rubber tube out of my belly. "Don't touch that," a voice warned. Dark came and light came and another voice, a gentle Southern voice that I mistook at first for Dr. Buckley's, was praying. "Dear Jesus Christ," it prayed politely, "please in your mercy let me have a B.M." "Who is that praying?" I asked the nurse. "He was shot in the stomach," she said. The prayer went on all that day and night, but growing fainter. Another voice was screaming in German. "That sounds like a girl," I said to the nurse. "They've been using children," she said. "He's scared, but it's only his leg." The doctor roared from a distance, "If that little Nazi coward doesn't shut up, tell him I'll personally tie his hands together so tight he'll have something to cry about. God damn it, *make him shut up.*" "I gave him my Luger pistol," I said, and began to weep. "Hush," the nurse said. "He's been operating for three days with hardly any rest, and the lieutenant just died." "What lieutenant?" "The one that was praying," she said. I asked, "Did the child kill the lieutenant?" "That child, or another," she said. "That's all they have left."

Because of a shortage of beds, I was evacuated by air that day to a station hospital in England. I was in a fever and drunk with morphine. The medical care was excellent and I recovered rapidly.

While I was driving to work, my car slipped just a trifle on the icy highway—it was late March, already spring, and I had not thought the rain would freeze on the asphalt—and immediately I was back on a German road and the jeep had just hit the trap and was veering into the field and rolling over. My foot trembled on the gas pedal. I make that response perhaps a dozen times a year, whenever a wheel slips on ice or gravel, and each time I am angry with myself. A person should carry away from a serious accident more than an instinctive response. But the experience had been devoid of meaning; in my role as victim I became simply what I thought was expected of me. As I knew even as I had them, my very nightmares were stereotypes. If only I could convince myself now that I had *imagined* the lieutenant's prayer, the boy's screams, the doctor's threat! Distortion of reality is at least personality. But I remain convinced of the truth of those events. Reflections of this sort I find strangely disturbing. They make me nervous, I pace about the room.

The writer who moves me most deeply is Chekhov. I like especially those tales of antithetical characters who meet by chance as they wander across immense plains, or as they travel upon the sea. In one story a wanderer wakes in the middle of the night in a strange room in a peasant village to see a white cow in the open door. She is banging her horn against the jamb. Such images remain forever in the mind. This is the story in which the wanderer is a dispassionate creature, a man of God who is traveling across Russia begging money to rebuild his burned church. The opposing character is a near idiot, a compulsive liar and thief. While the man of God is sleeping, the thief, of course, steals the rubles intended for the church; but he returns, full of vodka, to await his victim's awakening. He returns so that he may be accused of the crime; for clearly he finds his vindication, indeed his comfort, in the resentment he arouses by his transgressions, in the ensuing quarrels and the ultimate punishment handed out by his parents, the villagers, the political authorities. But the man of God does not care; he will not fight or even argue. The matter, he tells the other, is simply between him and God. And he leaves the village with his horse-drawn cart containing an ikon and the tin money box, the thief following after, trying to draw him into anger and debate. The man of God is as impersonal and as indifferent as the natural world, as remote and as austere as the sky above them both. He remains so even after the other confesses the theft and begs forgiveness. The thief falls in terror to the ground; he weeps, he calls the man of God his kinsman, his grandfather, his uncle. Troubled, he man of God looks for a moment at the sky and feels frightened himself. "He was frightened," says Chekhov, "and he felt pity for the thief"; and so he tells the other the conventional ritual that man has established in the face of the incomprehensible Authority. If the thief will confess to the priest, if he will make a penance, if he will do this and that. . . . It is noon at the end of the story; the two have reached the next town, where the thief, recovered, quarrels in the tavern with the drunken peasants and calls for the police. One can imagine the man of God moving onward into the immense afternoon landscape, a small figure growing ever smaller. Chekhov thought so little of the tale that he left it out of his collected edition. In another story, the antithetical characters are patients in a ship's infirmary on the long voyage from the Far East to their homeland. One of them is a discharged army orderly, a simple person who has been content to obey his superiors, who has no complaints and who accepts without question the most superstitious beliefs. The other is an irritable rationalist, an intellectual who rails against the injustice and tyranny to be found everywhere. Both die; their deaths are handled laconically. In the next to the last paragraph, the body of the orderly, covered in sailcloth and weighted with iron, sinks deeper and deeper as pilot fish circle about it and a shark rips the cloth; in the final paragraph the sunset above the waters is described. Chekhov imparts whatever human characteristics he can to the world of water: the pilot fish are in "ecstasy," the ocean "frowns." The clouds are given fanciful resemblances—one is an arch, one a lion, one something as domestic as a pair of shears. But all such attempts to find kinship and meaning in nature must fail, and the colors of the sunset, as they reflect upon the ocean, have a beauty—these are the last words of the story—"for which it is hard to find a name in the language of man." What does it matter, if one man accepts his condition and another protests against it? The conclusion of the story is terrible in its detachment and beauty, in its suggestion of an order far removed from human impulse and value. Whatever flaws I find in Chekhov I blame on his translators.

I have a retentive mind for wayward and useless things such as stray newspaper items, fillers among the daily reports of war and politics. One night twelve years ago, I ate dinner with my family at the Eagle's Nest restaurant on Main Street—Highway 60—in Morehead, Kentucky. I remember the taste of the chicken and hot biscuits and honey; I remember as well the display case with its Lifesavers and Beechnut gum. I remember the outline of the hill in the moonlight as we stepped outside, and I can tell anybody precisely where our car was parked. I remember all of this trivia because I had picked up a Louisville *Times* and read, while waiting by the cash register to pay my bill, the story of a Mexican who rented his town's bullfight stadium and then built a cross and had himself brutally affixed upon it. He was carried to the stadium, and his wife and children collected admission money at the gates from curious townspeople and tourists. Unfavorable publicity made the local officials cancel his contract, so his family carted him home on his cross and installed him inside. The curious still had to pay. He was, I believe, five days nailed to his cross, and came down prosperous. Reading the account, I thought, This is the end of something. I did not think of myself as a believing Christian, whatever I put down, for sake of identification, on the forms and questionnaires that all of us spend so much time filling out; and yet that news item was a personal threat—it diminished my personality in some subtle way and like an illness left me more susceptible to various kinds of contagion. I continue to hope the story false; or if it isn't, that the Mexican was desperate, that his family was starving. I hope he didn't do it for a Ford or a Chevy.

When I lived in Kentucky, I knew of a man who became so obsessed with the dual sense of the immensity of the universe and the smallness of our planet that he developed the fear that any sudden motion, even an unexpected hiccough, might send him flying into space. He walked gingerly, holding railings and touching store fronts as if he were blind, and finally was reduced to a baby's crawl. He was mad, but that is not to say his actions were beyond understanding to anybody who feels, as I think Chekhov did, that personality—whether one is a man of God, a thief, an orderly, or an intellectual—is a conscious and unconscious arrangement of attitudes and beliefs to serve as bulwark against the incomprehensible concepts of infinite time and infinite space. I consider myself a sensible person; and yet in moments of depression I can imagine the unique self to which I hold on so dearly in danger of being sucked off at any instant into the near vacuum of black space. Except, thank God, for a sense of horror, I once melted, vanished wholly away, in the swarm of a Long Island beach on an August afternoon, the quiet dispersal of my atoms accompanied less by the sound of the eternal wash of the sea than by the whisper of thousands of transistor radios each advertising the same used car. I like to look at the planets through a telescope of my own devising, because to so frame them within a magnifying lens is to make them one's own; and I highly recommend, for looking at the constellations, a plastic gadget called a Starfinder. It comes in a small cardboard box with a series of transparent discs, each showing a separate constellation and naming all the stars in it. The observer peers into the Starfinder with one eye, to see the constellation of his choice illuminated by a faint red light within the little tunnel of plastic. He holds the Starfinder upward, attempting to locate with the other eye the same constellation in the night sky. Suddenly, as if by miracle, the two eyes, which have been in danger of becoming crossed, come into focus and the observer discovers that high in the heavens the name of each star is printed beside it, and that the outlines of Bear or Hunter are traced in such a manner that the most obtuse can see the mythological figure. (Long before I knew about Orion and his hunting prowess, I was nearly killed by him. I was driving, alone, from Lexington, Kentucky, where my wife had just given birth to our second son, to our home in Morehead—a seventy-mile trip in an easterly direction—after midnight in late October. I was relaxed and happy. The three stars of Orion's belt, bright through the windshield, drew me toward them, emptied me of all feeling. I went off the shoulder of the road twice, drifted over the center line almost into the twin circles of a truck's glare, and finally pulled into the parking lot of a hilltop church to get out of the car and stare down those fierce and lovely and lonely stars.) A Starfinder costs a couple of bucks or so, a reasonable price for a device that can completely humanize the universe.

If I were Chekhov, I might have invented a character—let's call him Jimski, for my first name is James: I was named for my father's father and I have handed on the name to the third of my sons—who is, say, out for a walk in the country with a friend. Jimski tells his friend that his horse slipped and fell on the ice that morning, a trivial accident that immediately reminded him of the wound he received years before in one war or another, and of his inability to be profound on the occasion of his near-death. Jimski is in despair, conscious of the press of the universe upon him and of the shallowness of his own nature. He recounts a number of depressing incidents, each of which is intended to reinforce his view that personality is at best a precarious affair, a temporary expedient against negation. . . . Jimski wipes his nose and sighs. His friend Rodneyovitch—my middle name is Rodney, that being the name of the hero of an adventure novel my father read as a boy—is, while sympathetic, made of sterner and more practical stuff. He is, in other words, the antithetical character. "Jimski," he says, after shooting his gun aimlessly (for they are hunting quail), "what you say about the vagueness of our natures is false. Each of us has a built-in obsession, a monster within that shapes our facial expressions, that gives a special look to our noses and mouths and, yes, to the way we gesticulate and walk. We try to keep this monster hidden from the world and if possible from ourselves, even though its mark is every-where upon us and we cannot be free of it until we die. Don't you know of moments when this secret of another's identity has been suddenly revealed to you? Listen while I tell you . . ." And Rodneyovitch, that garrulous fellow, begins his own series of sad tales, two of which—taken out of my own experiences and not yet transformed into their Russian context—can be summarized as typical examples:

Item #1. Concerning a mail orderly of an anti-tank platoon to which I was assigned for several months in World War II. He had no friends and apparently desired none. The platoon thought him a sadist. Both in training camp and abroad he would postpone as long as possible the distribution of mail. Finally he would climb upon a table or file case and cry imperiously for silence. He dispensed the letters with a flourish, as if each were a token of his personal largess. If a soldier became angry at his tyrannical slowness, he was apt to leave his perch for an hour or so, taking all the mail with him; and he was known to have withheld letters for several days from any person who displeased him. His platoon wished to murder him; he was beaten up on at least one occasion. In eastern France he appeared late one night during a snowstorm at divisional headquarters, to which I had been transferred, to pick up some packages—a task anybody else would have delayed until the following morning. We saw him suddenly fall to the ground, threshing in helpless convulsions, his little packages skittering over the snow. A medic wedged open his mouth to keep him from biting off his tongue. The mail orderly had managed to conceal until that moment the fact that he was an epileptic. Afterwards, in tears, he begged that he be permitted to remain overseas with his buddies, to whom he thought himself of use; but he was immediately shipped home. I never heard of him again.

Item #2. Concerning a former field artillery captain. In my graduate school years, I lived for a brief period with my wife and infant son in a barracks apartment in a university housing area. Every adult male resident of that area was a war veteran and a father. Some families, of course, had two or even more children; the housing area, surrounded by a stout fence with self-locking gates for the safeguarding of the infants, was little more than a gigantic playpen. A rumor developed that two voyeurs, a Mutt and a Jeff, were wandering around the area after midnight. It was said that Mutt climbed on Jeff's shoulders to peer into the high windows of the barracks; Jeff apparently was so tall that he needed no assistance. It was also said that they were most likely to appear when a light flashed on in a bedroom late at night, for what they wished above all to see was a mother giving the milk of her breast to her child. Not much would have come of the rumors had it not been for a former field artillery captain, an older student of military bearing. He had two children. One of them, a girl of six or so, played jump rope by the hour just outside her door, but the other child, a son a year younger, was never seen. The notion of the pair of peeping Toms filled this ex-captain with a strange hatred. "Beasts," he would say of them with a snarl and a fastidious curl of the lip. "Dirty beasts." He lurked outside a friend's apartment all one night while the friend obediently clicked on and off the bedroom light. The friend's child screamed, waking the nearby families. There was quite a racket from the babies that night. Using his military experience, the undaunted ex-captain devised an elaborate communications network for capturing the pair. When any resident of the housing area saw a loiterer late at night, he was to call a certain telephone number: the person phoned was in turn to get in touch with another, and so on until the whole male populace had been alerted. Two men, designated in advance, were to conceal themselves behind the garbage cans at each of the three gates, while the other husbands were to form an advancing line that, moving from one end of the area to the other, would flush out the culprits. When this strategy produced nothing but false alarms and indignant protests from trapped but innocent prey—guests to the area, lost in the maze of corrugated huts—the ex-captain issued a daily password to all residents; and, with a few dedicated cronies, kept a vigil in the bushes at night. The loathing of the ex-captain for the Toms, the extraordinary measures he had taken (he had warned, in one of his mimeographed communiqués, that we were not to lose our heads and shoot to kill those who might turn out to be the wrong persons), kept us, even in daylight hours, from looking in confidence at anything but our own feet; no man dared to smile at a pretty girl without turning to the nearest bush and shouting, "Swallow of the north woods," or whatever the password happened to be. In short, husbands and wives began to feel guilt that they were male and female, sex itself became sinful. "Beasts! Dirty beasts!" That was all we could hear. Who were the dirty beasts? Were we? Was the ex-captain? I am sure that very few babies were conceived in the area for the month that terror reigned.

Finally, of course, normality returned. A little garbage collector was jailed for indecent exposure in another barracks area. "They've caught Mutt," the ex-captain crowed. I happened to be passing his apartment when he heard the news; the wide double doors were open, and standing within I saw, for the first time, his younger child. The boy's head was tipped, his thin little arms were extended before his body like an ape's, he was drooling. I said stupidly, "Is he sick?" "We love him," the ex-captain said angrily. "The doctors were at fault, though of course they deny it. We've checked the genealogy and for generations there's been no trace, I tell you absolutely no trace; it had to be the forceps when he was born," and he slammed the doors shut and stood in front of them, erect and alert as a sentry. "They've caught the small one, the pressure's on, and by God I bet the other beast has swum the Mississippi by now!"

As I say, these are stories of the kind Rodneyovitch would tell, and you must believe me when I also say he could go on with them all afternoon, quail whizzing to safety to the right and left of his boots as he and his friend Jimski plod on. Possibly such tales should be seen as unconscious distortions of experience, each made to fit neatly into a preconceived and melancholy idea about personality. And what of consequence distinguishes Rodneyovitch's view that the monster within gives us unique identity from Jimski's that personality is but a precarious stay against negation? Rodneyovitch's argument is hardly an optimistic one. Actually we can find more that is affirmative in the melodramatic remark we can attribute to Jimski that once when happiness made him unwary the hunter in the sky nearly bagged him: for is there not the implication that he was drawn upward in communion with those strange and distant jewels that are the hunter's belt? Jimski looks outward and Rodneyovitch inward, one haunted by vacuum and the other by viscera. What else is there to say? The two walk on, their debate becoming pointless, merging into one statement as they themselves shrink into a single dot on the horizon.

It was, you will remember, a trivial slip on the ice that set me off on this particular road. It seems to have brought me to the point where I exist as a brace of bushy-faced foreigners who, if they are to become one, must be viewed as the product of a Russian writer's synthesizing mind. This is odd, and I won't wholly accept it; but I suppose that if we pursue ourselves too far, searching for a personal truth, we are apt to become fictive. I once knew an eighteenth-century scholar, a man given to a blunt kind of self-searching, who ended up the very model of Boswell's Samuel Johnson, and whose last years were severely disturbed by his uncertainty as to who he was.

I, Jimski-Rodneyovitch or whatever, am defined by my contradictions. Given at times to violent passions, I nevertheless look forward as a clear necessity to a new political entity, one that encompasses a whole world at peace. Though a religious sceptic, I find Christian imagery diffusing into my thoughts and dreams. I know from experience that newspapers distort and sentimentalize—but for years I carried in my billfold a newspaper clipping, a photograph of two dogs crossing a street. The clipping has disintegrated, but I still remember the caption:

DOG'S BEST FRIEND—Flash, a blind greyhound, is led across a Southampton, England, street by his own "seeing eye" dog, a fox terrier named Peggy. The small dog's ability to serve as a guide for the greyhound has saved the latter from being destroyed by local authorities. Peggy, in turn, was saved from destruction several years ago by Mr. G. Corbin of Southampton. It is truly a new life for both dogs.

In short, I continue to believe, whatever the opposing evidence, in a universal brotherhood. Yet I have moved to a sparsely populated corner of a county in upstate New York, and I own nearly all the farm and woodlands surrounding my house. No poor farmer, no struggling graduate student, can build a shack or put in a trailer to disturb my view of the distant hills; and Cris, my son born in Kentucky, has already made "No Hunting" signs in his junior high print class to keep out those stout and fluorescent hunters from the city who clumsily commune with nature each deer season. Do these oppositions, as well as that related one between Jimski and Rodneyovitch, cancel each other out, leaving only the dry taste of irony as the heritage of the years since I lay in a field hospital in Germany?

Listen. When the cold spring rains ceased for a few days, my wife and I and our youngest son began to explore our new woods. Jimmy knows them so well that he will never be lost in them again. We found a grove of cedars, a stream full of rushing water from the still-melting snow, a deer trail leading down a slope into a glen that holds, in addition to a tiny field, cherry trees deformed by age—did a house once stand nearby?—and a marsh in which cattails grow. My wife cut red rags into strips so that, before the all-concealing leaves come out, we could mark the most accessible route for a path we will hack through the saplings in the long days of summer. The school bus had not yet brought our older sons home, so we left a note on the door telling them that if they wished to find us they would have to follow the strips of red cloth into the woods. We were in the glen in the center of the woods when we heard the first faint cries of Larry and Cris. We sat silently in a nest of dry weeds, listening to the nearby rush of the stream and the approaching sound of the boys as they crackled through the tangled underbrush toward us. Several burs were caught in my wife's graying hair. Our child's head barely protruded above the weeds; his eyes were round and glowing with the sense of our shared secret and with the expectancy that we would be found. For a moment I had the extraordinary sense of completion. I was a clear identity, a man of blood and soul, sitting with two of the people I loved and awaiting the other two. The glen did not become the center of the universe; from this secret navel no mystic cloak of unity moved out in waves to descend on every man and animal and tree here on earth or on the strange creatures sitting on their haunches or crawling across the plateaus of the dark and unknown planets circling Alpha Centauri. It was a limited victory, one that vanished as quickly as it came; but it was there, and worth the seeking. Between tasks more crucial to my survival, I can always hack a trail through my woods or re-read my Chekhov.

Listening on the Radio
to Late-Night Conversations

11 I FEEL THAT THE PAST HAS FINALLY caught up with the present, at least for this interval in time. I end, as I began, on a winter's night. The sky is clear, the ground is white. There is no wind to move the shutters. I end my account in my forty-fifth year, thereby managing to keep myself and my world reasonably intact, my wife at forty-two, my old dog Black Judy still alive, and my sons at home, unmarried, and too young for the draft.

I end too late to save my old barns, the ones my family and I worked on for most of the summer before last; this summer, they inexplicably burned to the ground, consumed in less than an hour. Neither my fire extinguisher nor the Enfield firemen were adequate opponents of flames feeding upon old hay and wood seasoned more than a century. Nothing remained at nightfall but a little universe of blinking red stars and a flaming pool that had been the silo foundation. A person who depends upon family relationships and a little world of possessions that he invests with a subjective value is apt to be severely disturbed when that world proves inconstant and as liable to destruction as the greater world beyond; I know that the night of the fire, as I stood by the pool of burning timbers—butt-ends of the hand-hewn beams I had admired so much when we bought the farm—I disliked everything I could see or that had the power to touch me through the dark with its presence. I disliked not only the desolation where the barns had been but the old house I had loved with the barns; and, across the road, the field of oats that not long before, as it moved through subtle shades of green and silver toward gold, had led me to think of continuity and an order in which I shared. I wanted to get rid of the property for whatever it would bring, I wanted to get the hell away from there, but it seemed as if there was no place to go. Some of the little stars in the ash heap went dead while others burst into flames that consumed whole galaxies.

It was but a minor disaster. For the past few months, until the weather brought us to a stop, all the members of my family worked together, building a new, smaller barn. We designed it ourselves and have made it as sound as a house, Larry in particular taking pride in his craftsmanship as a carpenter. Cris says maybe my wife and I will want to live in it when we get old, for the big farmhouse will be too much for us then. Perhaps, he says, he or one of his brothers—the first to marry and have children—can live in the farmhouse and mow the lawns and plow the garden and care for us and the dogs and the cats and the horses. It was something I thought about as I tried to make the barn sash plumb with the rough wood framing it. I like again what I see, but I know the limitations, the threat, of putting all of myself into the landscape, into the house or the new barn, into the family. One needs the personal world, but one also needs the public world. It is a profound pity that the two remain at such odds.

From my oldest son I have picked up the habit of now and then turning on a radio late at night, to listen to the fading and then blaring voices of the announcers in Boston and Philadelphia. Telephone conversations with members of the radio audience frequently supplant rock and folk songs. Like planes above a busy airfield, the callers wait in the complex electronic banks of Bell Telephone for their turn. In a farmhouse near Ithaca, New York, the voice of a woman calling from Newark to Philadelphia rushes in and ebbs and rushes in again. "I THINK," she says, "OUR GENERATION has made a horrible mess of things. But I keep saying to myself your life will be worthwhile IF YOU CAN ONLY LEAVE your corner of the world a little better than you found it. I believe in the U.N., support the N. double A.C.P., and am a volunteer aide Saturday night at the hospital." There follows a canned commercial for some prestige car. "I guess it isn't so bad to lust after a Caddy or a T-bird," says the announcer, "but such a goal sure won't bring you to the Holy Grail." A listener immediately calls in to complain; his urgency gives him priority. "LISTEN," he says, "FOR CHRIST'S SAKE don't knock the automobile. It's the last expression of independence we've got. Look, every weekend I take a little trip. I fix on a TOWN FOR A GOAL and estimate the ideal time. I know where the traffic tie-ups will be, and the same GOES FOR THE SPEED TRAPS. I take the back roads and try to make my estimate to the minute. My T-Bird gives me the only freedom I have, so DON'T KNOCK IT PLEASE."

It is now long past midnight. Even with the radio turned off, the dark air in the corners of my room and beyond the window remains electric with messages I understand. It is as if the expression late at night of one's feelings to an unknown public, to the heart of America, will close some gap, will heal some psychic fear, will bring one safely to earth.

~ II ~

The Stranger
at the Crossroads

1976

The Stranger
at the Crossroads

1 ❦ I LIVE BY A COUNTRY CROSSROADS, AND park my car in a barn, just across the dirt road from the old farmhouse. After returning from Ithaca late one overcast afternoon a few weeks ago, I crossed the road from the barn and was standing at the edge of the front lawn, feeling somewhat discouraged by, among other matters, the rapidity with which grass grows in wet and cool spring weather, when a small car with rusted fenders came slowly down the road and stopped at my side. I didn't recognize the car, and, since my head was higher than the roof, I couldn't see the driver. I assumed he was somebody in need of directions, and waited for him to speak. After what seemed to me an excessive period of silence, he said, "Do you m-mind if I ask you a question?" The stutter wasn't very pronounced.

"Are you lost?" I asked.

"S-sort of."

"The Mecklenburg road," I began, pointing in the direction of the state highway a mile away; but then I realized he couldn't see my hand, and I knelt on the grass—the lawn was about half a foot higher than the road—to peer into the window. The car had a console between the bucket seats, which kept the driver from sliding to the right window, but he was leaning across the console in the effort to see me. He was probably in his early thirties, a little pudgy for his age and already balding. His white T-shirt was smudged, and there was a smudge on his cheek as if he had rubbed at the skin with a greasy hand. One hand clutched the bottom of the window frame, so that he could support himself as he leaned in my direction, and I saw that the fingernails had been chewed down. The thumbnail was discolored, and little beads of dried blood lay in the cracks between the nail and the skin. He was wearing horn-rimmed glasses that gave him a mild, almost scholarly look.

"I know about the Mecklenburg road," he said apologetically. "That's not what I want to know, though I appreciate your wanting to tell me where it is. What I want to know is if there's anything w-wrong with me."

"Do you feel sick?"

"Not really. No, not s-sick. And I haven't been drinking. Not even a beer," he said, suspecting what was on my mind; "as a matter of fact, I don't drink anything but milk and soft drinks and water. Maybe a cup of coffee in the morning, sometimes two."

"What makes you think there might be something wrong?"

"Well, you see, I've been driving up and down these little side roads, where I can go slow and won't hit a dog or something if my eyes blur up. I've been trying to get myself to cry, but I can't."

"You want to cry?"

"I got this awful feeling inside me—a kind of emptiness—and I thought if I could only *c-cry*. . . . I don't have the best coordination, sometimes my body just won't do what my mind tells it to do, which might be the reason. Or maybe I can't cry because I know a man shouldn't cry, that it's shameful or something. Do you think that's what it could be?"

He spoke in a gentle, wondering voice that held none of the accents of self-pity. But how strange it was—as if I had been suddenly transported into the world of Russian fiction, where characters speak straight from the heart—to kneel on my front lawn in upstate New York, listening to somebody I'd never seen before, telling me that he couldn't cry! We tend in our embarrassment to laugh at people like that, to escape from them, to treat them like fools. He was looking into my eyes for some kind of answer, and for a moment I was unable to make the contact he wanted, and looked away from him. Over the hood of his car I could see the field—of clover, this year—bounded by the hedgerow and the creek, a plowed field beyond that (all my land, extending to the crest a half mile away); and, six miles distant, the misty ridge of Connecticut Hill. Swallows circled and dipped above the clover. Watching them, I said, "I don't think it's shameful for a man to cry."

"You're not crying."

"Why should I be?" I turned back to him in surprise. He was still leaning over the console, still searching out the expression on my face.

He said, "Just before I stopped, I thought you were sort of slouched. Crossing the road, you were kicking at the dirt. Down at the mouth, isn't that what they call it?"

"It's just the rainy weather, the damned grass," I said. My trouser leg felt wet, where my knee rested on the ground. "Some things, you know, just aren't worth crying about. . . ." I sighed, because such an answer seemed hopelessly inadequate; he was making some kind of appeal, and I was rejecting it. He irritated me—partly, I suppose, because he had made himself so vulnerable, and wanted me in the same condition. But why shouldn't I be more truthful, to myself as well as him? He was a stranger, someone I'd never see again. "And another thing," I said. "A girl I gave a low grade to telephoned me at the university just as I was leaving. She got very hostile. She told me what a lousy teacher I was."

"She didn't like you, and it made you feel bad."

"I suppose so." I knew my face had reddened: he had made it so simple I felt foolish. But he was wholly sympathetic. "In a nutshell, that's my problem too," he said. "That's been my problem as long as I can remember."

"That's why you feel so unhappy? Because people don't like you?"

"I was roofing with the guys today. My dad's a contractor; he saves the roofing work for overcast days, which means we've been doing an awful lot of it lately. I was roofing, that is, until I hit my thumb with the hammer. I mean, I hit it hard, because I was trying to drive this little nail not only through the shingles but through a couple of layers of crinkly flashing by the chimney. What I did was to drop the hammer to the roof and shout out, 'Golly darn!' The guys always laugh at me for saying 'golly darn' instead of some other word, but I had what I guess you'd call a good Christian upbringing—that was my mother's influence—and I can't help myself. So of course they laughed, but then Mike came over to see how bad I'd hurt myself. Mike's new on our crew, just out of trade school and sort of shy, and I thought he cared, I really did; but they'd put him up to kicking my hammer off the roof while he looked at my thumb—you know, by mistake on purpose. I didn't say a word. I just started down the ladder after it and the guys on the roof, Mike included, lifted the ladder just high enough so that the bottom moved in and the whole thing banged against the house and I fell off."

"That sounds pretty brutal. They might have broken your neck. Why didn't your father stop them?"

"Oh, he was off on another job. They never would have done it if my old dad had been there. He's as honest and good as they come, but he doesn't put up with any funny business."

"Wouldn't they know you'd tell your father when he came back?"

"I'd never do anything like that."

"Why not? If they knocked you off the ladder—"

"I'd just never tell on people."

"Why do you think they treated you like that? Were they jealous, because your father's the boss?"

"Well, I can be sort of clumsy, and wouldn't have a job roofing and carpentering if it wasn't for my dad, I grant you that. And he's always looking after me, like a broody hen. My dad and I bach it together, since my mom died. Do you know what he did for me Sunday morning, while I was still in bed? He took off my snow tires, without ever saying a word. That's the kind of dad I have."

"So the other guys probably *were* jealous."

"I couldn't say. Things like that have always happened to me. When I was a kid some other kids I liked—why, they tied me to a tree in the woods beyond school and forgot all about it. My folks went searching for me with a lantern and my dog. It was dark for at least an hour before they found me. A kid doesn't like being forgotten like that.

Why would they treat me that way? I always shared my lunch with anybody who seemed hungrier than I was. I still do. I give the other guys on the crew whatever they want—my cheese on rye, say, an apple or an orange....Today, lying on my back, the wind knocked out of me, and those guys laughing like crazy on the roof—it was sort of like a nightmare, you know?"

If he had been whining or demonstrating in some other way an obvious self-indulgence, if he had shown himself to be ungenerous or unkind, I perhaps would have known better how to respond. It is a simple matter to give advice to a person who strikes you as morally deficient, however useless such advice is. It is more difficult to talk to a person who is ingenuous, who has not learned about human nature despite the sufferings of experience. This young stranger, so gentle and so full of wonder at himself and other people, was clearly no idiot; but I spoke to him as if he were a very small child. I said, "People sometimes pick on a person because that person strikes them as—well, as being somehow *different*. It's not that being different is wrong; it's just that it gives them, the other people, a sense they have something in common. I guess everybody down deep is insecure, and that's one way to feel secure and part of a group—I mean, to pick on somebody who is, say, a little clumsy and doesn't swear the way the others do. And when that person who's somehow different, when he shows how much he likes the others, how eager he is to do things for them—why, that just makes them treat him worse."

"You mean, I shouldn't give away my sandwich or my apple?"

"Well, yes. And another thing. Are you as open with other people as you've been with me?"

"What do you mean?"

"I mean, do you blurt out with whatever's on your mind, like 'I can't cry'?"

"Well, that's the truth of the matter, you see. Listening to them laugh from the roof, I realized something. I mean, I realized that this was not only how it had always been but how it would be the rest of my life. And so I just picked up my hammer—you can see it in the back seat, by that apron stuffed with the roofing nails—and got into this

Capri that my dad bought me after my mom died, and I just took off. 'How it will always be,' I said to myself, over and over. I knew that when my dad got back to the job he would worry over me, he would drive everywhere looking for me like he and my mom did when I was a kid tied to the tree, and other times; only now he would be by himself because my mom is dead. I looked at my face in the rearview mirror, put on all the right expressions, but nothing happened. I had this empty feeling but couldn't cry. I can't tell you how terrible I used to feel—before today, I mean—if I made my dad worry, or if I hurt him in some other way! I used to be able to cry! That job I was on is over in Slaterville, and here I am at the other side of the county where my worried old dad nor nobody else will find me, but it doesn't seem to matter, that I'm hurting him; and maybe you and him are right saying, 'Don't give away your sandwich' and 'Don't talk about what you feel if you want to have friends.' Maybe you're both right, but what's the use of having friends then? Why should I care? And that I can't cry now—is that a good sign? Does it mean I'm learning how to behave? Or shouldn't I ask? Is it a bad sign that I would stop and ask you what's wrong with me?"

I told him that it wasn't a bad sign, that I was glad he had stopped to talk with me, and that I wished I knew how to answer the rest of his questions. I said that on occasion even at my age—I am fifty-five—I still felt the need to cry, but usually couldn't. "It was nice talking with you," he finally said; and I said, "Stop by again, any time you want to talk." We had been in our positions so long—for I had remained kneeling in the damp grass as he had remained leaning toward me, his body against the console—that we both had become stiff. We laughed about that, and then he started up his engine and went down the road—a little faster than he'd come, but more slowly than most people drive.

My own depression was gone; in its place I felt elation, as if more achievements were possible for me at my age than I had thought. And I felt that in recent years I had become too conscious of my dignity as a professor; that in keeping an emotional distance from others I withheld too often the urge to embrace another human, man or woman or child, for whom I felt compassion or the love that sudden understanding brings. Since my conversation with that stranger, I have talked about the encounter with many people, hoping that they, too, would see in it some need of their own. "It sounds like a story," they say, as if that dismisses its applicability to them. "Why don't you write it down?" He has passed by my house several times since our meeting—once on a sunny Saturday while I was working in the garden with my wife, once as I was sitting on the porch step at dusk, listening to the frogs in the pond and the marshy places beyond the pasture and waiting for I don't know what. He has installed on his Capri one of those reproductions of the old Model A horns you can now buy at the Ford agencies. He smiles and waves as he passes, and makes the horn sound a-woo-gah. The last time he passed, I called, "Hey, you," wishing I knew his name; and I gestured for him to stop, but he kept going down the road at his careful speed.

Mythology, Art,
and the Farming Life

2 I FIRST SAW JOAN WILCOX AT THE TOWN dump fourteen years ago, a few weeks after we moved to the country. She was a middle-aged woman, thin and fine-boned, wearing a dark dress considerably longer than the fashion of the period, and she was apparently delighted to have found in the debris of discarded metal a small, potbellied wood stove, which she and her young son hoisted into the bed of a rusted Chevrolet pickup. I was at a distance from them but could hear them talking, and I was intrigued by her accent, which to my ear sounded like that of an upper-class Englishwoman. I told my wife that I had seen at the dump a woman who had the bearing and voice of the Queen of England as well as the muscle to lift a cast-iron stove. Some weeks later, I learned that Joan and her husband, Hayden, were dairy farmers who lived a mile and a half from us, and that shortly before we came to the neighborhood their house had burned. They carried Joan's mother, who was paralyzed, out of the house in her wheelchair, but that wheelchair was the only possession they managed to save. The family had moved into a single-story chicken house—a long and narrow building next to the cow barn—and were converting it as best they could into a passable dwelling; at the dump, Joan had been looking for anything that might be useful in furnishing it.

Gradually, we learned some of the details of the Wilcoxes' background. Joan was born in Scotland but grew up in Australia. As a young woman she became a professional tea-taster in the East, but at the beginning of the Second World War she volunteered for service as a Wren. Hayden, born in the United States, had been a merchant seaman from his youth, rising to the captaincy of a ship. The two met in Liverpool, where his ship had docked to unload supplies during the war.

Their only child, Duncan, was the age of one of our sons, and because of the friendship of the children my wife and I became familiar with the Wilcoxes. Now that the boys have grown, we rarely see Joan and Hayden, for they are occupied with their dairy farm and the care of the mother (they can't afford a hired hand, much less a practical nurse), and my wife and I both work at the university. But for some years we did manage occasional visits back and forth. Once, my wife and I brought Hayden a bottle of wine for his birthday, and drank a toast with him in the barn as he was milking; Joan invited my wife for tea several times, and she came to the wedding of our oldest son. It was held in the side yard, with the paddock fence and hills for background—a casual affair in the modern manner, at which guests read poems, the farm bell was rung at the moment the ceremony was completed, and the groom set off a three-stage rocket that exploded streamers and pink talcum powder high above the pasture. One of the guests read a poem by a friend of his and ours, the ending lines of which referred to the "mystery in hay" and the "wonder in cows"; I was looking at Joan, who was listening intently to the words, and saw the absolute astonishment—for the lines of her weathered face betray her every emotion—with which she received those two phrases.

Perhaps one shouldn't expect such astonishment at the relationship of cows to the transcendent reality from a person whose own cows were named, as were Joan and Hayden's, for figures in classical mythology—from Ariadne and Athena to Urania and Xenoclea; but, on the other hand, perhaps only a person who had so named them and then daily had to muck the barn would be so conscious of the difference between ideal and real.

This summer Cris and I are building a barn for the goats he is raising, and we have fenced in a pasture for them. Cris is twenty-three and works for Morse Chain, in Ithaca; he moved back home this summer because we have the acreage that goats require. He will eventually earn his living from their milk and cheese. I suppose my wife and I—and now Cris—feel the pastoral dream. I know it has existed in me for as long as I can remember and has something to do with my liking for Cervantes. That dream lay deep within Don Quixote and was one and the same with his knight errantry: a belief that the Age of Gold could return, that all of us and all of our animals should be able to coexist peaceably, sharing our acorns, in a world devoid of injustice and cruelty and the distinctions of caste or status. Unlike Don Quixote, I have been cautious in pursuing such a dream, which means, of course, that I don't really believe in its achievement. Farming for me is a gesture, a respite, a refuge. A farm gives me a chance to be a carpenter, a mender of fences, a horseman, a gardener; to talk about the weather (the spring and early summer have been so wet the first hay has spoiled, the wheat has sprouted before it could be taken to market, the beans in low-lying areas have died) with the genuine farmers, including the one who rents most of our fields; to gather wild raspberries with my wife; to lie on my side, chewing a clover stem and watching the kids cavort and gambol (verbs that should be reserved exclusively for their actions); and to piss in the brightness of noontime on the despicable burdock, whose burs tangle the horses' tails and manes.

When we bought our farm, I told myself that I would like to be buried in the old apple orchard—a thought anything but morbid, for it really pleased me, like the occasional happy dreams I have and from which I am awakened by the sound of my own chuckles. Such a fancy implies, naturally, that one's children will stay on the land, and their children as well. The deed to our property shows that the land and house had stayed in the Kelsey family for well over one hundred years: farmers begot farmers; the rhythm of the generations was in harmony with the rhythm of nature, the cycle of the crops. But in the late nineteen-thirties all becomes chaotic: ownership passes quickly from name to name, sometimes twice within the same year. The slip of time the McConkeys have occupied the place is greater than that of any family since the Kelseys.

It is true that the freedom I have on my land and my staying power are possible only for people whom real-estate agents in their advertisements refer to as "gentleman farmers." The salaries we earn in the cities and towns support our indulgences; we would go bankrupt if our whole lives centered on our farms. The person most likely to take over our land is not our son the goat dairyman but rather the farmer who rents the fields, a wholly honest and reliable person, one with a shrewd business sense, mechanical aptitude, an instinct that tells him what and when to plant, and a great capacity for strenuous labor in the spring and fall—a farmer who has managed to beget three sons just like him, and who, in the past decade, has had the wit and resources to buy several farms surrounding ours, making our one hundred and seventy-three acres something of an enclave.

I suppose that whenever we talk about people we admire, as I admire Joan and Hayden, we reveal as much of ourselves as we do of them; certainly the people we admire often behave in a way that we would emulate had we more courage and less good sense. Joan and Hayden were possessed by the pastoral dream and abandoned themselves as recklessly to it as ever did Don Quixote. The dream has inflicted privation and suffering upon them to a degree that is presumptuous and perhaps even arrogant of me to write about. That they would escape the farming life now if they could is beyond question. One of their old friends—like Hayden, a former ship captain—visited them four or five years ago. He had stayed with the shipping company for which they worked until the year of compulsory retirement and was drawing a handsome pension. Hayden, though he quit a number of years before retirement, had made monthly payments into the company retirement fund while he was working; he and his friend calculated that he had sufficient equity in that fund to be drawing several hundred dollars a month. On the basis of those calculations and an early and encouraging reply to an inquiry the Wilcoxes made, they consigned their entire herd to auction. But the company that Hayden worked for had gone out of business, and the firm dispensing the pension checks had no record of his payments. Neither had he; all had been destroyed in the fire that burned their house. So they were forced to purchase a new but smaller herd.

I admire Joan and Hayden not only for their dream but for the staunchness with which they hold on to the pieces of it left to them. They gave the new cows the old names. Athena and Eurydice and Philomela are back in their pastures, and there are times when their names in the evenings resound in the dark woods, even as they did years ago when my wife and Jimmy (then about five) helped the three Wilcoxes round them up, after Hayden, driving his tractor through the fields, neglected to close a gate behind him. As the members of the search party entered the woods, our son somehow became separated from my wife. While she was searching for him, calling his name, the Wilcoxes were calling to each other and beseeching the supernal figures to return: "Hayden, where are you?" "Athena?" "Duncan, I think I've found Eurydice." "Come here, Urania, nice Urania." "Philomela!" It was almost dark before my wife found Jimmy wandering about, happily calling out the Greek names himself. They were near a strange road and had to walk a mile or more to get back to our car. The Wilcoxes were still in the woods, but my wife felt helpless to assist them. Early the next morning she phoned to see if the roundup had been successful. Joan said cheerfully, "Oh dear yes, I found some cows and drove them home, but they turned out to be the wrong ones. We finally sorted them out with our neighbors, though, so everything is perfectly all right."

Perhaps Hayden's absentmindedness about closing his gate, which seems to come upon him only when he's at the wheel of his tractor, is a consequence of a feeling of command, as in the days when he was captain of his oceangoing vessel and had a crew to look after the details. I'm absentminded, too. And I share with him and with Joan another trait not necessarily connected with successful farming—a love of reading, though their life is such that literature for them is more pleasurable memory than present event. Reading, in fact, had something to do with their marriage. They had met, that time in Liverpool, because she and her group of Wrens, who were stationed nearby in a facility without hot water, had requested permission to come aboard his ship to take showers. He had struck up a conversation about books with her, and found himself thinking of her as his ship returned to America. From New York he cabled advertisements to various English newspapers, asking that a woman whose name he didn't know but who had been a visitor aboard his ship on such-and-such a day get in touch with him at the pier in Liverpool on a designated day. Joan saw the little notice and met him when his ship docked; and so they were married. After the war, she lived with him aboard ship and explored ports throughout the world. The ship's library was a good one; at sea she read constantly, and he joined her whenever his responsibilities permitted. I have found it a remarkable experience, sitting in their converted chicken house, barn boots cluttering the doorway, a bit of manure on the floor (their life gives them precious little desire for tidiness, for putting on a show of order for late-night guests come to retrieve a son), to talk with that mustached man, tired from his daily chores but still holding himself erect in a manner almost military, and eager to discuss the life of Emma Goldman or the labor strife of the Depression years or any other knowledge gained from his shipboard reading.

At what point in their life Hayden and Joan decided to come ashore permanently I don't know. I do know that Hayden bought a pickup truck for Joan just before he set off on his final sea voyage, loosely tied a small anchor to its bumper, and told her to take rural routes across the nation and to buy land in whatever county of whatever state the anchor fell off—a nautical equivalent of Don Quixote's habit of giving Rocinante the rein at a crossroads to choose for him the future and whatever splendor it would bring. The anchor fell off near Slaterville Springs, Tompkins County, New York; Joan found the farm they wanted, at the opposite end of the county.

My wife told me that as she was leaving the Wilcoxes' home after her first tea Joan put a hand on her arm at the doorway and said, "We used to dream of a country estate, Hayden and I did, when we were on the ship. We read about country houses, the architecture and landscaping. We wanted a house with wings, kept up the way you manage to keep up yours; a stable for the horses; a grand lawn with trees; a flower garden—one with a pool. Of course all that was silly, for we'd made up our minds to have no servants. Well, there's my shrubbery"—Joan pointed to a few desolate junipers growing up from the foundation of the burned house across the road—"and there's my pool," and she pointed toward the muddy cow pond.

I'm always asking farmers I know to explain something about equipment, livestock, or farming techniques. I've learned, among other things, that dairy cattle are slaughtered in approximately their sixth year—at the optimum point, when milk production begins to slacken and the meat will still bring a good price. I imagine it must have shocked Hayden and Joan when they first learned this hard truth about their sleek and affectionate Athenas. And cows even in their most productive years can suffer from mastitis and ringworm and all the problems connected with calving. The other day, I was watching the farmer who rents our land as he was baling hay that had dried in the sun. A sudden storm of the sort we've been plagued with for months sent him home. As soon as the weather cleared, he returned, but with a different piece of equipment—something that chopped up the hay—and I figured that the rain had made him change his plans in midfield. I inquired the reason for this from another neighbor, who happened to pass in his truck—if you are standing on a country road, the neighbors all stop for a chat—and, after explaining about the loss of nutrients that occurs if you leave wet hay on the field (you can't bale it wet) and about how you have to make silage out of it as quickly as possible, he looked at me, understanding the motive for my question, and said, courteously enough, "Stick to teaching, Jim. You don't have the knack for machinery that farm work takes, any more than old Hayden does."

With help from my wife, I have installed an underground water line—four hundred feet of it, with a T and a shutoff valve at one end, where it intersects with the line going to the horse barn, and a frost valve and faucet at the other, inside the unfinished goat barn. It was the first major plumbing task we'd ever undertaken, but not a difficult one;

the pipe is plastic. Wood is the material I most enjoy working with, though. I like the grains and knots, and enjoy the smell of it when I saw. As Cris and my wife and Jimmy and I—abetted at times by youthful friends of my sons—have been putting up trusses and roofers, I have been looking down from the new height at the goats, all eighteen of them, in their pasture.

Working on the barn and looking at the goats have made me think of successful farmers like the one who rents our land; of Cris and of his chances; and of Hayden and Joan, who may be doing somewhat better in recent years but who have never been able to rebuild their house or to get sufficient help. Why should I feel a touch of envy of them, that pair of aging Don Quixotes, when my reason tells me their life would be for me a nightmare of entrapment? Is it their pluck, their dauntlessness? (A former student of mine, just back from a year in Israel, who stopped at their place to get directions to ours, said to us as soon as she got inside our door, "Who is that remarkable woman who lives down the road? I didn't know there were such *genuine* people in my own country. She looks and talks just like a woman on a kibbutz.") I come back again and again in my dreaming—it's no wonder that I hammer in the wrong size nail, saw the wrong board—to an August afternoon, an unusually hot day three or four summers ago. It was one of the last times that I mowed the weeds and orchard grass in the area around our half-acre pond, diagonally across the intersection from our house. I used to mow it regularly, using a sickle bar attached to a garden tractor—both scaled-down versions of real farm equipment—for we once thought of that area as a little park. Soon after moving to the country, we made a beach for swimming, covering the muck near the shoreline with bank-run gravel and sand. We planted highbush cranberries, multiflora roses, white pines, and willows nearby. But muskrats found the pond and burrowed into the shoreline, undermining a row of bushes; they snipped off a large number of seedlings. The runoff from the cultivated field to the east contained so many nutrients from the fertilizer the successful farmer uses that the pond began to fill up with algae and long strands of seaweed. Now that our children are grown—the youngest a high school senior in the fall—the pond is rarely used for swimming; weeds and tall grasses surround it.

On that August afternoon the pond was still halfway respectable, despite the algae and seaweed, despite the caved-in bank. As I was mowing, Joan came down the road in her old truck. She saw me and waved cheerfully, and suddenly braked, the tires skidding on the gravel. I left the tractor, thinking she had something to say. Apparently she had just loaded the truck—the bed was filled with rusty machine parts and garbage cans—for her face was flushed. She smiled at me, but she was looking at the water. Then, without saying a word, she dismounted from the truck—from the right side, since the left door wouldn't open. She was wearing a long, dark dress, much like the one she'd been wearing the first time I saw her, and she moved through the bushes and weeds with the same graceful bearing. She walked into the water until it was deep enough for that sort of curving plunge you can make even from the oozy bottom of a farm pond; and when she came to the surface I saw first her hair, wreathed in seaweed, and then her face and shoulders, green wreaths hanging from the shoulders, too. She was Botticelli's "Spring" and a draped version of his "Birth of Venus" as well. How odd it is that I, in fumbling for words to describe the effect on me of the Wilcoxes, look to art and literature and royalty, subjects that I am conversant with because of my profession, but that no teacher expects to encounter in his daily life! I really can't say what she was, caught up as I was by the gaunt figure rising from the water. All I can say is that I had never before seen such an expression of rapture—a look of joy so intense it struck me as mysterious. She stood upright in the muck, the water dripping from the seaweed in her hair, and she said, in that accent which years before had reminded me of the Queen of England, "There is more to life than suffering and taxes!"

Such a cliché! But it was as if those words had never been spoken before. I was astonished and had to look away from her. I didn't want her to see my face, to see the tears in my eyes, and I left her there and crossed the road to the safety of my old farmhouse.

1977

Fireflies

3   MY WIFE IS EDITOR OF A PROFESSIONAL
journal for one of the colleges at the university
where I teach. The people—deans, other admin-
istrative officers, secretaries—who work on the floor where she has her
office have a congenial and cooperative relationship, and enjoy gathering occasionally during lunch hour or at the end of the working day
to celebrate any of a variety of events in any of their lives: a marriage,
a departure for a new job, a trip abroad, a birthday, the first day of
spring after a hard winter. One afternoon early this spring, a former
administrator stopped by for such a celebration. As the group was
having refreshments at the large table in the conference room, this
professor, a man not given to personal reminiscence, began to tell his
neighbor about a bicycle trip he had taken with another student in
1936 in Germany. He was speaking quietly, but, either because of a
lapse in the general conversation or because of the nature of his story,
everybody listened.

The story was a simple one, told in a matter-of-fact voice, of what
he and his companion saw and did bicycling through Germany the
summer following the remilitarization of the Rhineland. Perhaps in
retelling his account I am altering it in accordance with my own feelings
and experiences, and it is likely that the people at the party, the younger
as well as the older, did much the same thing. The curious power of
certain stories comes from some unconscious invitation to the listener
to participate, to imagine himself an aspect of the teller.

These two students, the professor-to-be and his friend, had come to Germany to see the castles on the Rhine, the Black Forest, and the picturesque towns of the travel posters, but what they actually saw had little to do with quaintness or charm. In every town the buildings displayed swastikas on banners; loudspeakers in every town square amplified shrill voices and martial music; the major streets were congested with parades and the movement of military personnel and equipment. On their handlebars they had attached small American flags to identify themselves as visitors; their bicycles, so decorated, became part of the parades, were caught in the middle of convoys. In a populous town, they sat on their bicycles in the back of a crowd listening to Hitler give an impassioned speech in shouted words that they couldn't understand but that turned everybody except them into what seemed a single body, a single answering voice. Once, they rode through the gates, oddly open, of a camp for prisoners; guards rushed at them with rifles, forcing them back.

How do two young Americans respond to such nationalistic frenzy, to an evil they can barely comprehend? In Germany, the towns and villages nestle in the valleys, are rarely built upon the hills, as in Italy. Most castles on the Rhine have their towns far beneath them, and from the walls and windows of the towers one can see colored roof tiles and tiny spires beside the curving, glittering river. Those two boys would tour, say, some castle; then, removing their flags from the handlebars, they would hold them defiantly aloft and coast down the hill into the town, speeding through marketplaces and central squares. As they sped past the crowds and the swastika-decorated buildings, they sang together, as loudly as they could, the opening words of national songs of their own country—"O beautiful for spacious skies,/ For amber waves of grain," or "Oh, say, can you see by the dawn's early light,/What so proudly we hailed at the twilight's last gleaming?"— and, careering around processions of armored cars and troop carriers, they shouted "Heil Roosevelt!" to the soldiers, and then they pedalled furiously away, up the opposite hill. Usually they stayed in a farmer's barn or camped on the heights above a town. Never that summer did anyone pursue them, never were they molested or questioned, never—

except for that moment they had inadvertently strayed into the concentration camp—were they threatened. As they sat by their little
cooking fire, as they stared at the stars from their sleeping bags, they
spoke to each other of what they had seen, of what they had done that
day. And so each day went, that summer.

My wife told me the story some days after she had heard it, as we were
sitting at the kitchen table following a late supper. She was interested
especially in the effect it had made on the whole group—deans and
secretaries, younger people as well as older ones. I listened intently to
the story myself. I said that it held some of the qualities of those fairy
stories set in far-off times in which a virtuous youth enters a region of
dark enchantment but is protected by his innocence and by certain
talismans and magic words. As we idly made other speculations about
the story, about its relation to dreams we'd both had, the windows
began to darken, and the table, which I had made out of thick,
mellowed planks nearly a century and a half old, reflected the glow of
the lamp hanging above it. I was glad to be sitting with my wife at that
table in that old farmhouse of ours—the house in which we had raised
our three sons, two of whom were already out in the world, one editing
news film for a Philadelphia television station and the other working
the night shift in an Ithaca factory. I wanted our sons to find fulfillment,
to be content with their lives; and at the same time I wanted them to
return to their childhood selves and their childhood innocence, to be
sitting here at the table with us. I had all the conventional thoughts that
occur to parents, including the wish that the world were better than it
is. That was the effect of the story upon me.

I went to high school in a village in northern Ohio, about fifteen miles
southwest of Cleveland. I could recite the names of all the members of
the Roosevelt Cabinet like a litany, and I still can. In the eleventh grade,
I wrote a paper for my civics class in which I proposed an immediate
end to the Depression by means of a total price freeze, to be accompanied by the release of a large amount of currency and the imposition
of income and inheritance taxes designed to prevent that new money

from ending up in the pockets of the fortunate few. My teacher wrote on my paper, "Well, why not?" I was living in those years with an uncle and aunt, and worked evenings and Saturdays in my uncle's gasoline station, which sold ice and hamburgers as well as petroleum products. I had a recurrent dream in which President Roosevelt and Secretary Morgenthau, having heard of my proposal, came to visit me in the gas station. So that we would have more time for our conference, my two guests helped me with my tasks; while I pumped gasoline, President Roosevelt made hamburgers and Secretary Morgenthau put fifty-pound blocks of ice on automobile bumpers. After we finished our discussion, President Roosevelt smiled at me and said to Secretary Morgenthau, "Well, why not?"

Our village of three thousand inhabitants had a symphony orchestra, sponsored by the WPA, made up of professional musicians and anyone else who could play an instrument. The players came from the village and other communities in our part of the county. They practiced in the high school auditorium, and I sometimes sat in the back of that nearly empty room to listen to them. Normally, they played Beethoven and Mozart, but there was one elderly woman in the village who found so much delight in realizing an old fancy of hers—to sing "Flow Gently, Sweet Afton" with a full-size orchestra—that the conductor always obliged, at least at rehearsals. Her voice was untrained and full of tremolo effects, but what I remember best, beyond her obvious pleasure, is the absolute benignity and sense of well-being on the faces of the musicians who were helping her in the realization of a preposterous dream. I suppose an event of that sort was possible only in the Depression years; I realized even then that it wouldn't have happened had it not been for the WPA. But that it could take place at all affected my feelings toward myself, my village, and—for I was young and knew precious little about other events beginning elsewhere—the community of man.

It is late June, the season of fireflies. Even on overcast nights the country sky is riddled with comets, meteors, flashing stars, gauzy nebulae. Fireflies have the evocative power of certain aromas and fragments of tunes: they are what reminded me of my adolescence, which in turn reminded me of the story I had heard earlier this year. Standing on my porch, grasping the iron railing by the step and looking at the fireflies above the clover field, at the constellations receding above the clover, the fierce stars washing harmlessly past my speeding position on the porch to bob and diminish in the cosmic wake, I think that the magic of our talismans, the truths that perilously sustain us, the inviolability of our virtue are always a consequence of the power of our imagination. I also think this: Nostalgia is roused in us less by the memory of what once actually was than by the memory of what once was possible in our dreams.

1978

The Idea of Hawk

4 M Y GRANDFATHER SHUTTLED BETWEEN my parents' home and that of his married daughter, my Aunt Jo, from at least the time I was three. His early dependence upon his children never seemed odd to me, since it was a given in my life. I remember him as a small-boned, gentle, and uncomplaining old man whose long nose always dripped—doubtless from a sinus condition I was destined to inherit. I liked him for the stories he used to tell of his boyhood on a ranch, and for his ability to prepare meals, when my parents were away, in such a manner that there were never many dishes for my brother and me to wash. He died, of cancer, in my parents' house, after I had become a teacher who wanted to write; my mother and Aunt Jo nursed him in his last months. My father always accepted my grandfather's presence but appeared to have little in common with him. Six years ago, my father died, also of cancer. At the moment of his death my grandfather's unmarried daughter, my Aunt May, cried out in surprise at a sudden resemblance between my father and my grandfather, those disparate men. This past summer, Aunt Jo told me something about my grandfather's life that reveals something about my father's. The story I want to tell is theirs and mine.

Throughout his life, my father searched vainly for whatever it was that would constitute his "bracket." I never heard him attempt to define that bracket; perhaps he felt any effort to do so would constrict or destroy it. I know the difficulty, having sensed it frequently myself, so let me state it in terms that I understand.

One likes the idea, say, of *hawk*, and would aspire to it: the high freedom, the swift and effortless flight, the sharpness of eye, the vertical dive. For example, on a sunny day last spring, my wife and I, after planting our garden, lay on our backs in the grass, enjoying the warmth of the damp soil and the movement of a hawk far above us as it banked and climbed in the updraft. It became a dark point, a mote swimming with the others in the pools of our sun-blinded vision, and then it plunged. As it fell (for a moment I thought we were its prey), crows, those keen-sighted but heavier birds, slowly rose from various positions along the border of the woods that half encircled the horizon. The hawk was the tip of a diminishing stamen, the crows the end points of petals folding back upon the pistil. Hawk and crows composed a blossom so exquisite and inevitable in its movement toward enclosure that I felt the ache to be stamen or petal or—most crucial of all—seed of that pistil. But who in his normal mind would want to be hawk settling down with talons outspread to rake a tiny mouse, to be bird of carrion after a bit of pink intestine?

In a typically American way, my father confused a desired and idealized state with reality itself; and so he was perpetually disappointed. In the years of my childhood, he held any number of responsible and well-paying jobs, renouncing each of them as soon as he had achieved what in the academic profession we refer to as tenure—the moment that assures job security and clearly defined expectations until a scheduled retirement day. He became the hawk only to the degree that his motion was a dive from the rarefied air all the way to a pebble on the ground, followed by a laborious climb. In my opinion, the major pattern of his life forms the letter "V," even though the ascendant line wobbles here and there or drops like a graph depicting some corporation's uneven growth in sales or net worth.

His plunge began in the middle of the Depression, at that dark period of it when he lost the freedom to move from position to position. He deserted the family he loved (I would not have felt the extent of betrayal I did had he not obviously loved me, my brother, and our mother); asked for and received a divorce; and undertook a second, wholly unsuccessful, marriage. He ended up alone, and boxed in by debts. With everything lost, he gained in a tiny room or cell for indigent transients the freedom to hope for it all back, bit by bit.

And so he and my mother were remarried. Slowly he paid all his debts. Advancing to better and yet better jobs, he saved enough money and established sufficient credit to buy an automobile agency near Cleveland. But he had been easily deceived by the seller—the manufacturer went out of business shortly. His new debts were huge enough that his lawyer and even some of his major creditors advised him to declare bankruptcy, but he refused. To do so, he said, would hurt his good name and make it difficult for him to start another business. He was well into his sixties at the time; he was nearly seventy when he paid the last dollar he owed. Just before the onset of his terminal illness, he was accumulating capital to quit the reference-book business—he sold the books on commission to libraries—and become a consultant for small firms in financial disarray.

Not many years before his death, my mother told me that my father felt I had never forgiven him and that she hoped he was wrong. His feeling surprised me, and so did her uncertainty; I would have despised myself for being self-righteous, a moral prig, had I not long since *thought* I had forgiven him. And yet so much of my life had been and continued to be an attempt to persuade myself of my difference from him! In the back of my mind existed a kind of clock marking two or more times, somewhat similar to the watches worn by travelers who habitually cross oceans or continents. Regularly I had checked the present moment of my life against that of my father at my age. I congratulated myself as each of my children reached and then passed the age I had been when my father deserted his family. His rootlessness had made permanence itself a value to me; on several occasions, I refused outright and perhaps rudely to be considered for other teaching positions, at higher salaries. I had become inflexible and ungenerous in certain of my judgments. Whenever a husband and wife of my acquaintance separated in their middle years, I blamed the man and sometimes had difficulty speaking pleasantly to him; and because my mother had, of necessity, become a maid after my father deserted us, I disapproved of friends who hired maids as soon as they could afford that indulgence. Living in a large house I loved, one cluttered with the accumulation of the years and surrounded by farmlands and woods that belonged to my wife and me, I had spoken severely to my growing children of the danger of mistaking the quest after possession or position for the quest after happiness. And of course I hoped that none of my children would seek a career in business.

Such memories and feelings were much in mind during the long period of my father's illness—particularly on the occasions I drove alone from Ithaca to Cleveland to see my parents. The day after his second operation, six months before he was to die, I went to the office of the surgeon who had performed the operation and learned that the surgery had not slowed the growth of the malignancy. My father would experience a brief interval of returning health because of the removal of a blockage, but we should not be misled by that. Since he would require medication and nursing, the surgeon was willing to sign the paper necessary to admit him to a nursing home under the provisions of Medicare. The decision to have him admitted must be made immediately; if he were to be taken home for that brief period of seeming good health and then required the care of a nursing home, he would be denied all financial benefits. And what if he lingered on for many months? People like my father—those with a strong will to live—sometimes did that.

I said in anger that the Medicare legislation was cruel and unjust, apparently designed to push the elderly sick in our society out of sight as quickly as possible. The surgeon replied, kindly enough, that his job was to save or prolong lives and that the quality of the lives saved or prolonged lay in hands other than his own. He simply wished to stress that nursing-home care cost as much as fifty dollars a day, a sum beyond the means of many; that around-the-clock nursing care, which my father would ultimately need if we kept him at home, was much more expensive than that; and that my mother's size (she was less than five feet tall and weighed ninety pounds) as well as her age (she was in her eighties) obviously limited our choices. He believed that my mother and I should be as rational and objective as possible in making our decision.

The surgeon's office was three blocks from my parents' home. What I had just heard had altered my relationship with my father, in a way I could not yet consider. My mother would be sitting in the kitchen, waiting for my return with the news. Though her religious beliefs had been partially undermined as she grew old ("If there were a Heaven," she had said only half facetiously to me after the first moon landing, "those astronauts would have seen it"), I knew she would be praying. I walked several blocks in the wrong direction before resolving not to be a coward. I would tell her calmly and accurately everything the surgeon had said.

But when I actually saw her at the kitchen table, I burst into tears, and that was how she discovered the truth. She was the calm one. When I told her what the surgeon had said about the nursing home, she said, "But I want him *here*, Jim." She said it both as if it were the most important wish of her life and as if—like so many of her wishes, many years earlier—there were no chance of its being granted her. A sentence from an otherwise forgotten book came into my mind: *Memory is what we now have in place of religion.* At once I felt a happiness of a kind and intensity I had never experienced; for an interval I believed myself in possession of a truth beyond corruption.

I remembered an uncle—the husband of my mother's sister—rising from a chair, throwing down a fistful of cards on a table, and shouting at my brother and me, "You'll grow up worthless as your father!" Because we were as destitute as my absent father, because, too, we had arrived with our luggage at his door without asking if we might, my uncle the previous month had admitted my mother and brother and me into his home, even though his income in those bleak days was insufficient to support his own family. Wanting to be kind, desiring (perhaps desperately) not to be resentful, he had invited my brother and me to play a simple form of bridge with him and one of his daughters; he had been anticipating victory when the game neared its end, but with an unexpected card my brother had won for us. Later my uncle accepted and loved me like a son. I had suppressed the incident.

Such painful details from my past, all of them rising from buried grievances, humiliations, and victimizations for which I had blamed my father, now became available to me. Even while I understood my mother's resignation—in my adolescent dreams my father's desertion had become a barrier of cold but once molten material, a jagged and dark boulder that cut our hands as my mother and I tried to get around it—I understood my father's continuing need of illusions. I knew that from the beginning of his illness he had refused to acknowledge its nature; I knew that his expectation would be to come home, where, as he mended, he could make plans for his consulting business and discuss them with my mother; I knew that to commit him to a nursing home at this point of momentarily returning health would be to betray him as surely as he had betrayed his family. Memory—which works through connections, and which possibly may depend for its psychic energy upon its own faint memory of a union far greater than it can ever achieve—made me see that analogy. Memory also made me see that rough boulder of my dreams as the unjust and immovable obstruction before my father. And memory, which gives us our identities, can, by an act of grace, release us from ourselves through an outpouring of its most hidden contents. To remember my uncle's phrase was to take back my father. My past flooded out, into him, and was transformed; and so I was happy.

Still standing before my mother in the kitchen, I knew I would do anything in my power to put my parents in each other's arms again. "Of course he must come home, Mother," I said.

It turned out that there was very little I needed to do; both the surgeon and I had underestimated my parents' wills. My mother, with some assistance at first, gave my father all the care he needed. While he was regaining the strength to lift his pigskin satchel of reference books, he arranged a little office in the corner of his bedroom and had a telephone installed there. He sat before his card table, writing up a vita sheet and designing a letterhead and a business card for his consulting service, and acting as a volunteer telephone counselor for young people with drug and other problems: he liked to hear the telephone ring. He soon was able to drive his car again; the day before his death he took my mother grocery shopping. The only thing I did for him was to build a gate to protect his car. I had visited him in the hospital the day I was to return to Ithaca, to say goodbye and to find out if there was anything he'd like me to do before I left. "I've been lying here thinking of those damned cats caterwauling and coupling on the hood of the Chrysler, and it's driving me nuts," he said. "You know that lean-to or so-called carport where I keep it? Three sides are snug, but the cats get in at the front. What I'd really appreciate is a catproof gate, made of chicken wire."

With my father when he died were my mother; his younger sister, my Aunt May; and my wife and I. He died on his seventy-fourth birthday; because he enjoyed listening to classical music, my wife and I had brought a box containing an FM radio which he never had time to open. As I sat on the edge of his bed, he asked me what good books I had been reading lately. The question touched me, for it seemed to indicate that some barrier between us had dropped. Though he had always liked to read, he had shied away from literary conversations with me, as if he were afraid I might ridicule his tastes. I gave him some titles, and talked about two or three I thought he might want to read. He listened attentively. Then he gave me the titles of the books he had been reading or rereading; one of them, he said, was a sort of sequel or follow-up to *The Robe*. He asked me which of those books I liked. I told him all of them, but he knew me better than that. "I never could understand why you don't like Lloyd C. Douglas," he said. "I've been going through that one again"—and he pointed to the sequel, which lay on top of some other books on the nightstand I had made in junior high school—"marking passages I think are really just fine. Look at some of them and tell me if I'm wrong."

I was reaching for the book when he began coughing up blood. He tried to hide the fact, smiling almost shyly and holding his hand to his mouth as if to conceal the smile; and I tried to look at several of the passages he had underlined, so he wouldn't know I knew. They weren't religious or inspirational at all, but then my father had never been particularly religious. I couldn't make much sense out of the passages. The one I looked at most closely seemed to be a matter-of-fact statement about getting on with life. He began coughing more violently; the blood came up in thick strands. "Talk to me about this passage, Pop," I said, but put the book down and began to stroke his forehead. My wife came into the room. She cradled her arm around him, lifting him so that he could breathe, and holding a dish to his lips. My mother telephoned for an ambulance. There was uncertainty at the hospital as to who the patient was; my mother said in a low voice, "My husband. You know, Dr. Burmeister's cancer patient." My father heard her and cried, "I don't have cancer!"—his last words. He had ceased coughing; my wife plumped up his pillow and lowered his head onto it. My mother said clearly, "I love you, Clayton"; my Aunt May said, I love you Clayt;" and my wife and I said separately, "I love you, Pop." He heard us, for he smiled again and tried to speak but could not. It was at the instant of his death that my aunt, as I have said, cried out in surprise, "Why, how much like Dad he looks!"

While in Florida this past August, on a trip my wife and I had made to see her own ailing father, in Naples, we visited my Aunt Jo and her husband in St. Petersburg. I was curious about my grandfather, and asked Aunt Jo some questions. At first she was reluctant, but then she became eager to talk about him. She said that he and his two older brothers had inherited a large sum of money when their parents' ranch was sold. My aunt had heard that the brothers, who were more adept at physical tasks than her father, had teased him with any number of cruel practical jokes. They stayed in the West, but as soon as her father got his share of the money he came East, where he married and set himself up in the cigar-making business. "Oh, I used to *resent* him so," she said. "He was trusting enough to be a child—his partner cheated him, ran off with all the tobacco stock, cleaned the shelves and the till, and what did Dad do but take the money left him and set up a loan agency in the Cleveland Arcade until he simply *gave away* every cent he had! Then Mother died and Dad sent May and me off in the winter on the train to relatives in Michigan; we were wearing all the clothes we had—summer dresses. Clayton was older and stayed with him until he got through school, found a job, and married. When May and I were just out of secretarial school, living together and each making six or seven dollars a week, Dad moved in with us: he'd been peddling insurance door to door without much luck, and now said he would get a real job. But he had some high and mighty ideas of the sort of job a rancher's son and former owner of two businesses ought to have— your everyday factory job wouldn't do. So he'd be sitting at home in the evening when we came in with the bag of groceries. He would go through the bag. 'That's the wrong kind of bread,' he would say. Or 'You shouldn't have bought this pork, the bone's too big.' Do you know the moment I think he crumpled up for good? When I brought home a slab of butter, the kind the grocer weighed after scooping it from the barrel, he said, 'Jo, you shouldn't have bought so much, it'll turn rancid.' I picked it up and squeezed it between my fingers and held it under his nose and said, 'Dad, I bought this butter with my own hard-earned money, and I'll buy *twice* as much next time if I want to!' From that moment on and for the rest of his life, he never complained or asked for a thing. He just gave up pretending he was in control. The poor dear was ineffectual, a dreamer, that's all I can say. I don't think people can help being what they are, do you?"

She wanted my response; and so I said I thought some people try harder than others to get beyond what they're born with. She said that I was perfectly right, as if my remark were simply a confirmation of her view. I could understand how such a belief would be a help, especially in our later years; it makes us more tolerant of each other and less harsh with ourselves. And of course I was remembering my Aunt May's cry as my father died; and thinking of how much his two sisters as well as his son carried on in our bones the resemblance that had startled her. It made me feel kindly toward Aunt Jo, and indulgent toward myself, to see her broad forehead, her long nose, and her eyes that were a bit too large for her face. I remembered the strength of my happiness when at last I had forgiven my father. Surely in that happiness I had come close to whatever my father, without defining it, had always wanted from this world, and maybe what my grandfather had wanted, too. Such an instant may be the most important one of a lifetime, but it becomes in the following instant only the memory of a feeling, of a transient psychical state: a memory of how a long sequence of memories had coalesced to achieve, without any act of will, the transubstantiation of self into other. A recollection of this kind makes a pretty slender argument to oppose to the belief (with its firmer supporting evidence) that all of us are caught from the start. Still, I didn't want to agree wholly with Aunt Jo, at least not yet, and so I told her, *Well, yes and no; that is, I think you're both right and wrong*—the response that all professors experienced in the art of fudging can make in such a judicious manner that they appear to possess a more comprehensive insight into the problem than does the student who raised the difficult question.

Passages Early and Late

5 IN JUNE OF ONE OF MY FIRST YEARS AS A teacher, my wife and I and the drama teacher at my college and his wife made a daylong excursion from our eastern Kentucky town of Morehead to a state park. The children of both families had been left with friends. The spring term had just ended, and even Linda, the drama teacher's wife, was more relaxed than usual—she was normally the most intense and active of the four of us and was on medication for her high blood pressure. The day was cool and misty in the early morning, but bright and hot by noon: the kind of day in Kentucky in which meadowlarks sing in the hedgerows in the morning, wild roses bloom on the crumbling stone fences, and everything perceived between mid-morning and dusk is so sharply outlined that the viewer feels gifted with a strange power to look into the very essence of things—a bud, a thorn, a vulture on a rock, the rock itself.

We had brought food and cooking equipment for breakfast, but even hunger was pleasurable, something we didn't wish to satiate too quickly. And so we rented horses at the park stable as soon as it opened. We rode through the trails in the dark woods, trotting whenever we came to the sunny glades; and, in the green fields above the lake, we galloped abreast. The smell and warmth of sweating horses, the sound that hooves and leather make, the feeling that from the waist down the rider has become one with the animal while the chest and head remain free and wholly human—these sensations, so sensuous and agreeable, are particularly exhilarating for one who is young and a reasonably good horseman.

At a picnic site we finally dismounted, leading the horses back and forth until they were cooled enough to be tethered to saplings at the edge of the clearing. Linda and my wife walked to the car for the breakfast supplies while I gathered brush and branches into a pile for P.C., the drama teacher, who had offered to build the fire. P.C. was tall and thin and had the pale complexion of people who haunt dark theaters and basement studios. On his knees, patiently tending his small fire, he looked to me more an ascetic than an outdoorsman; but in his gentle voice he began reminiscing about his childhood in North Carolina, and about various experiences with bears and other wildlife in the Great Smokies. He spoke of moments of recklessness and danger. Once, as a boy, he had rescued a man whose car had plummeted from a cliff. . . .

It was characteristic of P.C. in his intervals of happiness—after, say, an opening performance of *The Tempest* in which his student actors from Neon and Salt Lick had conjured up more magic than he had believed possible—to talk about himself, to mention certain of his childhood adventures and to speak of famous actors with whom he'd had a beer or two during a season of summer stock; but he always did so in such a soft and apologetic voice that anybody not familiar with him would think he was telling one little lie after another. It is the fact of P.C.'s happiness, his shy garrulousness, that I remember from this day. I cannot remember what he said about bears, or about how he had managed to rescue a motorist whose car might or might not have been cradled in the branches of a tree; if he described for me some action of his adolescence in which his sense of abandon had nearly cost him his life, I have only a faint recollection that probably this is so.

For, while I can remember from this day everything that gave me a personal pleasure—including such a tableau as P.C. kneeling before a fire while four horses watched him—I can recall almost nothing of what any of my companions said, and nothing whatsoever of what particularly pleased them. What did my wife say, and what gave her the most delight? Did she smile at me? Was she wearing the boots and breeches from her high school days? My memory, usually so reliable in regard to what has made her happy, tells me much too little about my wife and the couple who for six years were among our closest friends.

I most regret my inability to recollect Linda's responses. She had wanted to be an actress. In a way, she was an unpaid drama teacher at the college, for she helped P.C. coach the student performers, designed costumes, and once or twice a year—whenever a play had a role for a woman that required a maturity and emotional response beyond the experience and ability of the available students—acted in the productions. Restless, she needed always to be planning parties or arranging social events for charitable purposes. A month before we went to the park, I had returned to my graduate school in Iowa to take the final oral examination for my doctoral degree. On the night immediately preceding my departure, Linda, aware of my anxiety, gathered all the members of my department and their wives before our front door to sing "Your Ph.D., your Ph.D., you're going to get . . . your Ph.D.," to the tune of "Aloha." Some years after my wife and I had left eastern Kentucky for upstate New York, Linda suffered a stroke that deprived her of speech. P.C. gave up the theater for less demanding work so that he would have the time to teach her word after word of her lost language. Following another stroke, Linda died, "knowing at least, thank God, how to speak," as P.C. told my wife and me in a late-night long-distance call following her burial.

On that day at the park, the four of us—after breakfast and further riding—walked the nature trails, dived into the cold water of a blue lake surrounded by green hills, raced our companions to the dam and back in foot-driven paddleboats, lay in the sand in our wet swimming suits and later in the grass of the meadow above the lake, and explored in the heat of late afternoon a cool cave whose roof was furred with sleeping bats. All day I kept saying to myself, "How happy I am! How good I feel!" My body felt lean and capable of the most strenuous physical task; at rest it was loose-limbed, drowsy, sensual.

Toward evening, we started home. I was driving; my wife rested her head on my shoulder. Nobody spoke, for we were all tired, but when I saw an intriguing road—the narrow kind, with gravel or sand only in the single pair of tracks, that curves as it climbs a forested hill—I swerved off the blacktop to take it. Roads of this kind often appear in my most mysterious dreams; and if I actually come upon such a road and do not take it, thinking that I can't spare the time or that my desire to follow it is merely superstitious, I suffer the nostalgia we feel for something of large value that we have willfully lost. I took such a road on that day at least partly because I didn't want my personal happiness to end. Not only was the term over, but I had just been granted my doctoral degree. Regardless of the lateness of the hour, of the fact that the families who were caring for our children were expecting us to retrieve them before supper, none of the others protested when I left the highway; perhaps they slept, perhaps they were as unwilling as I to admit that our excursion was almost completed.

I drove past several abandoned cabins. Beyond them, the road dipped to ford a rocky creek and climbed again into further woods. The uphill tracks had been eroded by the rivulets of the preceding rainy season; dry and snake-like channels now, they held large stones against which the frame of the car occasionally scraped. My companions had become alert. "Hadn't we better turn back?" my wife asked. I said maybe we could, at the top of the hill. At the crest, though, facing a huge sun just beginning to descend behind a ridge that paralleled ours, we looked down into a green and level valley. A wide stream divided the fields; and beneath us, at the edge of the stream, stood a small, white-painted church. Here the road stopped; there was no bridge. It was such an improbable destination for this rarely traveled and wretchedly maintained road that it reminded me at once of the end of such roads in my dreams; I wanted to see whether the church truly existed, and, if so, whether it really was as immaculate as it appeared to be from our height.

I remember no further ruts, no further rocky obstructions. By the side of the church, the road looped back upon itself like the terminus of a streetcar line. On the other bank of the stream, a somewhat wider and neatly-graveled road led to a parking lot. A barge—a simple ferry boat for passengers—was tied to the opposite shore; a cable fastened to trees on both banks and connected by a pulley and smaller cable to the boat obviously was intended to keep the worshipers from floating downstream during the flood season. How was the boat propelled? Did the worshipers sling a rope across the water to a solitary person who took our road for the purpose of pulling the others to his side? Were long poles hidden in the barge? While we marveled and built our theories, twilight came. There were no power lines in the valley—that was part of its charm—but such a lack meant no electricity in the church. Freshly painted, it shimmered and grew larger in the vanishing light.

The door unlatched easily; it had been kept shut by a hasp with a whittled stick through the staple. The interior was not yet dark; the walls and ceiling were white and the many-paned windows large. The unvarnished floor had the bleached and sanded look that comes from countless scrubbings. Six rows of pews faced the pulpit. Next to the lectern stood a bulky black piano and a stool. No religious objects or pictures decorated the little room; no sign existed outside or within the building to denote a sect. But the hymnals in the racks and on the piano were those of my childhood—and apparently of the childhoods of my companions too. Sitting on the stool, P.C. looked at the page to which the hymnal was opened and immediately began to play "In the Garden," and then "The Old Rugged Cross" and "The Little Brown Church in the Vale." Grouped around him, the rest of us, needing to see the words no more than he needed to see the musical notations, sang as if we had been invited into the church to do so; as if the purely physical and no doubt self-centered happiness we individually had experienced earlier that day had been an intentional and necessary preparation for this activity which otherwise was as isolated from everything in the past and from everything in the future as the church itself was isolated from our habitual world. The room slowly became one with the darkness gathering outside and each of the singers became only a face and a voice—a face almost indistinguishable from the other faces floating in the night, a voice merging with the melodic stream arising from a nearly invisible instrument.

In my sixth and last year of teaching in Kentucky, I gave a talk before a group of about thirty people, all of them considerably older than I, in the banquet hall of a hotel in Huntington, West Virginia. The occasion was West Virginia Poetry Day; I had been chosen to be the banquet speaker, and my wife had been invited to attend. I felt honored; not only was I a young and unknown teacher who never before had made a public address, but I had been plucked out of a neighboring state, as if nobody in West Virginia were quite up to the task.

The trip to Huntington took place in October rather than June, and my wife and I left our home in early afternoon rather than early morning—but this day, like the day we had spent in the state park, was one of unusual clarity. The trees were changing color; maples and oaks stood out sharply in the sunlight against the dark green of the pines. Our road led past the brick kilns and American Legion Post of Olive Hill and past the entrance to the park; a few miles beyond the entrance, it descended from the hills into a wide valley. Here the land was more fertile, the barns larger and in better repair. Steep-roofed farmhouses replaced the cabins with their rusty washing machines and refrigerators on the slanting porches. The streets of Huntington were broad and lined with trees; stately houses were set back in landscaped grounds. Our town of three thousand seemed a peasant hamlet to which Huntington was the provincial capital. The five-or-six story hotel with its uniformed porter waiting beneath the marquee was large enough to be the palace of an archduke.

Although we arrived on time, most of the guests were already seated at the U-shaped table beneath the chandelier, and were speaking to each other in subdued voices. A photographer wandered about, taking pictures. The president of the poetry society, a tall woman wearing a long dress and a corsage that matched the flowers on the table, introduced us to several people. One was the society editor of the Huntington newspaper, another the chairman of the English department at the local university. As my wife and I were escorted to our central places at the bottom of the U, I felt my new suit to be shoddy and ill-fitting.

The event began with a reading by the president of a poem written for the occasion by the governor of West Virginia; he was honorary chairman of the poetry society and had been responsible for the proclamation giving West Virginia its annual Poetry Day. Following his poem, which praised the state's beauty and its poets, the president began a roll call. As each named was pronounced, a man or woman would rise to recite a poem he or she had composed since the last banquet. Some of the members had memorized their work; others pulled folded sheets from pockets or purses, adjusted their glasses, and carefully read their verses. Halfway through the readings I realized that their own words were more important to the members than any speech of mine; I knew also that my prepared talk was much too long and full of quotations, and that to read it aloud would be a disaster.

Indigestion kept me from eating the fried chicken. I put my manuscript next to my plate; with a pen I deleted large segments, drawing connecting arrows between the remaining paragraphs, and put asterisks next to phrases I was so fond of that I wanted to make sure I would give them exactly as written. Once I began to speak, though, I abandoned the typed text almost completely. The subject of my address was "The Creative Process." I talked of divine and human love. My references were to Dante and Virgil and Beatrice and the stars that end each part of *The Divine Comedy;* to the speculations of the mathematician Henri Poincaré about the "aesthetic sieve" possessed by all creators, a sieve permitting only those combinations that are beautiful (and hence usually true) to escape from their dreaming to their conscious states; and to Hindu metaphysics. I was able to speak so readily, I think, because my subject, being both large and noble, assured me of the amplitude and generosity of my own mind. The occasional flashbulbs persuaded me of my status as a celebrity, and my voice became nearly as deep and resonant as that of Dylan Thomas. The ovation I received so gratified me that I immediately gave away my manuscript, though I had made no carbon of it, to the poetry society member who told me she regretted only the brevity of my remarks. For some years I kept a copy of the full page the Huntington newspaper had devoted to the banquet. In a note accompanying the copy she had mailed to me, the president of the society wrote that she thought the headline—"Mankind Equipped for Love, Poetry Speaker Says"—

somewhat unfortunate, but that she felt I might like to see the pictures. They included one of me, hand raised as I made a point. The brief text said that I had been inspirational.

After we left the hotel, my wife and I walked the streets of downtown Huntington, looking at the window displays of the now-closed department and furniture stores. Huntington, while still seeming exotic—the chairs and clothing in the windows were beyond our income—had managed to become friendlier; it was quite possible that someday we would be residents of such a city. Perhaps the chairman of the English department at the university had been so impressed by my talk that at this moment he was sitting before his desk in the study of one of those stately houses, writing me to find out if I would be interested in a position. Would it be in my best interest to accept such an offer immediately, or should I hold off while inquiring about possibilities elsewhere?

As we drove homeward, the wide valley was blue and shimmering in the light of a full moon. Mists rose from swamps and ponds, little exhalations of a drowsing and comfortable world tumbling through space with its moon. We closed our windows against the rapidly cooling night air and turned on the car heater. The large farmhouses with their brightly lit windows disappeared as we began the rise into the hills; instead we saw now and then a kerosene lamp glowing dimly in a cabin close to the road. Coming around a bend between Olive Hill and Morehead—we were that close to home—we saw what appeared to be a bonfire in the field to our left. I slowed the car and then stopped. Three figures stood before the fire. Beyond it, and illuminated more by the moon than the flames, a mule attached to a pole plodded in a circle. How marvelous to see, from this lonely road, a moonlit field with three men, a fire, and a mule!

"What do you suppose they're doing?" my wife asked.

"Why don't we find out?" I said. Normally I would never have suggested anything like that; I was usually too self-conscious, too uncertain of the propriety of intruding upon people I didn't know. I had never become acquainted with any of the hill farmers—nothing more than a word or two with them in the hardware or shoe store, a few phrases exchanged once with a family my wife and I had picked up after their Model A truck had broken down on the highway. The region was theirs, not mine, a fact I could tell simply by looking at the gaunt faces and bony bodies of the farmers who came to town: these men resembled the very fields they tilled. My clothes, my manner of speaking, my literary interests, my occupation as a teacher, all constituted a barrier I had never known how to surmount. I had been told by the older professors at the college that the hill people of our county were as proud as they were poor, and that their shyness or reticence was far in excess of any that I might feel; I had also been told that if they felt themselves victimized or insulted, particularly on a Saturday night in town, they were apt to respond with quick violence—among them were descendants of the survivors of the Tolliver and Martin feud, the most devastating in Kentucky history. Indeed, my college had been founded to bring understanding to these passionate families; the first president had almost been hit by a bullet as he stepped from the railroad car.

My wife and I walked slowly toward the fire. The men were apparently a farmer and his two almost-grown sons. The father, the shortest of the three, was bearded. They knew, of course, that we were approaching; but they never looked our way or gave us a greeting. We stopped a short distance from the fire and whispered to each other our conjectures about the equipment. The mule, as it plodded, was operating some kind of mill or press. One of the sons dropped an armful of cane into the hopper. A long and shallow cast-iron vat stood over the flames; two of its legs were shorter than the other pair, giving it a slight tilt. Much like the partitions in a labyrinth or maze, metal strips of various lengths welded to the floor of the open vat served to impede the flow of the dark liquid oozing from the upper side to the lower. Steam rose from the bubbling syrup.

"They're making molasses," my wife said. "It must be sorghum molasses. Look, they must have just cut the cane," and she pointed to the rows of stubble.

Slowly reaching into his baggy overalls, the father pulled a large knife from an inner pocket and unclasped the blade. He bent over and picked up a section of cane and cut two equal lengths of it; before handing them to the younger son, he scraped and whittled them a bit and considered them carefully in his open palm. These grave and deliberate actions were without seeming reference to us; but with an equal solemnity the son approached us and placed one piece of cane in my hand and the other in my wife's. At last the father looked at us, at our bodies and our faces; and we, in turn, looked expectantly at him, wondering what we were to do with our gifts. He said quietly, "It's better at the other end," motioning us to the lower part of the vat. The simplicity of the words gave the invitation the clarity and symbolic nature of a dream, and so we will probably remember it all our lives.

We dipped the cane into the heavy syrup collecting and cooling at the lower end, and sucked the sweetness from the surface of the cane and its pith. "Oh yes, this is *very* good," I said, dipping my cane again into the vat, and yet again. Our lips and fingers became sticky, but we found it pleasurable to lick our fingers, to run a tongue over our lips. When we had finished, we stood with the farmer and his sons, looking with them at the fire and the mule still patiently turning in his circle; listening with them to the crackling of the logs, the creaking of the press, the baying of a distant moonstruck hound. The taste of molasses lingered on my teeth and tongue. The fire warmed my stomach and thighs.

"You folks from up North?" the younger son asked.

"No," I said. "We've been on a little trip. We live in Morehead."

"Then you're almost home."

"Almost," I said.

Beyond our backs, a car droned past on the highway without slowing. After the sound had disappeared, I thought that the driver must have seen five figures and a mule. A few minutes later, we thanked our hosts and drove home in silence.

Our son Cris's thirty goats share a pasture with the two fat and elderly horses my wife and I bought when we moved from Ithaca to the Finger Lakes countryside in 1962. Eventually Cris would like to earn his livelihood through the sale of milk and cheese; for the present he works a late shift—3:30 P.M. until midnight—in an Ithaca factory. He does his chores, including the milking, in the early-morning hours, gets whatever sleep he can, repeats the chores, bathes, and dashes out the door to his pickup truck, buttoning his shirt as he goes.

For several weeks this past winter, during a period of the heaviest snowfalls, he was both nearly sleepless and always late for work. In August, the billy had managed to jump the fence and reach the nannies; eleven kids arrived in late January and early February, the worst possible season for their survival. Two of the births were difficult ones; Cris had to alter the position of the kids in the womb before pulling them from their mothers. Because the nights were too bitter for the kids to remain in the barn, he brought them into the house as they were born, one or two or three at a time.

All eleven were in the kitchen for a week. My wife and I fed them with nursing bottles or pans of warmed milk two or three times a day, and grew so fond of them that after the feedings we let them romp about the kitchen, all eleven at once, even though it meant a considerable amount of cleaning up with paper towels and pails of hot soapy water smelling of disinfectant. The one I liked best was a small white doe. If she were removed from her box, she would vigorously flap her ears and then jump as high as she could; because her muscles were still weak and the linoleum floor was slick, her legs would splay out and she would have to be helped onto her tiny brown hooves.

I have been on sabbatical leave from my university this academic year, and have been working at home, in my study. Several times (after my wife had left for her job in Ithaca and while Cris was still sleeping) I brought that favorite kid into the study, closed the door, placed her on the rug, and let her jump as much as she wanted to; I would lie on the rug and let her nibble at my hair and ears as well as my shirt. I was fond of that kid not only because she was alert and spunky, but because I had helped to save her life. Cris had brought her into the house early one afternoon. Still wet from the fluid in the sac, her body was nearly frozen. We filled the kitchen sink with warm water. While Cris prepared a mixture of glucose and water in a syringe, I immersed the kid: one of my hands supported her belly and chest, the other her limp head. The umbilical cord was still connected to her belly and floating, red and stringy, beside her. Some fecal matter that had been caught in her soft fur floated about, too. It seemed as if my hand were cupped against her heart, so intense was the throbbing.

And yet for a moment that heart faltered and stopped. I massaged the kid's chest while swishing her body back and forth in the water, and the beat came back into my palm as if it were the pulsing of my own blood. Cris pried open the jaws, inserted the tube of the syringe over the tongue and as far back as it would go and squeezed the warm syrup into the throat. In a few moments the legs jerked and the kid's eyes opened. My face must have been the first object she saw. The possibility that imprinting might work two ways has not been generally acknowledged.

That night my wife and I drove between high banks of snow the ten miles to Ithaca to hear a concert at Barnes Hall on the Cornell campus. The small auditorium, a former chapel on the second floor, has several stained-glass windows in the apse and organ pipes against one wall; the sloping sides of its high ceiling are connected by an intricate arrangement of wooden beams. It has become as familiar an environment to me as a room in my own house. On this evening, the selections were for violin and viola. The violist was a young woman I did not know, but the violinist was an old friend whose playing I always look forward to.

Despite the weather, the auditorium was filled. My wife and I sat in the tier of seats to the left of the stage. The occasional chattering of steam pipes, the single chime every fifteen minutes of the library tower clock, were subsumed into the rhythms of the more central instruments. I was attracted by the fluidity of the dresses worn by both performers. At some point I became aware that I was concentrating upon the slight indentation of the violist's navel; it came and went in the taut and silky fabric of her dress as her arm moved. Such a fixation bothered me; surely no other member of the audience could be so preoccupied. Two wholly serious and bearded youths nearby were following the score as best they could in the dim light; an elderly woman, resting her head within the furry nest of her coat collar, had closed her eyes either to sleep or the better to listen; a trio of girls in jeans in the front row leaned forward—chins cupped in their hands, elbows on their knees—in homage to such superb female talent.

During Mozart's Duo in G Major, the final selection of the evening, I forgot for a time both the audience and the physical presence of the performers and remembered—as I so often have done on this sabbatical leave, perhaps because it is my next to last before retirement—the Kentucky church, the ferryboat, and the faces of the singers (one now dead) in the dark; the circling of a mule under the full October moon and the figures before the fire. My body once had been young enough, my mind naïve enough, to permit me the illusion of self-containment, as if the external world existed for the gratification of my senses; and yet the very vigor of my responses had enabled me (so it seemed, listening to Mozart on a cold night in a warm hall in my fifty-seventh year) to vault beyond myself like an athlete of pure being. It was as if all that could be glorious for me had already occurred, as if my past signified far more than my future; and so I was returned to the violist and violinist in their sinuous dresses. Was it my sadness, my resignation, that made me aware then that my concentration on the violist all along had been caused by my feelings toward the limp and new-born kid I had immersed in the kitchen sink earlier that day?

The moment I saw, superimposed on the body of the violist, that of the kid—for I saw her drifting in somnolence there, the red cord streaming out, an image with the truth that dreams possess—I experienced an acceptance of pure physicality, a sensation quite unlike any of those of my desirous younger days; it permitted me an immediate tenderness for bodies, human and animal, in all their biological manifestations and changes. This acceptance altered the way I looked at the two performers, the older and the younger, and the way I looked at all the members of the audience, the children, the students, the middle-aged, the elderly; it was in harmony not only with the remembrance of warm molasses on the tongue and images of figures in a field, singers in a church, but with the fluid memories that must have been deep in Mozart's dreaming self as he put certain symbols on paper, symbols that these two performers now were faithfully recreating as spiritual sounds.

1979

Visitors from
the Fortunate Island

6 SIGURD AND JENNIFER, ON A VISIT FROM Iceland, spent two days with my wife and me this past summer. The four of us have been friends for nearly a quarter-century. I met Jennifer the day I began teaching at Cornell; she was then the departmental secretary. Sigurd, the curator of the Icelandic collection in the university library, occasionally taught a course in comparative literature or English. They had met—and married—in Berkeley. Jennifer was a Californian; Sigurd had come to Berkeley from Reykjavik for graduate work. He had planned to complete his dissertation in Ithaca, but never seemed to find time for it. Shortly before Jean and I moved to the region, Sigurd and Jennifer bought a dilapidated farmhouse on a hilltop near a stone quarry, an isolated and windy place that, except for its views of tree-covered ridges, reminded Sigurd of his native land. Though she had yet to see Iceland, Jennifer also was attracted by the austerity of the location, including its openness to sky, as if it appealed to some distant memory of her own. They spent their spare hours caulking the foundation, nailing down sheets of plywood over the splintered and shrunken floorboards, and plugging the cracks around windows. Using discarded stones from the quarry, they built a hearth, and kept it blazing with logs cut from the fallen timber in the wild ravine that was their back yard.

In those days, their two children, a boy and a girl, were of grammar-school age. Though their house was small, Sigurd and Jennifer were the kind of young couple whose affection for each other draws others by its hospitable radiance. Even their cat was friendly, rubbing against the legs of newcomers. Jennifer's voice had a pleasant depth; her laughter was resonant without ever becoming obtrusive. Sigurd's height, his soldierly bearing, and his dark beard made him imposing, like one's dream of a Viking marauder, and his accent gave to his English an unusual precision, as if words could be knives cutting to the center of the most intractable philosophical problem. His impulses, though, were toward kindliness and self-irony: his arguments might begin with metaphysical or intellectual premises, but were likely to end—especially if he were winning the debate—in a pun or some intentionally absurd final proof.

And so their house became the social center for a large group of untenured teachers, their families, and those visiting English scholars who preferred the casualness of the young to the perhaps more self-conscious professionalism of the tenured staff. I cannot remember a single vindictive remark directed against the senior professors at the parties, even though most of us felt our future to be in their hands; we came to that little farmhouse—sometimes, on winter evenings, backing our cars several times on the icy road to get the momentum to burst through a drift and reach the solitary house at the top of the hill—to be purged of pettiness and anxiety. Parking the car on the shoulder of the road and looking toward the lighted windows, I would try to think of something cheerful to say as Jean and I entered the house, something to make Jennifer and the others laugh.

Sigurd, always more concerned with books and ideas for their own sakes and for the conversations they could engender among friends than for the uses to which they could be put in advancing a career, never really wanted to complete the dissertation necessary for a tenured position in the United States. Instead, he applied for, and got, the job as director of a secondary school in the interior of his native island. Not long after he and his family left—by then Jean and I had bought our own farmhouse, as remote as theirs had been and just as open to sky—we had a letter from Sigurd in which he said he had been apprehensive that Jennifer might dislike a landscape devoid of trees, but that her first words upon descending from the airplane at Keflavik were, "Why, Sigurd, it doesn't *need* trees."

In those years during which our children were still young enough to want to accompany us wherever we might go, Jean and I and our sons visited Iceland on three occasions, either on our way to or from France and Italy, staying with Sigurd and Jennifer for periods of three days to a week. "Jennifer was right," my wife said to Sigurd, who had driven his Bronco more than a hundred kilometers over rough terrain to meet us on our first visit; and though nearly three years had passed since he had sent his letter, he understood her allusion at once.

I find it difficult to distinguish among the visits we made, partly because all of them took place in the season of incredibly long daylight, a season in which nobody feels much desire for sleep and a visitor to the island is surprised to discover that it is 3:00 A.M., the talk is as brisk as ever, and that through the window he can see a herd of horses galloping along the base of a mountain as well as a lineman climbing a pole near the house to repair a telephone wire: when the rhythm of life so slows that eternity seems a possibility on Earth itself, it is hard to separate one event from another. And each time we visited Iceland the sensation produced on me by the landscape was always fresh and yet the same, as if in some way I was being returned to a world I had known, though only in my imagination, as a very young child—or, more accurately, to a *feeling* for a world, since I had never imagined such strange rocks, such deep fissures, such moss-covered deserts, such blue lakes set before vistas of distant glaciers.

The toll road from Keflavik to Reykjavik is paved, the views extraordinary chiefly for the rocks, the sparsity of vegetation and the clarity of sky; but beyond Reykjavik—with its modern hotels and apartment buildings, numerous bookstores and small shops selling clothing and hardware—the asphalt ends; the road, winding up hills, becomes a country lane of a treeless Vermont. Fifty kilometers east of Reykjavik, the road overlooks the scattering of buildings at Thingvellir—a major historical site, since the original parliament, an open-air legislative assembly, met here, its first session held in 930—and overlooks as well the largest lake of the island, one with two volcanic islands of its own. Water of remarkable frigidity falls over a rocky cliff to flow within a fissure on its way through the lava plain to the lake. Glaciers are in the distance. Beyond the Thingvellir road juncture, the route that I recall is not much traveled; whenever it crosses sheets of lava it is little more than the eroded channels of an ancient cart path. Farmhouses, scarce before Thingvellir, now are nonexistent, but still flocks of sheep—to whom, if anyone, do they belong?—wander in the plains and on the gentler slopes. The road climbs, half-encircling a mountain; and suddenly Sigurd and Jennifer's town appears: the school buildings, a general store, some greenhouses, and less than a dozen dwellings. Beyond the town is another lake, beyond the lake the inevitable snow-covered volcanic peaks. The town is surrounded by a fence, to keep out the horses and sheep; the motorist must open a gate and shut it behind him before descending to that little world.

Sigurd and Jennifer's house was heated by boiling water that came—a wonder in itself—from a subterranean cauldron by means of a buried pipe; still gurgling and steaming, the used water had its outlet under the eaves, and spilled into the roof trough. From their kitchen window, one had a view of the lake and glacial peaks; from the living room window, a view of a level green plain beneath the rough mountains. To see any moving creature from either window—a distant human being, horse, sheep, bird—was to see what was rare, poignant, significant. I thought I'd be happy if I could live forever in that fence-enclosed town my friends had come to.

During the decade that had elapsed since Jean and I had last seen Sigurd and Jennifer, they had moved twice—first to Reykjavik and then to a fishing village on a harbor between Keflavik and Reykjavik; but my sense of who they were, my high regard for their separate personalities, was influenced in some measure by the memory of the houses I had known them to inhabit, with their house outside Ithaca serving as but the gatehouse to their true home, which lay at the end of a road that gradually lost its definition the further one traveled it, a home in a landscape that belonged to my own dreams.

"Oh, Sigurd," I asked, "why did you ever leave the school, and your house near the lake?"

He and Jennifer had barely arrived when I said that; having just brought in the luggage, Sigurd and I were standing in my study, where he and Jennifer were to sleep on the couch that converted to a bed.

"We all get older," he replied; for he immediately must have noticed—even as I had seen that he now walked with a cane and that his beard was speckled with gray—that I was bonier and that my hair, once reddish-blond, was well on its way to its destined white. "In winter, the road was usually impassable, did you know that? When the road was blocked, when the nights were so long, I thought of Reykjavik—the stores, the restaurants, the concerts, the *talk*—as something unbelievable, a fantasy city all lit up like a ship at sea . . ." He sighed, for he shared my obvious regret. "You're more fortunate here, you can get into Ithaca without trouble, even in winter. But aren't you sometimes lonely, with the children gone?"

I told him that so far, only Larry, our oldest son, had moved away; that our youngest, Jimmy, would be leaving for college in the fall; and that Cris, who worked a night shift in town, still lived with us, since we had land for his goats. Sigurd said that their daughter was a schoolteacher in Scotland, married and with a daughter of her own; that their son, who had remained in Iceland, was the father of a boy and a girl. Suddenly he laughed—that hearty laughter I associated with Iceland. "At least some things in life are harmonious! When you begin to look like a grandfather, Nature provides you with the grandchild you need to keep from being a fake."

"I'm still a fake, then."

"Well, no matter! There are plenty of people around. Too many, I thought, after we moved to Reykjavik. So much congestion! So much standing in lines! You can't imagine the bureaucracy. You have a simple request, so you are told to fill out a form at one office and take it to another. You're told you'll hear, just wait a week or two. You wait two weeks, three weeks. Tired of waiting, you go back to the second office and are told to go back to the first, where you're instructed—oh, politely enough: we Icelanders have good manners—to make a new application. If you've been accustomed to the freedom of the country, all that seems intolerable. And to be cramped in a fourth-story apartment!"

"So that's why you moved again?"

"Yes, it's a good enough compromise, a lovely village in easy driving distance of Reykjavik and where the officials are your neighbors and friends. We live in a little house—it's in an historic district, one of a row of old houses protected by law to keep them unchanged—on the harbor." As Sigurd was speaking, he was looking out the window, gazing beyond the road at the pond, the wheat field on the gentle hill, the weathered barn of our nearest neighbor. "You, too, have a pleasant view. We have a porch—"

He broke off, because Jennifer and Jean had come into the room. Jennifer put her arms on his shoulders and said to Jean and me in that low and tolerant voice that still was a pleasure to hear, "Sometimes Sigurd and I have supper on the porch, by candlelight. The fishing boats have lights; the harbor seems filled with little candles of its own. On a calm night you can hear voices coming off the water, and sometimes singing."

I said, "We're on a high plateau here. The road out there—that's the Waterburg Road. Two miles north, at Christian Hill, the plateau ends. Once—it was many years ago, the children were young—we had an ice storm, just here on the plateau. Then the sun came out. We could hear trucks on the highway, but the tires of our car just spun; Jean and I couldn't get to work, and of course the school bus couldn't make Christian Hill. So all of us—Jean and I and Larry and Cris and Jimmy—put on our ice skates and skated up and down the road. I've never known ice to be that smooth, that slick! You could glide maybe fifty feet with barely a stroke to set you off. A breeze came up. Cris got our old black umbrella and let the wind blow him down the road. We watched him get smaller and smaller until he was gone. By luck, the wind changed enough to blow him home again. He was so happy he couldn't speak at first, but finally he told us he'd met an old man also on skates, and they'd gone together as far as the ice would take them."

I knew that my words weren't a logical response to Jennifer's description of supper on a porch in Iceland; they were simply a description of a moment in my life in which my family had existed on a magical island of its own. I had been moved as much by the way her arms rested on Sigurd's shoulders as by what she had said; and so I simply spouted on, like the Great *Geysir*—the prototype of all those rhythmically gushing hot fountains—that Jennifer and Sigurd once had shown us. Sometimes to see old friends—to feel your affection for them and to sense their continuing affection for you and for each other—makes you sad and discontented. You want something that's buried in your own past, something so elusive you might have known it only in a dream, but which you associate with your friends, and your memory of them; and so you chatter on like that.

Sigurd needed the cane because of some trouble with his back; with the cane, he could walk well enough. Before supper, the four of us went out to the barns, to see Cris's goats and our two elderly horses. The goats were in the pasture, mostly concealed in the grass and hedgerow, but we could hear the tinkling of their bells. The day was humid, and the area around the goat barn smelled of musk and urine. The horses came up to the paddock rail as we approached their barn.

Jennifer asked, "Do you ride them very much?"

"They're fat, they need exercise," Jean said. "When the children were young, all of us rode. Now, nobody seems to have the time."

Flies had clustered around the eyes of both horses, always a disgusting sight. "How would you like to be bothered with flies like that?" I asked, brushing them away. I spoke of how much we used to enjoy the horses, and of the riding trails we had made through the woods. One trail, I said, went all the way to the tree house that Jimmy and I had built.

"Does Jimmy still use the tree house?" Jennifer asked.

"We built it to last," I said. "It has a room with two windows, a couch and a coffee table, and off the room a porch. . . .But no, he doesn't use it much. This summer, for instance, he's off on a wilderness camping trip in the Adirondacks. A tree house in a little woods can't compete with mountains and forests."

"It must be cool in the woods," Jennifer said. "I'd really love to walk one of your paths, just to look at the leaves." Her voice was so wistful that Sigurd embraced her. She stroked his arm. "You know, Siggie, that I don't *miss* trees when I'm home in Iceland. It's only here, where everything's so green, that I miss them there."

My mind was still on the tree house. "The chief fun was in building it. The day we finished it, Jimmy wanted to take off the roof, to build a second floor; and then he wanted to build a second tree house— there's a big maple nearby—and connect the two with a swinging bridge. I got indignant: but then I realized I was dreaming of getting a bulldozer to dig out the swamp—the tree house, you see, is on a hillside, above the swamp and the creek—so that we'd have a little lake there. 'Jimmy,' I cried, for I really was horrified at myself, 'you and I are like all the other exploiters, the people who turn orchards and pastures into one shopping mall after another!' And I think that's true of all of us. None of us ever can stop, nothing in *itself* is good enough anymore."

Standing by the fence, stroking the horses and brushing away the flies, we got into one of our old philosophical discussions. Was becoming always preferable to being? As for the "divine discontent" of mankind—how quickly the old wanting for God or Oneness could be supplanted by material desires! The Absolute may be infinite, but the desire for it is a single desire; the desire for material possessions is as infinite as things are infinite, and hence just as impossible of fulfillment on Earth. As young couples, we would have spoken with a greater ironic sense; instead of agreeing with each other, we would have taken opposing views for the sake of the argument. Nor at one of Jennifer and Sigurd's parties would I ever have declared so dogmatically that nothing was good enough anymore. My own vehemence had startled me. And yet—because we *were* in such agreement—I went on, "No wonder there's so much violence and theft! Even out here—can you imagine it, in such a rural setting?—somebody last month stole our tent from the pond area. Last year thieves broke into the tree house. They took just the Coleman lantern, but they overturned the bookcase for the hell of it and smashed the radio."

Sigurd said that vandalism and theft had increased in Reykjavik, and that the inflation rate in Iceland was averaging more than fifty percent a year. "'Fortunate island,/Where all men are equal/But not vulgar—not yet,'" he said, quoting W.H. Auden on Iceland, and causing me to remember—with such pleasure I forgot I was aggrieved—the importance of poetry to the people of his land, shopkeepers and politicians as well as teachers: at the last meeting of every session of the Althing, or parliament, Sigurd once had told us, the members compose their speeches in verse. "Clearly that's not a recent poem. . . . But you should be happy enough here," he went on cheerfully, waving his cane at the woods, the pasture, and the house, that old white farmhouse that both Jean and I *did* love and that was softly glowing in the evening sun.

"We *are*," I said. "Oh God, Sigurd, do you think a day passes that I don't know how lucky I am? To live in the country, to have a job that lets me do what I value doing, to love my wife even more than I did when we were first married?" But then I told Jennifer we couldn't walk the paths in the woods because they were blocked with fallen treetops. We had made the naïve mistake, I said, of trusting our government, of letting a conservation officer who looked like a kindly Boy Scout leader talk us into a selective cutting of the woods to improve the stand of timber. We hadn't known then, I said, that his job productivity—his *accountability*—was determined not by the trees he saved but by the board feet of lumber he managed to get consigned each month to the sawmills. "Come back in twenty years," I said. "Maybe by then we can take a walk in the woods."

After supper, we sipped Scotch in the living room and talked of our children, of their domestic and economic problems as well as their triumphs. Parents, we agreed, remain anxious about their children long after they've grown; the parents blame themselves, however wrongly, for their children's errors as adults, and spend fruitless hours regretting their anger years before, when a young child wouldn't put away his or her clothes.

I wanted, quite suddenly, to make Jennifer and Sigurd laugh, that old urge to tell some amusing anecdote as Jean and I, out in the winter dark, were about to enter the radiance and warmth of one of their parties. "Now here's a story, Sigurd, that any father would understand," I said, and told him about our neighbor Mike, a burly pipe fitter, a father of two children, a man of restless energy who used to spend his weekends constructing an addition to his house or remodeling a room or replacing a floor joist. He had bought an immense safe—it had come from a department store downtown being razed—and had it carted to the back of his house, by the exterior cellar steps. Using rope and a windlass, he tried to slide it down the stairs; the rope broke, and the safe, in falling, demolished both the stairway and the basement pump he'd installed the year before to handle the unexpected flow of water occasioned by the drilling of a new well that turned out to be artesian. Of course, the basement flooded, damaging his furnace; ultimately, though, he was able to dry the cellar, dig out a large number of foundation stones and the dirt behind them, wedge the safe into the opening, and cement it into place. I said that Mike had told me about his difficulties with the safe one Saturday afternoon when I went down to his house for advice on some problem of my own and found him replacing his still-splintered cellar steps. "'And what, Mike, do you keep in your safe?' I asked him. 'My hammer,' he cried. '*This* one,' waving it under my nose as if I were a fool not to have guessed. 'My sixteen-ounce Plumb claw hammer with the unbreakable fiberglass handle!'"

"It's too late for you or me to try something like that," Sigurd said thoughtfully, treating the account (just as he would have years before) with mock seriousness before breaking into laughter. He asked me whether Mike's attempt to keep the hammer had been successful; a child, after all, might search for the combination until he found it or make some dynamite with his Christmas chemistry set.

"Oh, that was long ago, Mike's our age and his son—the one who used to misplace his hammer—is in the Navy. Mike and his wife are divorced, and he lives alone. He doesn't remodel anything anymore. The other day I asked him what he now kept in the safe and he said, 'Still just my old Plumb hammer.'"

"Behavior conditioned by habit!" Sigurd held his hands palm up to signify his own helplessness before the habits of the years. He said brightly, "But I see that the experiment *did* work, the safe was a success." And then he sighed. "Nevertheless, I think your story a very sad one."

"I hadn't wanted it to be."

"Maybe," Jean said, "Mike just wants to hold on to a time when his children were young."

We were all silent, thinking of that useless safe. The failure of my anecdote to give pleasure, and the warmth of the Scotch, returned me to that strange state in which I felt myself deprived of something of extreme value that I could not define but that I associated with Iceland and my friends. I introduced a new subject (my words all that day were as discordant as my moods): the helplessness of any individual to affect the course of society, and how that helplessness influenced characterization in films and novels. Yes, Sigurd agreed, it now seemed sentimental to depict a character in control of his destiny, even to a limited extent. I said that, by God, the four of us sitting here knew that we were at least responsible for our own lives. How false novels and films were to actual people! I chose Jennifer as an example. Loving Sigurd, she had accepted Iceland and its austere beauty. As an adult, the mother of two children, she had learned a difficult new language, and had learned it so well that, with her children grown, she had become Sigurd's colleague in the secondary school in Reykjavik. And the two of them, having willed it to be so, now were living in happiness in a house on the harbor of a picturesque fishing village, listening in the dusk to the singing that came across the water. . . .

"Much too small a house!" Jennifer said, her way of shrugging off such compliments. "Our books are still in boxes, there isn't space. And the regulations won't let us build an addition. Visit us—I know you love Iceland and we have a bed for you—but if Cris or Jimmy comes along, bring a tent, a waterproof one. You remember how it rains!"

My lavish praise had disrupted our conversation and made Sigurd as well as Jennifer uncomfortable. The night breeze rippled the draperies of the opened window. A car droned past, a frog in the pond twanged like a rubber band. Sigurd yawned; all of us soon went to bed.

The next morning, after Jean had left for her job in Ithaca—she had come home earlier than usual the previous afternoon, to be there for the arrival of our guests—I drove Jennifer and Sigurd to a nearby state park, to walk a little-used path high above a gorge. Portions of the path went through woods where the trees—hemlock and beech and maple and oak—were unusually large for this long-settled land; other portions of it followed the gorge rim, and one could see the stream far below, tumbling over small precipices as if in preparation for the major fall, a drop of over two hundred feet. Ever since breakfast, I had sensed—an intuition, perhaps, since nothing in their voices or gestures betrayed it—a slight tension between Jennifer and Sigurd, as if they had quarreled over a trifle during the night: had I, by stressing their accomplishments, made them aware of some lack? On the path, Sigurd walked briskly ahead, using his cane for support while climbing over a fallen log or descending into a mossy ravine; Jennifer stayed at my side, naming the species of a particular tree I was unfamiliar with as well as identifying certain ferns and tiny flowers I would never have noticed without her guidance: she was delighted to find here so many of the living things that had grown near her old house by the stone quarry. She and I left the trail to get the view from a rocky peninsula jutting out from the cliff like a castle tower, with boulders for a parapet; Sigurd continued on alone, pointing at birds with his cane and cheerfully calling out *their* names—"Hawk! Cliff swallow! Gull! Bluejay!"— as he disappeared into further woods.

Jennifer and I climbed one of the boulders to stare directly down at the stream. In the distance, where it made its most spectacular drop, it seemed, from our position, either simply to end or to merge with the sky. Beyond and beneath that mystery lay the blue surface of the lake, its actual destination. The unexpected view of the lake caused Jennifer to recall the trip by car through Europe that she and Sigurd had taken the previous summer. They had visited cathedrals and museums in France and Spain, she said, but what had pleased them the most was the view from a mountain in Switzerland. They had found this par-ticular overlook on a topographical map with markings for unusual vistas; it was reached by a narrow road that climbed past a mountain village, became a cart trail, and ended in a farmyard. No view was obtainable there. They parked their car and followed a path that led upward, past several more farms with vegetable gardens, hens, and barns with roofs held down by stones. A grandmother, sitting on a doorstep in the sun and holding a baby, smiled and waved. Above one farm, a goatherd and his animals moved across a wrinkle on the mountain face. Then, quite suddenly, all of Switzerland seemed to open up before them—the system of valleys and snow-peaked mountains, the lakes and little towns huddled against the slopes. "Oh, it was so lovely!" Jennifer exclaimed, her eyes glistening with tears. "To find it like that, at the edge of a meadow, after it had become a lost cause! We never wanted to leave."

Sigurd had returned from the woods, to see what had happened to us; it must have seemed to him, as he came into the sunshine, that we were lost in conversation and about to step into the abyss. "Jen-nifer!" he cried. "Watch out! Get off that rock this instant!"

Without answering, Jennifer looked at the lake again, as if to recapture the much grander vista she had been remembering; and then she shrugged, climbed down from the rock and took the path away from Sigurd, back toward the car. He came toward me, using the cane for every step. He looked gray. "Lord, why did I become so angry? Of course it was safe enough, I knew you weren't children. I accept the equality of women! But when children are small, don't they turn to the father for authority? After the children are grown, a man is left with this dreadful habit, this wish to protect!"

I said that whenever I suddenly braked a car, my arm shot out to keep a long-gone child from bashing his head into the windshield; once, doing that, I had slapped Jean's face with the back of my hand. And I said that the last time I had been in a car driven by my father—he was in his seventies then, suffering from the cancer that was to take his life—his hand had reached out to keep me, still the toddler, safe. . . . Walking slowly on, we came upon Jennifer beyond a curve in the path.

She was sitting on a log and looking intently at a fern at her feet. "Don't we have something like this at home, Siggie?" she asked, and took his hand as he sat down beside her.

I wandered off, to let them talk quietly together. Jean and I, as close to each other as Jennifer and Sigurd were, occasionally had similar conflicts. To an outsider they would seem trivial, perhaps an indulgence in a world that knows as much about cruelty and terror as ours did; but to the partners of a long marriage who are still gladdened, at the end of each day, to be returned to each other and who always are aware, if but on some barely conscious level, that one of them inevitably is to be made desolate by the death of the other, the smallest of quarrels is violent and strange. Even I, as an old friend, was disturbed by this particular tiff; though less by it (they were intelligent people, they were talking it out) than by Jennifer's words from the rock. Her description of their search had been too close in spirit to a memory of mine of a road that gradually lost its definition as it led me into a landscape in which living creatures, animal and human, became poignant and rare: a road ending in a view of a lake and of distant, white-topped mountains. If the soul is desire, it cannot ever *have:* of course Jennifer and Sigurd would need to go to Switzerland to find what I saw as forever present in Sigurd's native land, what had made me wish to live there, a neighbor of my friends.

Eventually I returned, to sit beside them on the log. Once again—was this another vestigial response, another habit made useless by the years?—we became philosophical, exploring the various reasons that the natural world seemed a good, a quality enabling trees and birds and sky and water to work a therapeutic miracle upon us. Our origins, we agreed, lay in nature: volcanic action produced the first atmosphere, and in some watery epoch a bolt of lightning, striking the sea, had kindled the initial organisms to life. I said that once I had seen a documentary program about plate tectonics on public television. At the conclusion the narrator walked down a long sidewalk. Each slab constituted a geological era; the paint on the edge of the last slab represented the length of time that mankind had been on Earth. Then the narrator made a remark I would never forget: human consciousness, he said, was nature's faculty for apprehending itself. I asked both of my friends, "Do you believe that?"

Jennifer said, "Why, yes, I believe it," and Sigurd said that, yes, our consciousness made us able to distinguish one thing from another, to classify and organize; it kept us separate from each other and the natural world in order that we might try to understand ourselves and our environment. Jennifer said that at the moment our consciousness left us, the unity we spent our lives struggling to find and comprehend obviously returned; all of nature became One, as it had been before our birth.

"Is it enough to know that?" I asked.

Sigurd said it would have to do.

The Bullfrog Pond

7 IT WAS THE SECOND AND FINAL EVENING of a visit by Sigurd, the Icelander, and Jennifer, his California-born wife, who now taught with him in a secondary school in Reykjavik. As young men, Sigurd and I were colleagues at Cornell, but it was twenty years since he and Jennifer had sold their isolated Finger Lakes house near a stone quarry and gone off with their two children to Sigurd's native land, and ten years since Jean and I and our three boys had most recently visited them in Iceland.

The last decade had aged the four of us while bringing our children to maturity. Jennifer and Sigurd now had three grandchildren—two in Reykjavik, where their son lived, and the third in Scotland, where their daughter and her husband were teachers. Jean and I were not yet grandparents. Though two of our sons still lived with us, Jimmy, our youngest, would be entering college in the fall, and this summer was away, wilderness-camping with high school friends in the Adirondacks. Cris, who worked the second shift at the Morse Chain plant, in Ithaca, never got home until after midnight. He was twenty-five. Of our children, Cris was the one most interested in using the farmland surrounding the old country house that all three had grown up in. He kept a herd of goats that he milked in the early-morning hours, and he hoped someday to earn his living through the sale of dairy products; he spent his weekends experimenting with various methods of making cheese.

Waiting for our wives to return from Ithaca, where they had gone after dinner to see one of Jennifer's acquaintances, Sigurd and I sat talking in the living room. He was tired and vaguely depressed, as one is apt to be near the end of a long vacation. On a walk Jennifer and he and I had taken that morning along the rim of Taughannock Gorge, he shouted angrily at her for standing on a rock jutting from the gorge wall. They quarreled. He apologized, but he remained upset by his bossiness, his tendency to transfer to his wife the feelings of protection he'd once had for his children: it was, he said, the habit he would most like to break. I said that I, too, found it difficult to outgrow fatherhood. I supposed my inability to counsel any of my children, now that they were grown, accounted for the degree to which I remembered the days in which all of them had depended upon my sometimes faulty guardianship. For example, I often found myself reliving the events of the year I had spent with my family in France and Italy. One boy or another—their ages then had ranged from just three to thirteen—was always teetering in the window of a tower, balancing himself on a parapet, peering into a deep and unprotected well.

If I were to choose one day that seemed a perfect metaphor of fatherhood, I said, it would be our last full day in Europe. Jean and I and our two older children, helped by the desk clerk and porter and chambermaid, spent much of the morning extricating our three-year-old from the Naples hotel bedroom into which he had locked himself. We visited Pompeii in the noonday heat, and in the late afternoon climbed Vesuvius to walk the lip of the cone with a group of other tourists. It wasn't simply the height that I found frightening; it was a sense of desolation, emptiness, and waste. I felt I particularly had to keep Jimmy—he was so young—from that mammoth but constricting cone on one side of us, from the empty sky on the other; I shamed all my children with my panic and anger. Ultimately, Larry, the oldest boy, put Jimmy on his shoulders and—either to prove me too cautionary or just to get away—went right down that mountain of ash, sometimes standing, sometimes using his bottom for a sled and sending up great spumes of dust. "Look at that boy sliding down the mountain with a baby on his shoulders!" another tourist exclaimed, as if it were the chief spectacle Vesuvius provided. Covered with soot but behaving as if nothing extraordinary had happened, they were sitting next to the locked car and drinking from a shared bottle of Coca-Cola when Jean and Cris and I finally made it down the zigzagging trail to the parking lot.

Sigurd remarked that all fathers had some variation of that story to tell. "I'm not through," I said. "I drove back to Naples in the dark, the children in back and Jean beside me, with none of us saying a word. Then I got lost trying to find the garage at the hotel. 'A simple matter,' you might say. 'Here's the front of the hotel—just drive to the garage in back.' But get off those main streets, and Naples is nothing but a maze of branching alleys so narrow that the fenders of a VW nearly scrape the walls. I had to make three attempts—"

"And fathers, we know, aren't supposed to get lost."

"So our children think. On the first try we came around a bend to discover a family of six or so celebrating a feast day or some other occasion with a dinner on a candlelit table set out in the middle of the alley. They had to remove the dishes and the wine bottles and the candles and a vase of flowers—a lace tablecloth, too!—and cart the table and chairs partway up a staircase in the nearest building to let us by. They were singing and smiling; they bowed to us as we passed, they bore us no grudge. A fine Italian family. We felt almost as if we were part of the celebration. On the second try—"

"I can guess what happened."

"Of course. I entered another alley but came around a bend to see the same candlelit table before us. They weren't so happy this time to remove the dishes and flowers and candles and so on and to retreat up the stairs with the table and chairs. And then, when I took yet another alley and *still* found myself going around a familiar bend to see the candles—well, I turned off the car lights and tried to back up, but managed only to bash a fender in my nervousness. There was no turning back, Sigurd! Our children were all on the floor behind the front seat, piled on top of each other, and hissing at me; even Jean was slumped as far down as you can get in the front of a VW. As the rest of that Italian family moved everything away again, the husband put his head in the car window and asked, in English, 'Why? Why? Why?' "

"One 'why' for each attempt," Sigurd observed. He softly repeated the word three times himself, and then sighed.

I wanted to make him laugh, to return both of us to the light-hearted spirit of the parties he and Jennifer had given in their house by the quarry so many years before. But, as had been true of so many of our conversations during this brief visit, each of us, while feeling our old affection for the other, ended up solemn and discontented. Even to me my tale had seemed lugubrious. "You and I—at least we always tried to be responsible fathers," I said.

The windows were open; the breeze occasionally carried the tinkling of goat bells or the twanging of frogs in our pond. We listened to those sounds. "Tell me," Sigurd said. "Isn't it time our wives came back?"

But it was only ten. We had been sipping Scotch; I refilled our glasses. Idly talking, we wandered from room to room, upstairs and down, using one staircase or another—we have three in this sprawling house. I was more or less looking for an album of photographs taken during our three visits to Iceland, but it was nowhere to be found. Nearly every room in the house has at least one bookcase, and old school texts (Jean's and mine as well as those of our children), juvenile fiction, encyclopedias, scrapbooks, scholarly treatises, novels, and volumes of poetry are all jumbled together in them. At one time I carried a memory of the color and shape of each book and where it most likely had been shelved, but the constant addition of new titles, combined with the increased use of my books by the children as they grew, finally resulted in the same kind of disorder that had developed earlier in the closets. At the end of a second-floor hallway, Sigurd and I bent down to go through a small door to enter a large room with a platform; in the nineteenth century it had served as a circuit-court chamber for the judges who traveled about on horseback.

"When the boys were small and had disobeyed Jean or me, I would say to them, 'Let's go to the judge's chamber so I can try the case,'" I said as Sigurd and I sat down on the edge of the platform. "Now look at the room," and I pointed to the various unmade beds. "It's become a bunkhouse!" I told him that Cris often brought out young people in need of guidance or just food; they helped him milk the goats and clean the barn. Sometimes they stayed a night, sometimes a week or longer. One boy named Sam, who frequently returned, was adept at fixing farm machinery, but equally adept at breaking things with it. "Even worse than that, Sigurd, Sam loses all my tools. Not just my hammer. The socket set, the wrenches, the screwdrivers—they're all rusting out there somewhere," and I gestured in the direction of the dark fields.

"A house the size of yours needs people," Sigurd said reasonably. "What would you ever do with a place like this without Cris? You're lucky to have a son still at home, one interested in putting a farm to its proper use."

When Cris was a young child, I said, he helped Larry and Jean and me build the horse barn to replace a much larger barn that had burned down. He remarked at the time that he thought we should construct the barn like a house, so that Jean and I could live in it when we got as old as his grandparents; Larry or Jimmy or he could then live in the farmhouse with a wife and children, and look after us. That a boy hammering next to his father would be dreaming such generous thoughts had given me the kind of happiness that makes one's eyes too blurred to drive a nail properly; but Jean and I, in our late fifties, certainly found no pleasure in contemplating some future retirement to a horse barn while goats wandered about eating our shrubs and the house became a deteriorating and untidy commune.

"Since I became a grandfather, I think in platitudes," Sigurd said, with another sigh. "Still, it's true enough that we can't impose our sense of what's fit on the younger ones."

I felt threatened by the reverse of that, I said. Not long ago, an editor had wanted to know if I would do a book. What she had in mind wasn't quite *Zen and the Art of Goat Raising*, she said, but such a title might suggest certain possibilities. . . . "I'm a professor of English," I said to Sigurd, "with courses to teach, with programs to direct. I don't look to goats for spiritual sustenance! When I was younger I was in control of my life. If a roof needed replacing, I replaced it. I built barns, I could pull a screw out of a horse's hoof when my boys weren't strong enough to do it, I painted one side of the house every summer. Now things are getting out of hand, and I *don't like it at all.*"

Jean and Jennifer had come back and were chatting in the living room with Sigurd and me when Cris arrived with Sam, whom he'd found at a downtown corner. Cris had driven directly home from his job—without even washing the grease from his hands—just in case we might still be up. Smiling, he was full of memories of our visits to Iceland—of the sheep and horses that wandered on the mountain slopes and seemed so free; of the lava flow from Hekla that had ponderously moved forward, bathing us in its shimmering heat as we watched; of cold lakes set in volcanic basins. If discontent had led me from one long story to the next, simple happiness had loosened Cris's tongue; he usually came home, as he told Sigurd, to a dark house. He spoke of the sagas he had read as a child, after our first stay in Iceland, and of parallels between them and Greek myths; the latter brought him, by way of Pan, to the subject of goats. As he talked, his excitement and pleasure made him pace the room and pull at his reddish beard—a beard not yet so luxuriant as Sigurd's, which he had always admired. Suddenly aware that he had forgotten the conventional amenities, he introduced Sam to Sigurd and Jennifer and asked us all what we had been doing, how we had been passing the hours.

I said that Jean and Jennifer had been away and that Sigurd and I hadn't done much other than to listen to the sound of the bullfrogs.

"What bullfrogs?" Cris asked.

"The ones in the pond," I said. "Listen," and we all sat quietly until we heard a twang, as if a rubber band had snapped, and then another.

Sam had remained standing uncertainly in the doorway even after his introduction, but now he laughed, contemptuous of the sound. "Them ain't *bull*frogs," he said, with a knowing look at Cris.

Sam often contradicted me, and everybody else. He was a pudgy boy who had spent his childhood in a series of foster homes. That spring, after quarreling with a teacher and other students, he had dropped out of his senior year of high school. I could understand his need to be stubborn and assertive; still, his dismissal of that twang irritated me, and I said that for twenty years I had told people bullfrogs twanged like that, and nobody had argued.

Cris said that Sam was right: he and Sam had found a pond with genuine bullfrogs and would be happy to lead us there, if we would like to hear them. I asked him where the pond was; he pointed out the window at the lights blinking from the radio tower on Connecticut Hill, six miles away. "You go almost there, turn right on the Cayutaville Road, make a left, and—well, none of the roads have names."

It was 1:00 A.M. Sigurd and Jennifer would be leaving for Iceland soon after breakfast. I began, in my old fatherly manner, "I really don't think, Cris—" but Jennifer said she wanted to go. Though she was fond of Iceland, I knew she still had strong attachments not only to her relatives and friends in the United States but to the natural world she once had known—the trees and plants and animal life. (That morning, on our walk along the rim of the gorge, she had stopped to touch and to name ferns and wild flowers that she remembered from the ravine behind their old house by the stone quarry.) Sigurd said he would also like to hear frogs that did more than just twang; he had been cheerful ever since Cris's arrival, and now, eager to be off in search of frogs, he reached for the cane he needed because of back trouble.

"Don't you need to milk your goats?" I asked Cris.

"Never mind!" He was laughing and already heading out the door with Sam, beckoning for us to come.

Cris took Sam in his pickup truck; I followed with the others. Our route consisted chiefly of a succession of roads barely more than fire trails or cart paths, the trees and underbrush so close that branches occasionally scraped the car. Most of these roads, I had been told, were once surrounded by pastures and cornfields, but the land, never very productive, had gradually been abandoned, the owners leaving during the Depression or in the later years of urban prosperity brought about by the Second World War. The New York Department of Conservation managed thousands of acres here, permitting the habitat gradually to revert to its original state. Three or four old sugar maples in a row, their thick boles illuminated in our headlights, meant that a house had stood behind them: how odd that houses and barns, and all the life they had contained, could be gone—and so soon! Though all of our children were fascinated by the region, Jean and I never much liked it; the young trees blocked the views and made us feel uneasy and confined. Even the vaguest memory of the Connecticut Hill area, as I mowed a field or replaced a section of rotten house siding, would give me the awareness of both the urgency of my task and its ultimate uselessness.

Now Cris drove through it, flashing his lights to indicate for us passages of some danger or difficulty—a fallen tree partly obstructing the road, a washed-out section, a boulder. Two or three miles into that wilderness, he stopped the truck and came to our car to say apologetically that he had made a wrong turn; he guided me back to a gap in the underbrush, where both vehicles could reverse their direction. After leading us along another road, he stopped again, at what might have been the identical place. "Lost forever!" I said to my passengers as Cris approached once more. He said, "We're here. Turn off your lights."

Then, in the darkness, we stood with Cris and Sam by the side of the road. "Be careful of the drop-off," Cris whispered.

"What drop-off?" The question was a chorus.

"Well, don't move until you can see."

Slowly the blackness took on various unfamiliar shapes. Below us, a few feet away, tiny lights began to shimmer and to spread, as if over a large field.

"What's that, shining everywhere?" Jean asked.

"Glowworms, I think," I said.

"Stars, on the pond," Cris said; and even as he was saying those words I felt as if all of us had moved an immense distance away, and were staring down at our universe. On a summer's night at our farmhouse, one can see friendly lights on distant hills and hear many sounds—a truck backfiring, a dog barking in the hamlet of Mecklenburg, the twanging of *our* frogs, and, of course, the comforting tinkling of goat bells. Here the absolute stillness and tiny points of light were frightening.

"Your frogs, Sam—" I began; but Cris hushed me, a hand on my arm. Then a horn blared: though we were miles from the nearest railroad track, I thought for an instant that a diesel locomotive was bearing down upon us.

"Lord!" Sigurd cried.

"Bullfrogs!" Sam said triumphantly. "I told you, didn't I?"

The horn below us blared again; another replied from the opposite bank. "Cassiopeia answering the Dog Star," Cris said.

The fancy so pleased me that I smiled at the mirrored stars.

"You were scared, weren't you?" Cris asked, his hand still restraining me.

"Oh, not really. Not much. It was Sigurd who cried, 'Lord.'"

We stood on the bank, teasing each other like that and listening. Jennifer said she would remember this pond and its sounds during the long nights of the coming Icelandic winter. As for me, I was, for the moment, happy as a child.

Bodiless Guests

8   LAST SPRING, WHILE LISTENING TO A young woman, a scholar from England visiting at Cornell, speak about Wordsworth's complicated and ambivalent attitude toward books, as revealed in Book V of *The Prelude* and elsewhere, I found myself only partly attending to her words, and then only to the degree that they carried me back to my experiences following the death of my brother nearly five years earlier. At the wine-and-cheese reception after the lecture, I spoke with an undergraduate student, a girl I admired for her vitality and genuineness. I asked Buffy if she had liked the lecture; she said that her brother had died unexpectedly during the winter, and that she chiefly had been thinking, throughout the talk, of how in the weeks after his death she had not felt alive. "During all those weeks I was nothing but one character or another in books I'd read," she said.

I told her I had not really heard the speech, either, and for the identical reason. Clearly, a remark by the lecturer, or one of her quotations from Wordsworth, had set each of us off like that.

"When did you begin to *feel* again?" I asked.

"At a movie. It wasn't what you'd think of as a good movie—good the way literature can be. It was supposed to be funny, and everybody was laughing, but I thought it pretty sordid—I mean, the jokes were cheap and obvious. Suddenly it hit me that my brother was dead, and so I sat there in all that laughter just sobbing away! Do you know that two of my friends, both English majors—one who had lost her mother, the other her father—told me they couldn't feel grief afterward, either, for the longest time, because they felt that they were living in books?"

"Books protect us, maybe."

Her eyes widened. "Who wants that? Did you?"

"No. To tell the truth, I felt drugged at first—"

"Wiped out?"

"Well, yes. And then more and more like a walking corpse, a zombie."

Buffy said, "It seemed to me, listening to the lecture, as if Wordsworth, whatever his praise of literature—remember that line in the handout?" She stopped and unfolded a copy of a passage from *The Prelude* that the lecturer had given each member of her audience, and quoted the phrase "a joy, a consolation, and a hope" before going on. "As if Wordsworth felt that books held some threat he didn't really want to confront."

Carrying our wineglasses, Buffy and I moved through the crowd to an antique sofa in an alcove, in order to talk further about these curious feelings, to see if we could understand the menace lying deep beneath the words on the pages of the books we respected and even loved.

What compelled Wordsworth, we wondered, to recount at length the dream of a friend who falls asleep after reading a portion of *Don Quixote?* In that dream, a spectral Don Quixote has the task of burying two books, apparently because the eternal truths contained in them are dangerous. One of them is Euclid's *Elements;* the other, a book of poetry, foretells the annihilation of mankind through deluge. The dreamer wants to accompany the phantom on his errand, but the sea rises quickly toward both, and the dreamer wakes in terror. Although our discussion of that ambiguous dream was inconclusive, it led me to remember more sharply than I had in years the details of my own submergence at the time of my brother's death.

When the telephone rang at 3:00 A.M. on July 15, 1974, I felt at once like a fictional character caught in some as yet unknown circumstance of fate. My heart beat violently, and it was only with the greatest difficulty—as if part of me were dreaming the story—that I could pull away from the arm of my sleeping wife and the restraint of the sheet. I stumbled over my shoes and into the hallway, bright in the reflected glow of the bathroom night lamp.

"Hello," I said.

"This is Captain Borklund—"

"The police?"

"No, of . . ." and he mentioned the airline that my brother, also a captain, piloted airplanes for: airplanes so immense that the captain and his co-pilot walked up a spiral staircase from the passenger compartment to reach the cockpit. "You're Jim, aren't you? I'm Tom Borklund, a friend of your brother Jack. I thought you should know he's been in a serious accident—"

"A plane crash?"

"No, a limousine. The one bringing him and his crew from the Palmer House to O'Hare."

"You're calling from Chicago?"

"No, from Miami. We've sent out a couple of other captains to talk to his wife, in Fort Lauderdale; I've already contacted his daughters, in Gainesville and Atlanta. Your mother lives with you, doesn't she?"

"Yes. How serious is it?"

"*Very* serious." There was a pause. "The co-pilot died. I'm sorry to have to tell you that Jack's dead, too. Can you and your wife and mother fly tomorrow—not this morning, the day after—to Fort Lauderdale to be with Jack's family for the funeral? You can pick up round-trip company passes at your airport in Ithaca just before the flight. I've been checking schedules—"

"My mother?" She was ninety-one. How could I ever tell her that Jack was dead?

"Wouldn't she want to come?"

"I don't know. I really can't think." For all that came to my mind, other than the thought of my mother asleep in the downstairs bedroom, was a memory of my brother very much alive. He was running out of a house and down a street to protect me from a gang of boys on bicycles who had knocked me off mine; Jack rushed at them, but before they fled one stabbed him in the palm. He helped me to my feet, the blood dripping from his hand. We were living then in Normandy, a new subdivision of Little Rock. I was maybe twelve, Jack maybe sixteen. The week before, that same gang, from a rundown nearby neighborhood, burned the shack I had built in the woods behind our house. Jack found their tree house, smashed the lock on its door with a bullet from his rifle, and left a note telling them to stay out of Normandy.

"Would you like to call me back in a few minutes?"

"Yes, thanks, I would." I wrote down the number. Jean was sitting up in bed, the light on. "Jack's hurt?" she asked.

"Jack's dead."

She reached forward to embrace me, but I moved away: I didn't want sympathy for a death I didn't yet feel. I told her the little I knew, and said that I had to call back soon to let the captain in Miami know if she and my mother would be going with me to Florida for the funeral.

"Grace is still weak," Jean said.

"I know." My mother was recovering from a kidney infection. And anyway, wouldn't the funeral be more than she could bear, at her age? Two-and-a-half years earlier, as my father was dying of cancer, she had said to me, thinking of her life with him, "I never knew it would end like this, Jim;" but, frail and tiny—she was less than five feet tall—and old as she was, she nursed him to the moment of his death. For the following year she lived with her widowed sister, who, in a stubborn and touching struggle against arthritis and senility, rose at dawn to weed her vegetable garden and clean her house before sitting down to read the great works of Western culture that she had wanted to read ever since she was a young woman. She went through book after book, living so fully within them that they isolated her from my mother and helped to intensify the debility she wanted most desperately to avoid. She would bring a book to the dining-room table, which was set with empty plates and empty cups for bodiless guests. While reading, she could, by raising her eyebrows, lift Aristotle and Socrates or Sir Walter Raleigh and Queen Elizabeth from their texts and plump them down beside her for a lively conversation; when she tired of them, she raised them from their seats with her eyebrows and dropped them back into print. Now my aunt was dead. Only a few days after she came to live with us, my mother, equally resolute, surprised me by coming out to the barn, where I was using the power saw, to see if she could help me with the carpentry. She reached to hold the board I was sawing, lost her footing on the uneven floor, and tumbled over, hitting her head on the concrete curb that served to guide the sliding door. Carrying her light body into the house, I thought, This, then, is how she is going to die. I placed her, just as she was regaining consciousness, on the bed and ran to phone for an ambulance; but when I returned to the bedroom she was standing upright, holding the bedpost for support, raising and lowering her leg in an exercise I remembered from my childhood. It was her leg that hurt a little, she said, not her scalp, and she didn't want it to become stiff. "If I'm going to live, I have to be in a condition to help," she told me later that day, after X-rays showed a hairline crack in her hip. She had mended from that fall as quickly as she was recuperating from her present illness. But how could one who lived to help others continue to carry on, if those she loved and wanted to help were nearly all gone?

"I don't think she should go to the funeral," I said to Jean.

"If she doesn't, then I should stay with her," Jean said.

"We might be able to get a nurse."

"Would you want to leave her with a stranger at a time like this?"

"No, we couldn't do that, could we? If we were careful and had wheelchairs waiting at the airports, maybe it would be all right. Should I ask her in the morning?"

"She would say she wanted to go."

"That means she ought to then, doesn't it?" I said.

"But what if . . ."

"What if something happens on the trip?"

I couldn't bear to think of losing both my brother and my mother. And yet my mother, wisp though she might be, was resilient as Phoenix Jackson, the old black woman in Eudora Welty's story; that parallel had often occurred to me. I couldn't make the decision—it was part of the dream from which I had not yet awakened—and so I phoned that kindly presence in Miami without knowing yet what I would tell him. I asked him for details that he might not have revealed in the earlier conversation—for facts about the accident. He said that the highway apparently had been deserted—the accident had occurred at 1:45 A.M.—except for the limousine. The driver had been going very fast; perhaps he had swerved too sharply when he saw the exit for O'Hare. The only known fact was that the vehicle had hit a concrete barrier. Facing backward in the fold-down seats, two of the stewardesses had been hurt, not seriously, by the bodies flying past them: Jack and the copilot had been catapulted into the front. Jack had died either immediately or in the ambulance taking him to the hospital.

I told the captain I would be coming to Florida by myself.

The sky began to brighten. Birds bathed in the pools in the roof gutter above the open window in the bedroom, the scratching of their claws intensified by the half tunnel of tin; they sang from the roof, the trees, the bushes. I dressed slowly and, while Jean was making coffee, wakened my mother by bringing her a glass of orange juice and an antibiotic pill. Then I lay beside her on the bed.

"You must have something to tell me," she said.

"I do," I said.

"What is it?"

"Something so bad I don't know how to say it properly. At three o'clock I had a call from a captain in Miami. Jack—"

"Jack," she repeated.

"Jack is dead."

"Jackie," she said, as if she were seeing him as baby or young child.

We were both silent. She stared up at the ceiling; I turned away to look at the photographs on the wall—the ones she had brought with her when she came to live with us. She had arranged them in the same order they had been in on the wall of her bedroom at her sister's house—the same order that they had been in on the walls of all the bedrooms she had shared with my father during the later years of their married life: on the left, paired oval pictures of her mother and my father's mother; then a picture of her sister, a corsage on her dress, at the wedding of some relative; then one of my father in profile—a young man with brushed-back hair who looked vaguely like F. Scott Fitzgerald; then one of Jack and me as children; and, finally, a picture of my father, Jack, and me standing before the grandest house I had lived in as a boy, the one in Normandy.

"How did it happen?" my mother asked at last.

"He was in a limousine with his crew, on the way from the Palmer House in Chicago to O'Hare airport. It was one-thirty in the morning—*this* morning—and there apparently weren't any other cars on the road. The driver must have been going too fast. He may have swerved too sharply when he saw the exit to the airport. In any event, the limousine struck a barrier. Jack and his co-pilot were thrown into the front seat. Jack died either immediately or soon afterward, in the ambulance taking him to the hospital."

"He used to laugh and run away so!" my mother said. "One time, just after I'd given him a bath and left to get a clean towel from the line, he slipped out the front door to go running and laughing, naked and wet, down the street! Another time, soon after you'd been born, I really didn't know what to do. . . . I tied him by a long rope to a tree in the front yard."

"I know." She often mentioned she had done that; she obviously regretted it. "You did that only once."

"Yes." She reached for my hand. "But I really can't understand about this accident," she said apologetically. "Would you mind telling me again what happened?"

"Of course not," I said. "Jack was in a limousine with his crew; they were on their way from the Palmer House in Chicago to O'Hare airport," and, as I repeated the description of the event as I had heard it, I entered a world not my own: I was remembering the nearly deaf grandmother in James Agee's *A Death in the Family,* whose son-in-law has been killed in a car accident and to whom certain excruciating details of that accident must be repeated, the words shouted into her ear trumpet. I had been speaking in a low voice to my mother, for her hearing was remarkably acute; none of her faculties was impaired. She was having trouble simply because long ago she had accepted her own death as a possibility at any moment and believed without think-

ing of it that her two children would outlive her for decades. It was
Agee's novel in which I was existing, not this present moment at all,
and in repeating the story of Jack's death I realized I had raised my
voice slightly.

"Tell me again," she said when I had finished the second time, and
I did. "Tell me once more," she said, and once more I did; and then she
said quietly and with dignity, still looking at the ceiling, "There, that's
enough, you needn't shout. I think I know."

But I was a boy named Rufus who lived long ago in Tennessee,
and it was my father who had died, and it was my grandmother who
mercifully at last understood.

My tickets were waiting for me at the Ithaca airport the following
morning. "You must know somebody important," the agent said,
handing them to me. "Somebody got bumped for your sake." At
LaGuardia, awaiting the connection that would take me first class—I
had never flown first class—to Fort Lauderdale on my brother's airline,
I felt a sense of mysterious importance, as if my journey were far more
significant than that of any of my fellow passengers. *A Death in the
Family* remained with me: now it was the scene in which the boy,
permitted to stay home from school because his father has died, leaves
the house to stand in the alley as his schoolmates go by, and is unable
to control the wide smile that comes to him because destiny has made
of him something special. More than thirty years earlier I had driven
Jack to LaGuardia from the Flushing apartment he had rented as a first
home for himself and his bride, and had stood with him as he looked
at weather data in preparation for a flight to Dallas on the DC-3 he then
was piloting. (The information came from a Teletype in an office down
the hall from the waiting room.) My memory of LaGuardia as a much
smaller terminal than it now was, one to which I had come with my
brother, a recently appointed captain who had decided that the thun-
derstorm over the Gulf and much of Texas would have dissipated by
his arrival-time and that he would not cancel the flight—"The decision
is mine," he had said—also set me apart.

The stewardess on the Fort Lauderdale flight who brought me a

Bloody Mary, that fringe benefit for first-class travelers, had seen my name on the manifest. She asked me if I was Jack's brother, and when I said yes she said he had been a lovely man, happy and always joking, and the most capable captain she knew of. At the Fort Lauderdale terminal I was met by one of Jack's married daughters—he had three girls; I have three sons—and by an official from the airline, a former captain with silver hair and a soldierly bearing. "Are you Uncle Jim?" my niece said doubtfully. "You don't look at all like Daddy!" While she went for the car—Jack's Cadillac—the official handed me an envelope. "Give this to Jack's wife," he said. "We don't know how much money she may have on hand, and don't want her to worry about expenses at a time like this." He told me of the death benefits and pension that she would receive. "Of course she's broken up. The captains who brought her the news saw to it that she was given sedation and stayed with her until the older daughters came. But it might help, just a little, if you could let her know, when she's ready for it, that Jack made sure she will have an adequate income. And here"—he gave me a sheet of paper with names and telephone numbers—"is a list of people from the airline she or you can call if there's the slightest worry about anything."

I said that I thought the consideration shown by the airline and the captains was remarkable—something beyond my experience. I couldn't imagine the university where I taught behaving so to my wife, were I to die. What I didn't say was that I had never spent a night trying to solace the wife or husband of a recently deceased colleague, though a number had died during the years of my teaching career; I was at once too distant and too shy, perhaps too busy as a humanist in a large university to know my equally busy colleagues and their families as well as I ought.

"We're always ready for emergencies, in our business," he said soberly. "It's true, though, that pilots have a special bond. And Jack—well, of course, everybody liked your brother." He smiled and shook my hand.

Driving me to her mother's house, my niece at first said nothing; I, too, was quiet. She was a slim young woman, with her father's facial features and curly blonde hair; she had been, I remembered from letters, a model for a time, and now was a buyer of women's clothes for a chain of department stores. Glancing at her now and then, I regretted that our families lived so far apart; over the years, we had visited each other so infrequently that this girl and I had barely recognized each other. And yet, in my mind, my brother had always been "there"— somebody I could count on. In the days before airlines took to the stratosphere, before traffic in the sky became congested, Jack once obtained permission to fly over our house—we lived in a remote Kentucky hill town then—and took a picture from the cockpit. On the print he sent us, he had circled in black the rectangle of roof that he rightly identified as ours. Soon after we moved to upstate New York, he sent us a photograph of our new neighborhood, but in that print the roofs were tinier, for he was already higher up. My sense of him as a comforting presence, somebody winging along above me—after all, he might have been contained in any of those points of light that one finds at night by looking half a sky in advance of the area from which a faint rumble seems to come—obviously was related to those photographs from the fifties, but its intensity was a result of my childhood memories. During the Depression, my father had deserted my mother, brother, and me; though he ultimately returned, that act remained for me, even after my marriage, a betrayal of nearly inconceivable dimensions. Jack, who had wanted both to go to college and to learn how to fly—from his second year in high school he had kept a framed photograph in color of an early Douglas airliner on his bedroom wall— worked, instead, at a hamburger stand in a Cleveland dime store, bringing his weekly pay to our mother; later, just as if he were the husband and father, we accompanied him from Ohio to Michigan, where, as a student in the work-study program of an engineering institute sponsored by an auto firm, he continued to buy our food.

Well, Jack was strong and determined enough to get beyond all that, I thought, pleased by the cool smoothness of the leather seat of his air-conditioned car—pleased, too, by his attractive and well-dressed daughter. But then, as I relaxed, that memory, forgotten until his death, of Jack and me and the gang in Normandy returned. I was entangled in my fallen bicycle; my knee was bruised, and I was crying.

Jack rushed out of the house to save me from the boys, all bigger than I, and one of them stabbed him in the palm with a tiny knife. He helped me to my feet, blood dripping from his hand. . . .

My niece had been thinking of the past, too. While we were waiting for a traffic light, she said that one of her childhood memories was of her father celebrating, maybe with a bottle of champagne, the publication of an early book of mine—a study of an English novelist; I must have sent him a copy. What she particularly recalled was her father telling her mother that what I did would last after my death, while what he did vanished with his vapor trail.

"Nothing lasts," I said.

"Daddy was too much an optimist ever to have believed *that*."

I still wanted to shy away from the praise. "It must have been Scotch he was drinking, not champagne. Scotch always made Jack sentimental."

"He was very proud of you."

I said, "Sometimes I try to imagine what it's like to land one of those monster airplanes at night in a fog or snowstorm, the passengers asleep or reading magazines, maybe a mother giving a baby a nursing bottle. And do you know that sometimes students would come to my office who had flown with Jack to Puerto Rico or someplace? Jack had asked those students to say hello to me. How do you suppose he found out they were from Cornell?"

"It wouldn't be on the manifest. He liked to talk with his passengers, though. Probably he was on the lookout for Cornell students."

"Well, I've always been proud of him, too."

"The two of you are so different."

"I'm smaller."

"It's not that! You're more—more contemplative or scholarly, maybe. It's written all over your face."

"You're seeing me at a sad time."

"I can imagine Daddy looking down at us and laughing so hard! He's telling some joke, telling us to cheer up. Oh, *damn it all!*" she cried, her face contorting; the spasm of grief had caught her at the moment she obviously least expected it to. The light turned green, and she slammed her foot against the accelerator.

Despite the passage of time, I do not want to intrude more than I already have into the feelings of Jack's immediate family in the days following his death; my concern is with my own responses, especially with the way in which another work of fiction—Joyce's *The Dead*—had begun to supplant Agee's novel before I had reached the house, perhaps even before I had arrived at the Fort Lauderdale terminal. For I saw myself within the story of Gabriel Conroy, that self-conscious literary person who longs for something beyond the hubbub and gaiety of the Christmas party, who longs, perhaps, for death; Gabriel Conroy, who is no match in generosity and love for a dead boy, Michael Furey. However distinct my story was from Gabriel's, I felt that I, too, was in competition with one who had died before me, and the knowledge that this was so, and that I was but living a truth of human relationships long since made evident in literature, dulled my sense of loss.

At the memorial service in the funeral home the evening before the funeral, I talked to many of my brother's friends, including those who had served with him during the Second World War as instructors of RAF cadets at an air base near Clewiston, in the interior of southern Florida. One of them, who had remained in the Clewiston area as a cattle rancher, had no telephone; another of their group had flown low over his ranch in a private plane to drop him a note attached to a stone to let him know of Jack's death and of the time of the service. I stood at the center of that group of men—all of them tanned and athletic-looking, most of them veteran captains for one airline or another—listening to their stories about Jack from those Clewiston years; of how he had taken his golf bag along in the airplane and landed with his cadet on a fairway of a country club to play a hole before taking off again, an act for which he had been reprimanded by the colonel. And of how he, in turn, was constantly reprimanding a cadet, a careless young British aristocrat who ignored all the rules. On one training flight Jack asked him on the intercom connecting the two open cockpits if he had buckled his seat belt, and the cadet said yes. After repeating the question and getting the same bored, monosyllabic answer, Jack turned the plane upside down. "Do you see what would have happened if you hadn't buckled your seat belt?" he asked, but heard no reply. Looking over the fuselage, he saw a parachute drifting toward the swamp.

I told them that before the war, while I was still a college student in Cleveland and my brother an instructor in acrobatic flying in Baltimore, I had visited him one weekend. He took me for a flight, first making sure that both *my* seat belt and parachute were fastened securely. He flew upside down over Baltimore before going through his complete acrobatic repertoire. As he pulled out of a power dive over Chesapeake Bay, I thought I had blacked out; after we landed, I still couldn't see. "Jack, I'm *blind* and I think I'm going to throw up," I cried. Laughing, he lifted off the helmet with the goggles he had earlier placed on my head: the leather had slipped down over my eyes. But mine was the anecdote of a nonflier; it was a story to be listened to politely and with pity (or so I thought as I was telling it) for all the experiences I could never know.

The name "Gabriel Conroy" again echoed in my mind during the clergyman's address, as he praised my brother's zest for life; images from the story—of Gabriel's wife, Gretta, standing above him on the staircase as she listens to the husky tenor voice singing "The Lass of Aughrim," of Gabriel lying in the bed of the cold hotel room and looking out the window at the snow falling against the lamppost— seemed to represent my own pale existence. Afterward, at Jack's house, I joined my nieces in diversions designed by them to ease their mother's grief: pastimes that Jack had enjoyed with his family—charades, word games, riddles. I tried to be outgoing, funny, to be as much like my brother as I could, but I felt nothing but a numbness to life. I couldn't remember certain ordinary words, and was forgetful even of the names of my three nieces.

At the suggestion of a family acquaintance, who told me that it was a tradition in Jack's neighborhood, I arranged for a luncheon party to follow the funeral. Twenty or so people from his block filled the little room at the restaurant. As soon as the cocktails were served, I rose to offer a toast to Jack, saying that it was helpful to remember that he had died not following a lengthy illness but quickly, and on his way to pilot an aircraft—an activity he loved nearly as much as life itself ("Hear! Hear!" somebody cried), and that we should follow the example of his life and make this luncheon a pleasurable occasion. No longer was I trying in the slightest to resist Gabriel Conroy: in behaving in a way so foreign to my nature—since childhood I have preferred silence and privacy after any large loss—I felt as though I had given up my identity to a fictional presence, as though I were offering a toast not to my dead brother but to my two living maiden aunts at their annual Christmas party. I made suitable references to *carpe diem* poems, and sat down to applause and laughter.

Early the next afternoon, I left Fort Lauderdale. My return ticket, as I discovered upon boarding the plane, was not first-class and was valid only to LaGuardia. The trip to Fort Lauderdale had been non-stop; the return flight stopped at several cities. My brother, who as pilot had particularly enjoyed landings, once told me that they were similar to sexual intercourse, in that no two were ever alike; following his virginal flight as captain, he confessed, he remained in the cockpit until not only the passengers but all the crew members left, for he knew that if he were to talk to anybody his voice would tremble. I remembered that remark during the landings of the homeward journey, as I have always remembered it as a passenger in any gently descending plane; in the past it had made my heart beat rapidly, but now I felt just a vague regret that I did not value my life enough to be afraid of losing it. At LaGuardia, I found I would have to wait a number of hours for a plane to Ithaca; I bought a ticket for a flight to a nearby city, Elmira, which would depart within the half-hour, and called my wife at work to ask if she would meet me there.

"What's wrong?" she asked, responding immediately to the deadness in my voice. I said nothing was wrong, I guessed I was just tired.

Jean was not at the Elmira terminal to greet me. Other passengers met their wives or husbands or children, embraced, and quickly left.

That late afternoon was sunny and pleasantly cool, a relief from the heat of Florida in July, and so I took my bag and sat on the bench in front of the building. Another passenger—a woman my age—joined me; we were the only ones left. Both of us watched the cars and taxis that occasionally approached. At last I smiled at her and made some remark about the two of us being the forgotten ones. *"I've* not been forgotten," she said, glancing at her watch. "My husband is leaving the plant right now. He'll be here in ten minutes."

Much later I was to realize that her words had begun the process of releasing me from the second of the two works of fiction: in refusing the connection with me, she had thrown me back upon myself. After the woman left with her husband—"I hope your wife comes soon," she said, waving goodbye—I paced the sidewalk. Jack had been killed on his way to the airport; what if, by that dreadful irony of the gods and Greek tragedians. . . . I couldn't complete the thought; it lay, a heavy and undigested piece of foreknowledge, in my stomach and head, and I began to perspire and to feel giddy, feverish. When our VW convertible, that flout of the riskiness of life, appeared, its chrome wheel-covers and orange fenders glittering in the sun, I felt as if I had been granted a double miracle, as if Jean and I alike had been plucked from our graves. "You're so damned late," I said huskily, throwing my bag in back.

"I left in time, but I've never driven to this airport before," Jean said. "I made the wrong turn onto the expressway—wouldn't you *think* you should follow the arrow to Elmira?—and got partway to Binghamton."

"Oh my God," I said, reaching over to embrace her—or, rather, to accept and complete the embrace she had offered me the morning of the phone call. Then I began to sob. Never have I wept so convulsively and for so long; I had been freed from the permanence and truth, from the consuming power, of literary works. My anguish was for the loss of my brother, that moving point of light or vanishing jet trail high above me, that sixteen-year-old whose bleeding hand once again was helping me to my feet; it was for my sister-in-law and my nieces, whose desolation I finally could respond to, in the newness of my own grief; it was for my wife and children and their vitality, which, as I tried to control myself by looking directly at Jean, seemed to shimmer in my eyes like a lovely spiderweb spanning a sunlit forest path that deer or bears have made and constantly traverse; and it was for a mother who, blessed at more than ninety with sharpness of eye and ear and recall, was waiting at home for her surviving son to return with news of the funeral of her firstborn, the naked baby who constantly eludes her to run, always laughing, down the street.

1980

Redefining a Word on Independence Day

THROUGHOUT MY CHILDHOOD, I WANTED to be liked, and my conscience was a kind of ear trumpet directed toward noises of apparent social approval or disapprobation; its distortions, which were many, were simply a consequence of its sensitivity and amplifying power. My recurrent discovery that I had exaggerated a disgrace gave me an equally exaggerated feeling of grace. For example, as an eighth grader, I misjudged a fly ball that cost Pulaski Heights Junior High School in Little Rock the baseball game. If only I had not moved! The ball was hit directly to me in right field, and of course everybody jeered as I ran this way and that in my eagerness to catch it, to save the game. The next day, I passed the baseball coach on the narrow back stairs of the school building. "Hi, Jim," he said, smiling and giving me a pat, a greeting so profound that I can still see his face and the wall tiles, glossy beige squares, behind it.

Certain of my childhood shames not so released by word and gesture remained with me for years, however buried they might be. In my late thirties, while attending a reunion of my father's clan, I overheard my Aunt Jo tell my mother how much she had always admired me. Her words bestowed on me an extraordinary sense of well-being, for, in my tenth year, visiting with my parents at the home of my uncle and aunt, I had disgraced myself by frightening their six-year-old daughter, Connie. Sitting with my cousin on the upstairs landing, I made up a ghost story that so fascinated her that I embellished it with ever more grisly details. Suddenly she began to sob loudly, as if I had done her physical harm; my Aunt Jo came running up the stairs. "He scared me," Connie whispered, pointing at me. I said I had been telling her a ghost story. "Don't ever, *ever* do anything like that again," Aunt Jo said severely, soothing Connie while leading her downstairs. I stayed on the landing, listening while my aunt, now in the living room, explained to the other adults that somehow I had badly frightened Connie, though I admitted only to talking to her about ghosts. "Jimmy never lies," my mother said; but she and my father climbed the stairs to hear my explanation. After they completed the interrogation, I left the house to sit in my father's Packard, where I immediately broke the dashboard light—it was something like a night lamp, a bulb built into a little hood above the gauges—by poking at it with my finger. Then I climbed into the rear seat and lay down, waiting for my parents; as soon as they entered the car, I sat up to tell my father that Connie had broken the bulb. He believed me, which increased my guilt; after all, an hour before my mother had said I never lied, and, indeed *this* lie was the first I remember making. Had I intentionally broken the bulb, to incriminate my cousin Connie, the cause of my shame? Or was that little destructive act as well as the lie an attempt to prove myself as unworthy as my Aunt Jo thought me? It was even possible that I broke the bulb in anger at my father for his questions; and then, not wanting to be accused of yet another wrongful act, lied to extricate myself. In any case, I was a sneaky fellow, one whom my uncle and aunt had even more reason to disapprove of than they knew; and the events of that afternoon were the reason that my aunt's praise more than twenty years later came to me as a benediction.

In the summer of 1958, I directed a writers' conference at Antioch College. It was an unusually successful affair, for the students were all talented and at that level of competence in which they recognized the offending word or phrase in their manuscripts while the critic was still pointing a pencil at a stanza or paragraph and preparing to explain what was wrong with it; within a year, nearly every student began to publish, and a few went on to gain major reputations. At the local tavern, students and staff drank beer together and sang bawdy songs and swore eternal friendship; and I was wondrously pleased and half in love with everybody there, including myself. The Antioch professor who had hired me was pleased, too, and on the Saturday morning following the conference he and my wife and I lingered in our farewells. On impulse, he offered to lead us out of town by a special route—perhaps the first time a visitor to Yellow Springs, Ohio, had been given a guide to direct him out of that hamlet. He stopped his car at a country crossroads, gesturing in the direction we should take. As our car passed his, he smiled broadly and waved, and then cried out to me, "You really want to be liked, don't you?" I waved back, smiling too, pretending not to have heard him; but ten miles later, I asked Jean, "Why do you suppose he said that?"

"Maybe because it's true."

"But it sounded—well, almost like a taunt."

"Some people, when they want to praise somebody, have to make it sound like that."

"Then you think it was praise?"

"I think he wanted to tell you that your friendliness helped to pull all those strangers together."

"I don't like people saying I want to be liked."

"Don't you want to be liked?"

"Yes."

But the remark bothered me all the way back to our home in Ithaca.

The act that I feel to be the most shameful of my adult life is seemingly more trivial than the theft of pears that some readers of the *Confessions* think Augustine made too much of. I stole nothing; nor did I unwittingly make a fool of myself or frighten a child or tell a lie. What I did was no more than this: in walking out of an auditorium in the middle of somebody's speech, I stopped to bend over a still-seated student of mine to murmur a few now-forgotten words.

The gathering in the auditorium occurred at the tag end of a year

of racial upheaval at my university. As a member of the faculty committee most concerned with issues of this kind, I had been involved
from the beginning of the fall term with attempts to resolve the
underlying problems. I disliked both the rhetoric and the eagerness to
assume personal power of certain black activists and their white supporters; but, like most of my friends among the faculty, I understood,
or thought I did, the resentment of those blacks who, brought from
urban ghettos to a predominantly white upstate New York community
out of the university's well-meaning attempt to redress racial imbal-
ance, termed the institution racist. I felt a spiritual kinship with a black
leader who had spoken to me about the relationship between Camus's
argument in *The Rebel* and the black movement; and I saw myself, my
own yearning to be liked by those I respected, in the girl who, as part
of a black strategy to obtain courses for minorities, stopped coming to
a class of mine in which she was the only non-white—but who spent
the hour in my office, making order out of everything I had neglected
because of the press of events, and who awaited my arrival in order to
turn in her assignments and discuss the work. She brought me file
folders for student manuscripts and a cork board to which I could pin
telephone messages and notices of upcoming meetings. Whenever I
was walking across the quadrangle and heard her voice in the distance,
calling my name, and saw the arms of her dashiki waving like sema-
phore flags, I knew that the university could expect, on that day, some
new form of protest.

But now it was May, and the major events—the classroom dem-
onstrations, the building takeover accompanied by the appearance of
guns—were over, leaving behind chiefly a residue of bitterness. The
university was fragmented; because of its inability to act, the administration had lost the trust of all groups, each of which had called for
its own type of action. Isolated instances of violence had recently
occurred—a white student, for example, had been found bleeding and
unconscious; apparently he had been bludgeoned during the night
with a weapon that had protruding nails or studs. As for myself, I was
suffering that kind of exhaustion or spiritual paralysis in which a

person, desperately desiring truth, listens with complete concentration to others and believes without question in what they say, so long as they speak from the heart.

Being anticlimactic, the meeting in the auditorium attracted few of the activists become instant celebrities; to my surprise, it brought together, at last, on the platform and in the audience, both blacks and whites, and mainly of the sort I admired—those (or so I thought, listening to the faculty and student speakers) who would continue to struggle, without demagogy and despite weariness, for the principles of equality and justice upon which our country was founded. The question at hand concerned the implications of the president's edict forbidding ingress to the campus by a registered student, a black suspected of bludgeoning the white. The act was abhorrent; still, no legal charges as yet had been filed against the black, and didn't such an edict declare him guilty in advance of any court trial? Why had there been an immediate assumption that the attack was the work of a black? Had the anguish of the year taught the community nothing?

I would have asked similar questions, had I not come to the auditorium from another and much smaller meeting—with the president, several other administrators, and a campus patrolman—to which I had been invited as the acting chairman of my faculty committee. I heard a wholly reasonable patrolman explain that on the evening after the attack he had been part of a stake-out by officers in various isolated sections of the campus where further violence might be expected; hidden behind a bush, he had observed a white male approaching on the asphalt pathway and seen three black males suddenly emerge, one of them bearing a spiked club, from behind the trees on the opposite side of that walk. He had saved the white male from injury by calling for the blacks to surrender and had recognized the identity of the one with the club—he was the student to whom the president had denied campus ingress; unfortunately, being under orders not to use his revolver even for a warning shot, he had been unable to prevent their escape.

Given the location—a poorly lit section of a campus walk—a positive identification of any of the thwarted assailants might have

been questioned; yet the patrolman obviously believed he was report-
ing the truth, and I believed at once in his belief. Knowing of the
forthcoming assembly to protest his edict, the president had called us
together to explain his reason for it and to gain our support. I said the
decision seemed the least that could be done for public safety, and that
I thought a university official should attend the assembly, to counteract
any new outcry of racial bias; but my suggestion was met with hopeless
shrugs from all the administrators. To mention the patrolman's testimony in advance of trial would be unfair to the defendant and put the
case in jeopardy.

So, in all that audience, I was the only one who knew enough to
agree with the president; and yet I was powerless to intervene. Why had
I come? Could I have possibly thought my silent presence could lessen
any new sense of outrage against an institution whose recent and
frightening vulnerability made me aware of how deeply I cared for it?
Whatever my reason, my presence simply provided one more body to
a group that believed it was behaving responsibly in protesting an edict
that had just won my clearly voiced support elsewhere. I grew more
and more upset by my immobility, which seemed at one with my
spiritual state; I needed, for my salvation, to break free from this
mannerly and attentive crowd. Abruptly rising from my seat, I dropped
a book I had forgotten was in my lap; searching for it, I disturbed the
nearby people and momentarily distracted the speaker.

Halfway up the aisle, I saw my student. Who he actually was
matters even less than what I said. I felt myself surrounded by people
who desired, with me, a brotherhood that transcended color; I felt
myself unfairly separated from them by a secret that forced me into a
rejection of our common bond. As we sometimes do in dreams, I
perceived myself as the single focus of attention, even though the
speaker had resumed; and I stopped before that nameless student to
signify to everybody who happened to be in the audience—including,
if they were there, the black girl who had waved the colorful arms of
her dashiki and the black boy who read Camus—that I was no racist,
that I was a friendly guy who considered them all O.K. That was what
I wanted my self-conscious smile and my words to mean.

Even as I was speaking, a sense of humiliation struck, a shame for my weakness in wishing to be favorably viewed by others; but not until that night, tossing in bed, did I understand what had happened to my psyche. I had left because I thought, on the basis of my privileged knowledge, that the protesters were wrong; and I had discredited myself in my own eyes by attempting to prove I was still with them. Nobody in the auditorium could have had the slightest idea of my inner conflict; my departure, which to me had seemed so dramatic, had meant nothing to anybody but me. My shame was for an inner betrayal only. At the moment I was bending down to speak, shame was already losing its public dimension to become what I now knew it to be: something wholly internal, a violation of my ideal conception of myself. I couldn't even unburden myself by waking my wife to confess to her, for what, after all, was there to confess? That I had smiled and murmured a few words to a student?

That gathering in the auditorium took place more than twelve years ago. The present moment is the morning of July 4, 1980. The air is cool and dry, and from the study window of my farmhouse I can see the separate trees at the end of the cornfield almost as distinctly as I can see the wild roses blooming just beyond the pane. My youngest son, who is on Cyprus, has already been at work for hours, there being no American holiday for undergraduate archeologists on a dig on a foreign island whose inhabitants have, at best, an ambiguous feeling for our country. My oldest son, a film-maker, probably is still sleeping off a summer cold in his Philadelphia bedroom. He phoned late last night—he calls my wife and me nearly every holiday—to say that he was fine despite a stuffy nose, that he had just filmed a television commercial for an automobile manufacturer, and that he believed the funding would come through for the documentary he wished to make. Just beyond the rear yard, at the edge of the old apple orchard, my third son and his partner are hammering away at the second addition to their goat barn, a wing designed to increase the efficiency of their dairy operation. My mother, now ninety-seven, is eating Grape-Nuts in the kitchen and talking to the six-week-old kitten that apparently wants to share her breakfast. My wife, having picked the first crop of sugar peas (she just brought me a pod, to taste), is hanging the wash on the line and singing. I am fifty-eight, and my world is orderly enough for me to look back at that revelation from my forty-sixth year—surely it was late in coming!—as if it had the quaintness of a maxim or bit of scripture embroidered on linen.

For I had learned on that day what all of us have come to learn, the loneliness of the battleground on which we win or lose our self-respect; in our age such knowledge is the token of our maturity and the cause of our incommunicable anxieties. Perhaps my insight was belated and painful because I have always wanted to place my trust in something greater than myself—God, the natural universe, the collective wisdom of an enlightened people, the judgment of an incorruptible friend. I have looked for hints even in the courage of swallows, the magnanimity of horses and dogs.

But my reason, a cheap psychiatrist, tells me that an explanation of this kind is as absurd as the response it would justify; that the intensity of my shame for a trivial act was only the symptom of a neurosis brought on by fatigue and problems beyond solution. I was closer to a breakdown than I realized. At term's end, hadn't I escaped to Italy, to sleep, at first, twelve to fifteen hours every day? By such arguments our reason would put down as excessive all those pains that harm nobody but ourselves, would bury them as unworthy of its consideration. The burial, though, can be accomplished only within our memories, and the deeper the grave within us, the more securely we make the feeling ours, a part (however submerged) of what we are and would be; and I am glad that this is so.

One of the senior lexicographers of my favorite desk dictionary is an acquaintance of long standing; as young college instructors in Cleveland, we often struggled together over the murky intricacies of Conrad's prose in *Heart of Darkness* as we followed Marlow's self-revelatory journey up the Congo. In looking up a definition in that dictionary, I feel myself in a suitably obscure communication with my friend. The first definition of shame in his dictionary ("a painful feeling of having lost the respect of others . . .") is implied in the subsequent ones, none of which has paramount application to our present condition, whatever its relevance to our youthful past. Perhaps civilization so far has survived disorder after disorder, I would tell my friend, not because sidewalks and policemen and gossip are restraining forces, which was Marlow's view as it once was yours and mine, but rather because individuals have said, *I must become better than I am; everything depends on me.*

1981

The Windows of the Mint

$\sim$ **10** WHILE SIFTING THROUGH THE litter in my desk drawer a number of years ago, I came across two brittle pieces of a picture postcard. I taped them together and then taped the card onto the glass of my study window, where it remains. It depicts an urban scene from which only a portion of sky and the end of a boulevard in the foreground are missing. The major building is intact: a three-story, block-long structure in an austere classical style which hardly needs the flag on the roof to denote its governmental nature. A man with a stovepipe hat, swallow-tailed coat, cane, and protruding stomach is leisurely crossing the wide street at the intersection, the focal point of the picture. Walking the opposite way and about to pass him is a wasp-waisted woman in a long dress and feathered hat—she is as obviously a lady as he is a gentleman—who is holding the hand of a fat child in a red coat. At the center of the intersection a man somewhat lower in the social hierarchy (for he is in shirtsleeves and his hands are in his pockets) trudges forward. Behind him a bicyclist is about to enter the boulevard. A woman in red—she is outsize, like the statue of a queen—has just crossed the side street. Her hands rest on her wide hips; the hem of her gown still drapes over the curb. Other figures, more nondescript, stand or pace nearby. An open touring car with three passengers has already passed the intersection, leaving behind a jaunty trail of white smoke. Approaching from the other direction—apparently at so moderate a speed that the pedestrians needn't bother themselves with a glance that way—are a three-wheeled motorcycle van and a streetcar. If the piece of sky missing from the upper left corner were to be found, it would contain these words printed on the clouds: "U.S. MINT, PHILADELPHIA, PA."

I have kept this card for more than half a century. It was already old—the date on the postmark is August 31, 1912—when my mother removed it from an album so that I could look at it during an illness in my fourth or fifth year. A slight fever can cause a child's mind to concentrate so fully on a specific picture, or on a single detail in it, that his actual surroundings—a bedroom, say, with its familiar bureau and wallpaper, its closet door partly ajar—become the less substantial reality. This picture held a particular appeal for me because it was capable of transformations.

For the card has been cunningly fashioned—with two plies of cardboard, apertures in the heavier ply, transparent paper in several colors between the plies—to permit changes in the time of day. Looked at in ordinary light, the scene represents morning or late afternoon; the figures have shadows, and a pale crescent moon floats above the flag. But if the card is held against a sunny pane or lampshade, the moon brightens and the corner street light glows. The windows of the Mint possess a splendid yellow-gold incandescence, those of the streetcar and more distant buildings a fainter yellow. The headlights of streetcar and motorcycle shine, and the area immediately before the touring car (its headlights being hidden from view) turns a gauzy white. The taillight of the car is a tiny ruby. Objects—buildings, the larger trees—take on greater mass, as they do in the actual world at dusk, just before solidity begins to melt. It becomes difficult to separate the rich and the regal from the poor and the nondescript. All of the pedestrians simply seem caught in the act of hurrying home, to the security of their own homes.

As I child, I would hold a flashlight against the back of the card after my room became completely dark. Everything in the picture would be invisible except for the variously colored lights and a single figure—that of the streetcar's motorman, outlined against the windshield, peering into a street so black that his headlight illuminated nothing whatever. The windows of the Mint blazed but were empty of life, and the brightly lit streetcar carried no passengers. With a second flashlight, of the pencil type, I could focus the beam on the streetcar alone, thus endowing it with imaginary movement through the dark. I thought of the motorman as pulling the throttle to allow the rails to carry him around bends and over the clack-clack of crossings to a deserted terminus that glowed—larger flashlight again—just like the Mint it actually was. The terminus, each window a golden bar, was a treasure so vast that I knew the motorman must be both lonely and full of that kind of happiness indistinguishable from wonder. Though I experienced his happiness as if it were my own, I was not the motorman. I don't think children ever put themselves into the little worlds that fascinate them. To do so is to turn gold into dross; to enter a world is to lose it.

I have been out in the world quite some time: it is January of the year that will bring my sixtieth birthday. Earlier in the month, my wife and I, both longtime employees of Cornell, attended a three-hour seminar, sponsored by the personnel office of the university, called "Planning for Retirement." The audience was composed of silver-haired men and women, some of them friends of ours, most of the rest acquaintances or at least people whose faces were familiar—vice-presidents and other administrative officers; librarians who over the years have located elusive books for me and fined me for not returning them on time; mathematicians, physicists, biologists, engineers, and fellow-humanists, many of whom have made distinguished contributions to their fields. We were the students; our teachers, who were more fashionably dressed than any of us, were, it seemed to me, a group of earnest and well-meaning kids just out of business school. Though the cause—how to survive inflation after our paychecks cease—was wholly in our practical self-interest, I felt the seminar to be an initiatory rite into the secrets of old age, a rite as disquieting to me as the first orientation lecture I had attended as a private in an Army reception center during the Second World War. A sense of an unavoidable future violation of my freedom and dignity linked the present orientation to the earlier one. Sitting beside my wife of thirty-six years, aware—even as I was watching slides and listening to statistics of one financial strategy or another—that in some corner of her mind, she, like me, was conscious of our life together and of the comfortable old farmhouse in which we raised our three sons, I was also feeling the heaviness in my arm from a typhoid injection and hearing a lieutenant read in a monotone the grave penalties for desertion in wartime and wondering about what lay ahead for me, a recruit soon to become a rifleman in an infantry platoon.

The following weekend, both Jean and I were still depressed, a condition unrelieved by the common sense telling us that we have many useful years ahead: it was simply that kind of weekend in which the winter seems unendurably long, one's own life doesn't add up to much, and nobody wants to think of tomorrow. Two of our three sons—Jim, a junior at Cornell, and Cris, his older brother—continue to live with us, as does my ninety-eight-year-old mother, and normally we are gratified that they do. But the washing machine broke, and then the oil furnace. We have a wood furnace as a backup, and though we have enough logs to last through the winter, many of them have not been split and piled in the basement. I resented my sons for not having accomplished that chore in October, even as Jean resented the disorder of their rooms. One of them, irritable all morning because of our gloom and perhaps some undisclosed personal problem or loss, spilled a glass of chocolate milk at lunch and said, with tears in his eyes, "Life is just too much"—an overreaction that nevertheless stirred in us feelings of love and guilt.

After lunch, we decided to varnish the worn floorboards in the dining room, and Jean immediately began to clean out the buffet so that we could more easily move it. (Discontent of one sort or another underlies nearly all of the home repairs and improvements that she and I make.) As the most convenient receptacle in the house, its drawer was jammed with inoperable watches, eyeglasses that corrected a younger vision, instructions and guarantees for already discarded household appliances and garden tools, road maps, subway tokens,

French centimes, old passports, color slides from the various trips we took when our children were small, and an accumulation of all their school report cards. Jean had been at work half an hour before she came into my study, wiping her eyes. "I feel so unhappy I've got to do something else," she said, embracing me tightly; and later, in looking at the still open drawer, I saw that she had worked her way down to some small photographs in flimsy gilt frames. With the weight of everything she already had sorted through, she must have found the picture on top—one of Larry, our oldest child, taken in his sixth year at his first piano recital—too much to bear.

We were living then in a small town in the hills of eastern Kentucky. I was a young professor at the college; Jean, though her graduate degree was in biochemistry and her previous job that of a research chemist, taught the journalism course and handled the college publicity. Larry was still too young for school and Cris was an infant, and Jean often wrote her news stories at a typewriter on the dining-room table, in view of the playpen. To occupy Larry's attention, she bought him an old typewriter and installed it on the opposite side of the table. Not all the keys worked, but he would type out lines of "z"s and "x"s and ampersands. My department chairman and his wife, a fine pianist who gave lessons to adults and older children, lived nearby, and one morning when the wife stopped by for coffee with Jean, Larry's typing caught her attention. In a low voice, she said to Jean, "It's amazing how strong his fingers have become. I believe he's ready for the piano. Maybe I can see how it goes, early some morning before my first student comes." The following dawn, Larry, wearing a suit we had recently bought him, came into our bedroom, carrying my graduate-school briefcase. "Tie my shoes," he said to Jean. "I'm going for my piano lesson." We managed to hold him off until after breakfast and a warning call to the teacher; but in a month we bought a piano that cost almost a third of our combined annual salaries and that we paid for, with difficulty, over a three-year span. Now Larry is thirty-one, a busy cinematographer in Philadelphia who enjoys playing Mozart and Beethoven on his own piano in his spare moments. In the picture, he sits upright and self-possessed on a dark stage—a tiny figure between a Steinway concert grand and a spray of flowers, his fingers properly arched at the keyboard. He is dressed in the suit, its coat sleeves already too short; at his neck, a bow tie is askew. His head is turned toward the camera; the eyes of his too-white face (the colors of the photograph have faded) reflect the glow of the flashbulb and the triumph he has just experienced.

In looking at the photograph, I felt such love for my wife that I had to search her out, to return her embrace; and then I went for a walk, alone, in the snow, asking myself why it should be that a happy memory often cannot dissipate or even alleviate a present disquietude, but instead turns it into grief; and, furthermore, why it should be that the bond—the understanding and sympathy—between a long-married husband and wife depends so greatly on the shared knowledge of that miserable truth.

It is now a Thursday morning late in the long Cornell intersession; the spring term starts on Monday, and I should be preparing my first lectures for the students who will be returning with the sun of Jamaica and Florida on their refreshed young faces. Jean, who is not a teacher, left for work two hours ago. As is my custom, I stood by the window, watching as her car slowly went down the snow-covered country road, saying to myself, as it disappeared over the crest half a mile away, "I love you; be careful"—words whose magical protective power is doubtless a vestige of the beliefs of our most distant ancestors.

I have been sitting at my desk, looking at the postcard of the Philadelphia Mint, caught by some elusive connection between my childhood response to it and a kind of happiness that endures without contamination through our adult years, that never reverses into grief or pain. In particular, I have been remembering the July day four years ago that Cris and I drove to Montour Falls, a village about fifteen miles from our house. We had gone there to order roof trusses for a small barn Cris was building for his newly purchased herd of goats. Jean's birthday was only a few days distant, and, after we had purchased the trusses, we stopped at a drugstore, where I bought her a Timex watch— a slightly better model than her present one, which no longer was reliable; at a hardware store, where Cris bought her a dozen Corning tumblers, to replace the set that had shattered, glass by glass, over the past few years; and then to a grocery store, where we bought birthday candles and a box of Betty Crocker chocolate cake mix.

There is, certainly, a simple pleasure in making such purchases with one's son, and in contemplating both the upcoming birthday of a wife and the completion of a structure felt by the son to be part of the fulfillment of a dream. But my happiness that day was so extraordinary that for months afterward I thought of it as a gift that transcended physicality. I had been in Montour Falls once before, to haggle with an automobile dealer over a car beyond my means, and I have been there since. It is an attractive little place, situated in a valley, and its main street ends in a tiny park where water tumbles down rocks— the falls from which the village gets part of its name. A small manufacturing plant, where Shepard Niles hoists and cranes are made, stands at the edge of the village. The central blocks show the ravages both of age and of the enclosed shopping malls in the nearby cities. But on the day I visited there with Cris, the village was charming and inviolate, a tidy collection of tree-shaded houses and old-fashioned stores in which the floorboards creaked as they ought to—a suddenly-stumbled-upon Eden of the American imagination, one that still had its *grande dame* in the great house which, with the falls, overlooked the village, but also one in which the mayor, the farm worker, and the lathe operator joined in an easy, genial relationship, solving their problems in the downtown café over cups of Maxwell House. Without exception, the shopkeepers were friendly and honest folk, patient with us as we examined every possible gift on their shelves, glad to bring from the storeroom some dusty item that might be just what we were after; and, as I pulled out of the municipal parking lot, the policeman smiled and waved me on, as if we had been friends forever. It seemed to me that in a sense we had, and that I obscurely knew his village—not so much through the illusions of a *déjà vu* as through the truth of a *déjà connu* (if there is such a phrase). For I believed I had been returned to an authentic state of being, one experienced I didn't know when, an island of feeling toward which I had ever since been swimming.

What was that earlier event? In looking at the postcard, it too has returned to me, as if both it and the visit to Montour Falls were prefigured in my childhood wonder at the picture. That earlier event—which also included a visit—is tangled up with a period of my life I normally choose to forget. In my fifteenth year, having said goodbye in Flint, Michigan, to the mother who could not support me any more than I could support her, I moved to Chicago, to live for some months with my father and a stepmother I wouldn't accept and who naturally enough returned my coldness. I worried about my sexuality, partly because one day I was accosted by a middle-aged man as I walked through Jackson Park on my way to school, partly because my father or stepmother, or both, left a pulp-paper pamphlet titled *Masturbation: A Youthful Folly* on the kitchen table for me to peruse while they were away on one of his business trips. My naïveté was monumental, even for that era, and my sexuality had no clear expression. In my loneliness I had developed the habit, mainly on weekends, of sitting on my bed and looking out my first-floor window at the streetcars and pedestrians. Each streetcar carried a number on its side. I began to jot down the numbers, and to keep a record of the length of time it took each trolley to reach the end of the line and return. One of them came back much earlier than my schedule called for; it was empty, and though would-be passengers stepped into the street to board it, the motorman disdained them, clanging his bell as he traveled past the intersection at a reckless speed. (The link between that streetcar and my childhood contemplation of the postcard never occurred to me.) Such a variation in the schedule simply gave me an odd, quasi-sexual excitement, and in the following days I sat before the card table my stepmother had put in my room for me to do my homework on and wrote several little stories to explain the mystery. As voyeuristic in those months as the boy in Joyce's "Araby," I was perhaps sublimating sexual desires into a conscious dreaming, for I constructed a number of further little tales from what I saw in the sad face of a passerby, in the sweep of a cloak.

One time, my stepmother read a story of mine while I was in school and showed it to my father. They held a conference with me after dinner: did I, they wanted to know, plan on sending my writings out for publication? The *Daily News*, I said, prints vignettes like mine. They both said that real authors never use family names, only pen names, and that I should choose one; and they suggested that then and there the three of us might find one, as if it were a warm family game from my early childhood, like "I Spy" or "Ghost." I had mentioned the *Daily News* because my father knew some of the executives there, but it was obvious to me that both he and my stepmother wanted to divorce themselves from my efforts. In such a rejection I felt my very imagination to be diseased. "Thank you," I said. "Maybe we can talk about it later," and I fled to my room. As the school term drew toward its end, I could concentrate on neither my stories nor my homework; though previously I had enjoyed mathematics, now I couldn't solve the simplest problems in geometry.

Such an experience is an old story, and not only for me: variations of it lurk within fables, and echoes of it can be found in the bedtime tales I once read to my own children. In any event, it was followed by a storybook inversion. One summer day, my father asked me to go with him on a selling trip to a town called Oregon, Illinois, both because he would like my company and because my constant presence, now that school was out, had a disturbing effect on my stepmother, who was having (he said) woman troubles; perhaps I had noticed that he as well as I was having difficulties with her.

And so I went. I remember it as a lovely afternoon in late June or early July, and I remember that my father almost at once became as carefree and affectionate as I had known him to be before he left my mother. Driving along, he talked about the meaning of life and the importance of the college education he'd never had and all the professional fields I someday would need to choose among. The possibilities that lay before me gladdened him, as if they widened or extended his own future.

I don't think Oregon, Illinois, has much in common with Montour Falls, New York, though I saw it for only an hour or so, walking its streets as I waited for my father. It is, I believe, much larger than Montour Falls. It doesn't have an agreeable natural spectacle at the end of its main street, but, in my memory, it does have a factory, by a stream, in which pleasant objects—pianos or some other musical instruments—are built. I had a Coke in a drugstore, and the waitress smiled at me. This was the extent of my contact with its inhabitants; and yet I was fonder of Oregon than of any place I ever had lived in or visited before, believing that eventually I would return, marry somebody like the waitress, and have children who loved me as I would love them. I would run the hardware store or build pianos or become editor of the newspaper. My happiness in Oregon was a miraculous glow in the dark as my father and I traveled homeward in his second-hand Packard; though it was behind me, it was ahead, as mysterious and incorporeal as the nature of God.

Today is one of thin gray clouds, with sudden cascades of snow giving way to bursts of light. Whenever the sun shines, the windows of the Mint respond as if an electrician in its basement had flicked on the master switch. My childhood wonder at those golden bars is one with my adolescent happiness in Oregon, one with my middle-aged happiness in Montour Falls, and is a quality or state that never can change into a baser form through any reverse alchemy of the human spirit. For I have memories of two sorts of happiness, only one of which is the food of present discontent: the other is its antidote. The first is based on events leading up to actual moments of fulfillment—Larry at the piano—whose remembrance tells me of times and conditions lost; the other, like my response to the Mint, is separate from reality. Based on imagination and desire, immune to time and vicissitude, it is the happiness we sometimes hear in music and find in certain books and paintings, even though we can discover no particular melody or words or images that convey it. At the very least, the recognition of this kind of happiness within his own life reconciles a man in his sixtieth year to the child within him, enabling him to join his wife in sifting through memorabilia in order to move a buffet and varnish a worn floor.

The Laughter of Zeus

11   I LIVE IN A GREEK REVIVAL FARM-house ten miles from Ithaca, where I teach at the university. My office is in the basement of a building that was constructed in the mid-nineteenth century as a stable, but soon metamorphosed into a three-story structure with Doric columns at its main entrance. In a sub-basement directly across the hall from my office is a high-ceilinged coffeehouse that at one time was a museum of plaster casts of Greek and Roman torsos, busts, and semi-divine beasts. The coffeehouse is named "The Temple of Zeus," for it still contains casts of the statuary that once adorned the west pediment of that temple at Olympia.

The eastern part of the United States—particularly in its towns and villages—is a repository of classical-revival artifacts and architecture, but I know of no other region in which place names are so resolutely those of Greek and Latin cities, statesmen, writers, soldiers, and mythological figures as is my section of the Finger Lakes region. Although the lakes retain the names of the Indians who once roamed their shores, townships and towns near the city of Ithaca are called Ulysses, Hector, Ovid, Romulus, Etna, Marathon, Virgil, and the like.

In moving with my family, in 1962, from a house on a busy Ithaca street to a farmhouse at a country crossroads, I was responding to a desire for spiritual belonging that was more romantic than classical. But I suppose that in America the romantic and classical have always been mixed. It gets very difficult to separate them in our heritage, for romanticism provided men like Thomas Jefferson with a deity—"Nature's God"—more amenable to human reason and a classical conception of order than is the Christian and Hebrew Jehovah. In a sense, my Greek Revival farmhouse is a romantic construction—a dream of order and balance and proportion set down, in 1831, in a rude wilderness to represent its original owner's sense of himself and what he could achieve as well as a spiritual attitude that justified his striving. Certainly its appeal to me, at the time I first saw the house, was that of a dream —one intensified by my inability to find spiritual meanings through reason, as Jefferson could, even as whatever faith I had in reason made me too skeptical for the simple Christian religiosity of my mother. All I had was a large capacity for wonder. While we still lived in Ithaca, I spent many hours at night looking at the stars through a four-inch telescope, wishing to be drawn up into them in some miracle of union.

Indeed, the first possession I brought into the farmhouse was that telescope, and I put it in a corner of the parlor that was to become my study. The windows of this room—the most formal in the house—are framed at the sides and top by wood that has been fluted to resemble Greek columns. After positioning the telescope on its tripod, I looked out the window at the wild-rose brambles just beyond the glass and at a field of corn whose dark-green leaves were shimmering in the August sunlight, and I was caught by the sense of a lovely strangeness that yet was familiar—a response so intense as to be astonishing, and of the kind that perhaps comes only when the outer eye perceives what the inner one, which is blind to everything but the ideal, has all along visualized as the omphalos of the universe, as its long-sought home.

I think a response like that is possible only once, and then in a person's younger years. But its memory can persist. For a long time I believed that, through place, I could become whole, achieving that balance of mind and spirit, of body and soul, that we ascribe to the Greeks. Over the decades I have come to know my land through a kind of amateur archeology. I have found the eroded remains of a couple of dams—one near a seasonal stream deep in the woods, built perhaps by an early settler (for, though there is no puckered hole to indicate where a fruit cellar might have been, a line of rotted cherry stumps suggests that a cabin had once been close by), and the other, much larger and on a stream that runs even during the summer months, at the spot where, according to early county maps, a sawmill stood. It would have been the sawmill to which the logs to make the planks of our house were carted, as the lands were being cleared for crops and cow pasture. And I have come to know my house the way anybody does who raises three sons in one and who jacks up beams to straighten slanting floors and tilting door frames, tears out improvements of previous owners and adds improvements of his own, repairs siding, and yearly coats a fourth of its exterior with white paint. Without barns, a farmhouse is forlorn, devoid of its justification; and many years ago, after our cow and hay barns were destroyed by fire, my wife and our older sons and I began the task of constructing smaller new ones, the first for the family's horses, another for our son Cris's goats, and a third for our growing collection of second-hand farm equipment—tractors, manure spreaders, and plows.

To all members of my family this farm has been an agency for much happiness, and I would choose to live nowhere else; and yet on occasion—the first in my mid-forties, as I was straddling a barn ridge, nailing down metal roofing and enjoying the view of my property on a sunny day—I have been surprised by a sudden sense of unreality, as if all my efforts at wholeness through belonging were a kind of playacting, and I a person without substance. And then, three years ago, in the spring preceding our youngest son's entrance into college, he and Jean and I spent a month in Greece, seeing the remains of the temples whose pediments the twin pairs of wooden gables of our house simulate; and nothing at home has since been quite the same.

On our first complete day in Athens—we had arrived the previous afternoon, and that night had walked up to the Acropolis, lit not by the artificial illumination our guidebook had promised but, more graciously, by the full moon—we looked up a Greek architect who had been a visiting professor at my university. He told us that we would be seeing the beauty of his country in the process of being destroyed by a plague of concrete and commercialism—a virulence spreading from the major cities to the farthest islands, where its first symptoms were jerry-built white cubicles built poxlike on hills and in coves for the tourist trade. Of what value are good architects, he asked bitterly, in a society that wants nothing but another fast drachma? That midnight, at dinner at an outdoor restaurant, I sat next to a Greek poet about my age who said that his serious work had never received much attention and that in recent years he had chiefly amused himself writing parodies of T.S. Eliot's religious verse. Although he had lost one lung to cancer, he smoked cigarettes while we were waiting to be served and between courses. After drinking some wine, he suffered such a paroxysm of coughing that he put his head on the table to recover his strength. "I have an allergy to wine," he said apologetically, as soon as he could speak. "I should never drink, my doctor has warned me; yes, I shall give it up," and he emptied the bottle into my glass while lighting his next cigarette. I already had drunk too much, and so I toasted his health, the friendliness of all Greeks, and the loveliness of the Parthenon in the moonlight. I said that people in my region of the United States felt a special affinity for his land, and that nearly everybody I knew had visited it at least once; my wife and I had wanted to come sooner but decided to wait for the Fascist colonels to get booted out. Before taking the last sip, I added a final toast—to democracy. He gave me an ironic smile. "Let me tell you a secret about all Greeks today," he said. "We are incapable of governing ourselves. To put it frankly, we were much happier under the colonels."

As I age, my spirit seems to travel ever more poorly; I was depressed by these opening contacts with Greeks to a degree that jet lag couldn't explain. I suppose I had expected the past to have a greater influence upon the Greeks than apparently it did: I wanted them to be the living part of that museum which is the heritage of us all. Walking back to our hotel at an early-morning hour with Jean and Jimmy, feeling those pangs of indigestion that resemble a heart attack, I complained that we had come to Greece to see the past, not to be reminded of the present—a remark that in retrospect has, for me, at least a vestige of the dramatic irony of the Greek tragedians, for the past in all its dying strength was to impinge upon me in a manner I neither expected nor desired.

We spent the greater part of our first week on the Peloponnesus, following the Sacred Way out of Athens and the modern world (the sulfurous industrial region which that desecrated Way borders) and into the past, as it is revealed in such customary attractions for tourists as Corinth, Mycenae, Olympia, Epidaurus, and Delphi; and then we spent three weeks on the islands, visiting Mykonos and Delos and Rhodes, but staying mainly on Patmos and Crete. Jimmy, who had been on his high school cross-country team, ran the stadium course at Olympia; he and I ran the one at Delphi while Jean took pictures of us; and, at Epidaurus, she and I and a dozen other parents sat in the highest rows of the theater while our offspring, collected in the center of the arena far below, tested the acoustics by clapping and speaking—sounds that reached us as a confusion of German and Japanese and English syllables interspersed with the popping of firecrackers. In short, we did, saw, and heard nothing uncommon; and, I suppose, my growing awareness of the intensity of the Greek spiritual belief was not an unusual one for pilgrims to the past.

It first came to me in climbing the many steps to one acropolis or another as a sense of how far the citizens of any polis had to climb to reach these places of worship, these sacred strongholds. A religious aura seemed still to emanate from the ruins not only of Delphi—that remote and romantic site that once was the center of the world—but of every place we visited. At Olympia, only the foundation stones remain of the building for which the coffeehouse opposite my university office was named; once, it contained a statue of the seated Zeus so huge that, had the god stood up, his head would have burst through the roof of his temple. Delos, the smallest of the Cycladean islands, at one time contained an oracle second in fame only to the one at Delphi, and a great temple to Apollo built by a consortium of Greek states. According to myth, the island floated about until Poseidon anchored it as a haven for Leto; she, made pregnant by Zeus, had been fleeing his wife, Hera, and on Delos gave birth to the divine twins Artemis and

Apollo. So holy was this island to the Athenians that, as the dominant power of the Delian Confederacy, they forbade any births or deaths on it, and for a period—by a decree even more cruel—banished its natives as impure.

How deeply did the Greeks believe in their gods? Before visiting the various ruins, I thought that the myths were, to them as to us, fables pleasing to the imagination; that in filling the sky with Andromeda, the Dioscuri, Cassiopeia, and so on, they were simply humanizing their wonder at the unknown. On clear nights at my farmhouse, nights in which the stars were far more radiant than the glow of Ithaca on the otherwise dark horizon, I used to focus my telescope on Andromeda, our sister galaxy, or search for Castor after locating the brighter Pollux. I also had a little plastic tube (equipped with a battery-operated red bulb and a series of discs of the constellations) called a Starfinder. By looking with one eye into the tube while focusing the other on the proper constellation above, I would find the names of stars and the dotted outline of a mythological figure inscribed in the very heavens. Telescope and Starfinder were instruments helping me to feel that I belonged to my house and land much as my saw, hammer, and paint-brush were; or, for that matter, early county maps and books about the history and geology of the Finger Lakes. Standing at the top of windy Mt. Kynthos on Delos, though, or looking beyond the tumbled stones at Delphi toward the sea, I realized that the Greeks belonged to a cosmos in a way that I never could. Values and attitudes alter for an individual in his lifetime, and even more so for the society of which he is a part; no generalization will hold for any epoch, modern or medieval or classical. And yet I knew, looking upon the ruins at one site or another, that at an undetermined magical moment the intelligence of the Greeks fused with their apprehension of the sacred; that moment had nothing whatever to do with balance or proportion, or any wish of later people to heal their divisions. Zeus lived, and the universe was One. Such belief takes long to ebb, permitting civilization, but the very attempt to hold on to it ultimately does it in.

It was not until we were on Patmos, a small island whose soil is unimportant to archeologists, that I felt the psychological or spiritual impact of my realization. While still in Athens, we found that the Greeks we met considered Patmos, not Delos, to be the "most religious" of their islands: a special place. In a grotto here, the banished St. John the Divine, who may or may not have been the Apostle John, underwent his Revelation; and the island is dominated by a mountaintop monastery whose monks are revered by the farmers and fishermen and merchants. Patmos is more popular with Athenians than with foreigners; though small concrete cubes and a scattering of hotels have been built, the new construction does not yet seem an excrescence on a pastoral landscape. I asked the taxi-driver who found us tiny twin apartments—one for Jimmy, the other for Jean and me—on the second floor of a cube overlooking the bay at Grikou if he liked his island home, and he answered, "Why, of course!" with the only partially feigned astonishment at the naïveté of the question which is my response to similar queries from city visitors to our farm.

I intended to keep a journal of our visit to Greece but managed only one complete entry, written soon after our arrival on Patmos. It reads:

J U N E   4   (O N   P A T M O S)

The atmosphere here is clearer than anywhere else we've been in Greece, giving a sharp definition to hills, goats, houses (and the donkey I'm looking at from the terrace of our little apartment). The people of Patmos are friendly, and their smiles the kind that give happiness to the recipient. I feel more relaxed than I did in looking at the antiquities elsewhere—so often they gave me first a melancholy (which is pleasant enough) and then a sense of futility. The remarks in the *Blue Guide* about the statue of Zeus (p. 337) are illustrative of what I felt. The statue was the masterpiece of Pheidias, one of the Seven Wonders of the ancient world. The ivory had cracked by the 2nd c. B.C., and had to be repaired; in Julius Caesar's time it was struck—what irony!—by lightning. The Roman emperor Caligula "wanted to remove it to Rome and to replace the head of

Zeus with his own, but every time his agents came near the statue it burst into a large peal of laughter." That laughter—can I ever explain why?—seems an analogy of some of my personal feelings. Of course it expresses the difference between the God and the pretensions of a vain and corrupt emperor—but isn't the laughter, the scoffing, the only thing left of a civilization's spiritual impulse? Laughter of this sort seems finally directed against the scoffer himself, against a Zeus frozen on his pedestal, and so marks the very end of any myth. On Patmos, Zeus's laughter doesn't bother me—though here I think about it in a way I didn't at Olympia.

As I was writing that, evening began to set in, and I couldn't read the small print of the *Blue Guide*. I went inside for my glasses and a candle, returning to the terrace to copy the passage on page 337 and complete the entry. Music started up at the taverna on the shore soon after I finished writing, and a brightly lit cruise ship passed by, beyond the entrance to the bay. My very sense of peace must have made me vulnerable to the words I had written—much as, on the barn roof, it had left me unguarded enough to wonder if my life was only a pose. I have never thought of any deity as other than an expression of a human need, but I believed at that instant in the reality of the dying and immobilized god, and in his laughter. That laughter was real enough to be echoing still. It reached out to encompass the passengers on the cruise ship, the revelers in the taverna, and me, sitting by my little candle under the stars; and I knew the flimsiness of all my protecting values and beliefs, and saw all the illusions that my desires had invented. "Why be buried there?" I asked out loud, thinking of my long-held but secret wish that my grave might be either in the old apple orchard at the rear of our yard or in a glen in the woods which a tree house built long ago by Jimmy and me overlooks. But chiefly I was conscious of my triviality. I had no desire to belong anywhere.

This year marks the sesquicentennial anniversary of the construction of our house by Thomas Kelsey, whose faded name is stenciled on the inside of the loft door of his single remaining outbuilding, which he used for carriages and we use for automobiles. In addition to Jean and me, our son Cris lives at home, as does my mother. In September, I will be sixty; in November, my mother will be entering her centenary year. She has been living with us for nearly eight years—a long period for her to remain in one place. Both her parents died before she entered school, and in her childhood she was handed from relative to relative (she remembers an unknown male voice shouting one night, "If that child continues to cry, throw her into the street!"); and my father, throughout their marriage, moved from city to city in quest of a success beyond his grasp. Occasionally, Jean and I take her to a restaurant. As the returning car approaches our crossroads, she invariably says, "What a lovely home you have," and, just as invariably, Jean or I respond, "You mean *we* have, Mother: it's your home, too"; but she refuses to be bothered by notions of belonging anywhere. When I was a child, though, she dreamed of a home of her own, where she could raise her family and where the picture she most valued—a reproduction of the famous Raphael Madonna in an oval Victorian frame—would find its permanent wall. Briefly, she thought she had that home, for my father purchased one in a subdivision of Little Rock called Normandy by its developer; but then my father left us, we lost the house, and my mother had to sell every piece of furniture, every painting.

Had I not gone to Greece, the knowledge that I neither could nor desired to belong to my farm or any other place would eventually have come to me—though perhaps too slowly for conscious recognition, as I think it has come to my mother. In my early twenties, soon after the Second World War ended and I was a civilian again and back in school as a graduate student, I read an essay by Francis Bacon which contained the passage, "A certain rabbin, upon the text, 'Your young men shall see visions, and your old men shall dream dreams,' inferreth that young men are admitted nearer to God than old." The view struck me as so curious that the words have stayed in my memory. I had many dreams—that is to say, conscious wishes or daydreams—for my life was before me; I thought visions available only to the elderly, if to anybody at all. Now I understand that our apprehension of the sacred does diminish in our later years, as not only the prophet Joel but the Romantic poets knew; and with it our need for spiritual belonging. Though the loss is a major one, it at least gives us the freedom to enjoy small things for what they contain in themselves.

And yet how the real-estate metaphor hangs on, in my subconscious dreaming! In one dream that recurs, Jean and I are an indeterminate age; our children are either not yet born or have all left. She and I go for a ride into the country, far out on a narrow, black-topped road we've never known about, looking for a house to move into. It's quite lovely on this road; there are hills in the distance, or maybe mountains with snow. In a wide valley, we see a large white-clapboard house set far back from the road, and behind it a red barn. The house is for sale. The door is unlocked, and so we enter. Downstairs are several rooms—beautiful rooms with marble hearths and floor-to-ceiling windows. But they are empty of furniture, and our voices echo against the white walls. On the second floor we find a ballroom with a chandelier, a raised stage at one end, and chairs lined up against a wall. The echoing is even more pronounced here. There is a small, closed door at the far end of the room. I open it and go down a long corridor alone. It leads to many other rooms. They are dark and dusty. The floors are sloping in these rooms, for this wing is very old—much older than the rest of the house. This long-unused part of the house, which seems so enormous, is even more fascinating than the ballroom; it is also what makes us decide that the house would be impractical for us. It would be impossible to heat, for one thing. We buy a cozier house, in town; but sometimes we drive out into the country just to see that other house. It is always there, unlocked and waiting, and we are always attracted by it.

I think this dream is a sublimation of my earlier desires and is cautionary. The yearning to belong, I realize, has hidden deep within it a longing to escape, as if the self were the ultimate barrier to union. I want to hold to my identity. My mother, though, doesn't worry about holding to hers. She lives without much thought to herself, refusing even to discuss her health. Asked how she feels, she says, "With my fingers"; asked if she's all right, she says, "No, I'm half left." She spends a great deal of time in a bedroom filled with photographs of her parents, her young husband, her sister, and my brother and me as children; here she often rereads (but I think no longer with grief) the last letters her sister and my brother wrote her before their deaths. I believe she lives for what the past contains, and for the love she has for Jean and her grandchildren and particularly for me; but other people matter less and less. When she was almost ninety, she told me (in that humorous manner we use to reveal our disbelief in what was once a crucial truth to us) that she no longer believed in Heaven, because the astronauts had reported nothing about its existence, but it seems to me that in the diminution of her personal desires she is achieving that state which to Eastern religions is the necessary condition for blessedness.

My brother, Jack, who was an airline captain, knew more about the stars than I ever have; on long flights over the ocean he used to put his plane on automatic pilot and look at them, and he often spoke to me of how much brighter and more sharply defined they become the higher one rises into the frigid stratosphere. Cris also knows more about them than I do. One night in June, he dusted and recollimated my telescope and took it into the back yard to show Jean and me certain nebulae and star clusters. After a half hour or so of watching, I became bored, and, while Cris was adjusting the telescope to view another cluster, I took the flashlight—he had been using it as a kind of celestial pointer through the dust of the atmosphere, those acidic motes that are a gift of my native state of Ohio to my adopted homeland—and directed its beam in a semicircle across the acre of grass, briefly lighting, at midpoint in the arc, the base of some of the trees in the apple orchard. Shortly afterward, a blade of thousands of little lights swept in the same arc across the lawn, much like a jeweled windshield wiper. "Look," I said to my wife and son, repeating the movement with the flashlight but not believing that the phenomenon would recur or even that I had seen it. But once again it took place, like an echo of the beam. Miracles, however slight, require rational explanations, and we decided that the jeweled blade was caused by glowworms—those wingless females or larvae of the firefly—each of which was chemically responding to the flashlight. But how precise that individual response, to produce the illusion of a moving blade! Again and again I flashed the beam across the grass, though the time between flash and response lengthened, and the blade itself grew fainter.

Finally, Cris complained that I was more interested in bugs in the grass than I was in the universe. I stayed out late with him and Jean to prove him wrong, and also because it was a pleasure to be alive with my wife and son beneath the constellations and to sense the dark presence of a comforting house behind us—one whose twin roof peaks only seemed to reach the stars. But, of course, Cris was right.

Sleeping in the Study

12 ALTHOUGH MY WIFE AND I HAVE THE largest of the six bedrooms in our farmhouse, we have been sleeping for more than a year on a convertible couch in my first-floor study. We bought the couch to accommodate our annual influx of summer visitors and used it for that purpose for a couple of seasons before deciding to try it out. It was more comfortable than we expected; and we liked waking up to different cracks in the ceiling and to windows that faced the morning sun.

On occasion, the mechanism jams, or a rivet works loose. Another inconvenience is that the study has no place for clothes storage, which means that upon rising we must walk upstairs to our bureau and the two wall-length closets I built for our bedroom fifteen years ago. But sleeping downstairs, we say, makes us closer to my mother, in case she needs help; the study is separated from her bedroom only by a bathroom, with doors opening to both. It is a spurious reason, or nearly so, since my mother (although she is almost ninety-nine) neither wants nor requires anybody's assistance. We sleep here, we also say, because in winter the downstairs is warmer than the upstairs, and because here one is in better control of all the basement humming that is heard only at night—from the wood and oil furnaces, which share in turn the task of heating us; from the various pumps as well as the water softener. We can more easily let in an errant cat or dog; be ready to repel a burglar or save family, guests, and pets from fire; or get a glass of milk for the insomnia that afflicts us more frequently with each passing year.

In thinking of the matter, I have decided that most of these reasons are as quixotic as the other members of the household—in addition to my mother, two of our grown sons are presently living with us, as is the partner of one of them in his goat dairy enterprise—take them to be. Another reason exists. I believe that sleeping downstairs reminds Jean and me of our days as young parents, when we were guardians of infants and school-age children, finding at least part of our meaning in that responsibility which a father and mother must ultimately relinquish, though slowly and only after painful conflict; and of the days even before that, when she and I were graduate students—Jean in biochemistry and I in English—living in a trailer set on concrete blocks in an Iowa field and sleeping on a similar, if much bumpier, convertible couch. To me, the world does seem younger, somehow, in my study become a bedroom, with our clothes thrown on the chair or on the cushions we must remove before pulling open the bed; and with a wall of books overlooking us and an untidy desk at our feet. And I know that sometimes, in reaching from bed to turn on the FM radio—we bought it nearly a decade ago for my father as he was dying of cancer—on its bookcase shelf, I am reminded of the Philco, borrowed from my parents, which sat on the little bookcase by the couch in our trailer. Returning with Jean to our warm Masonite shell after a walk on those quiet winter nights in which the magnified stars were ice crystals in an atmosphere frozen elsewhere to a transparent glass, I would tune that Philco to distant stations, wondering whether one of them was in the mysterious city we eventually would call our home.

Recently, I woke at 3:00 A.M., that hour of dread (seven years ago, I received a telephone call at that hour from a stranger, who told me that my older brother and only sibling had been killed in a car accident), to a repeating sound that I thought too uncertain and deep to come from any clock. In a country house, any unusual noise before dawn is omnipresent; barefoot and wearing shorts, following the beam of my flashlight, I tried to trace this one to its source. I pattered from room to room and then into the basement, a region I normally enter wearing an old shirt, jeans, and boots (for the cellars of old farmhouses have earthen and sometimes muddy floors, low beams festooned with cobwebs, and connect with crawl spaces in which cats, invisible except for eyes glittering like phosphorescent growths in the damp soil, keep vigil for their soft-furred victims) before discovering that it proceeded from a clock, after all—the battery-powered one in my mother's bedroom. A failing power supply—the clock was four hours slow— had imparted to its ticking the hollowness of a terminal despair.

An acceptance of the most primitive beliefs lies beneath my reasoning cortex and at that hour of the morning can jut above it, like an emerging tectonic plate; my first response was to believe that my mother was dying. Rushing to her bedside, I cupped the flashlight to make a diffuse glow. She was sleeping peacefully, a small and white-haired child. I took the clock from the wall and carried it into the dining room, remembering that somewhere I had read that Jung had investi-gated the correlation between the cessation of life and that of grand-father clocks, a kind of research so singular that it had caused me to suspect either the book I was reading or Jung himself. Still, if a man of his stature *had* believed in the possibility of such a correlation, it would be imprudent of me not to replace the battery of my mother's cheap little clock before it wore out completely. By such partial agreement with my instinctive and irrational self does my reason mollify it and slowly regain ascendancy. Rummaging around until I found a new battery in the drawer of the buffet, I replaced the old one and returned the clock to its wall, pleased by its regular, quiet ticking; but by then my mind was rarefied beyond desire for sleep. As I was searching for a title in the study bookcase, my flashlight woke Jean. "What are you doing?" she asked. "Looking for something about Jung and grandfather clocks," I said. "Oh," she said, as if nothing were more reasonable.

Not finding that text, I picked up from my desk the unfinished pages of a chapter which would be the penultimate one of the present book, and brought them into the kitchen, thinking to reread them while drinking a glass of my son's goat milk in that heart of the house, whose thick plank table (which I made from the house's own flesh, from the wood of a closet wall that Jean and I long ago, after much deliberation, removed from the living room) and whose pine cabinets, and appliances scarred by years of servitude, were the customary nursemaids to my insomnia. But death—the imminence of it, and not only for my mother—still lay heavy in the damp, pre-dawn air, and perhaps was the agent curling the pages of my manuscript and otherwise preventing me from attending to it.

My entire professional life has been devoted to literature, absorbing me to such an extent that my personal values, actions, and even most intimate feelings have been influenced by it; whatever it is that I am includes Levin scything a field, Don Quixote facing the Knight of Mirrors, and any of the lonely and dissatisfied peasants on Chekhov's vast steppe beneath the indifferent stars who, having just lost themselves in tales of supernatural terror while seated near two crude burial crosses, see something quite as extraordinary as anything in life or legend—a smiling stranger: a happy man!—approach their fire. In recent years, though, I have on occasion felt that literature can become (especially to the degree that it reflects ultimate matters, prophesying between the lines each of our tiny deaths in that instant which will stop time forever) a threat which is intensified by my knowledge that Wordsworth, before me, felt a similar threat. Such a fear is, of course, no more rational than the one occasioned by the slowing of my mother's clock. On this morning, it was attached—despite my efforts to subdue my instincts—to my own writing. My chapter, when complete, would tell of the end of something within me whose loss, however clear to my analytical mind, I found difficult to acknowledge to the rest of whatever I was. To finish the chapter and then the book constituted a frightening closure to my life. I had defeated the implications of the failing clock by transferring them to my own life and work.

At the instant of recognition of what I had done, the name "Evelyn Beale" was offered up to my consciousness from the recess where it had rested for nearly half a century. Although as an adolescent I had briefly lived with her and my father during the final year of their marriage, I never spoke her first name nor cared what the last had been; to my knowledge, the only place I ever saw her full name was on the letter I found in my twelfth year in my mother's dresser drawer as I was trying to discover the reason for a silent grief in her more profound than any I had felt or witnessed. At that age, I already had learned to read the ending of any missive if I was eager for its major argument; the conclusion of this letter was, "Obviously, if you love your husband as much as you say you do, you will agree to a divorce out of the knowledge that he finds a greater happiness with me. Yours sincerely, Evelyn Beale."

These words arrived in my conscious mind with much else dealing with love and betrayal and, perhaps surprisingly, the attractions of death. At such moments, certain selected elements of one's life constitute a continuum, or the finale of a Fourth of July celebration in which the entire sky is interlaced with all the glowing umbrellas that earlier had come individually, caught in that chronological movement from expectation through awe or fright to regret.

The centerpiece of my inner display was made up of my father's various departures and apologetic returns. As a high school senior, I was the sole witness at the remarriage of my parents; and, as a college sophomore, I drove my mother in my second-hand Ford, my first car and a gift from my father, through the morning rain of Ohio and the gray drizzle of an Indiana afternoon, to a small hotel in an Illinois town to prevent him from repeating his old mistake. That night, seated alone in my Ford, surrounded by the marvelous old-car smells of damp engine grease and exhaust fumes absorbed into upholstery, I watched the rain on the waxed hood form into globules that reflected the neon colors of the hotel sign while listening to Joe Louis defeat Max Schmeling—my 1934 V-8 was one of the first models to have a built-in radio—as my mother and father patched up their lives in his hotel room, to live henceforth in fidelity and much happiness until he coughed up blood and died, his head cradled in my wife's arm, as my mother and my aunt and I helplessly watched; and, as I remembered all this, remembering too that his death had presaged to me my own, I also was a child, running off into a ravine in the woods to be alone, for my mother's grief had now become mine, and I had no idea as to what would happen to her, my brother, and me. In that ravine, I asked myself, "What is the worst possible thing that can happen to you?" and replied, "Your own death, you dope," an answer that gave me, however false it was, a sense of solace and even of peace, as if God had touched my forehead with His hand.

Seated at the kitchen table in my sixty-first year, I realized how often I had assuaged grief or despair by such means, reducing my emotions or those of anybody who might have trespassed against me through that foreknowledge which makes betrayal, as well as all feelings of love and hatred, trivial. Had my memory called up Evelyn Beale to give me, as comfort, precisely that which had just been a threat? But even as I was wondering that, I was hearing my mother say, shortly before my father died, "I never knew it would end like this, Jim," and I was grasping her arm and telling her, with all the fierce conviction that comes when one knows one's voice is simply the instrument of all the truth that has ever been written or felt by individuals since time began, that "this" was no ending, that everything she and my father had experienced together still existed—"Remember, Mother, how you used to tell me that before I was born and Jack was a baby and you were washing diapers or something in that basement in Cuyahoga Falls, Clayton would come home from the tire plant for lunch and rush into the cellar to hug you so tightly you could barely breathe?"—and would continue to exist, so long as memory endures; and that it was the very endurance of memory which makes life at once so terrible and yet so incredibly precious.

My own memory, having relived the past as if it were the present in order to give to an old knowledge the immediacy of revelation, became quiescent. The house with its sleeping occupants, though, had regained the holiness I had felt for it in those years in which I had been a young father, a guardian against the dark; and the pages on the table before me no longer held any intimation of my end.

Finally, I became tired, my world the habitual one. On my way back to bed, I let in the cat mewing at the front door, telling it that if it pissed again on the bathroom rug I would cut off its offending parts, words it took with as much equanimity as ever. Then I felt my way through that narrow aisle between my desk and the opened couch to climb into the bed of that changing but constant room which Jean and I have shared ever since we were graduate students; and embracing her, I slept.

JAMES McCONKEY

has written novels, stories, and criticism in addition to autobiography. Born in Ohio, he has lived for more than thirty years in a farmhouse in the Finger Lakes countryside. He is Goldwin Smith Professor of English Literature, emeritus, at Cornell University, where he currently is Advisor on the Arts to the Provost.

COURT OF MEMORY

has been set in Minion, an excellent example of how far digital typesetting has progressed in the past decade. Designed by Robert Slimbach of Adobe Systems, Minion is a modern interpretation of a classic Renaissance "old style" face. All the faces in this family have their origin in the humanistic script developed and widely used in the late fifteenth and early sixteenth centuries. Scholarly publishers such as Aldus and Jenson converted the calligraphy of contemporary scribes into readable, elegant book faces, incorporating lively italics, ligatures, and "small capitals" as integral parts of the fonts.

Slimbach's design is especially suited for the demands of modern offset printing. It is even in color, calligraphic in spirit, and contains *(deo gratias)* a full range of italics, old style figures, ligatures, and genuine small caps, necessary appurtenances not often available in modern "re-cuttings." A successful synthesis of both historical precedence and contemporary design, Minion is perfectly suited for book work demanding a classic face designed for digital setting.

This book was typeset at The Typeworks, Point Roberts, Washington and printed by and bound by Haddon Craftsmen, Scranton, Pennsylvania.